D1094965

Tampa Review 55/56

❖ A GALLERY OF LITERARY AND VISUAL ART IN PRINT FOR 54 YEARS ❖

Tampa Review is published twice each year by the University of Tampa Press. Founded in 1964 as *UT Poetry Review*, *Tampa Review* is the oldest continuously published literary journal in Florida. Subscriptions in the United States are $25 per year; basic subscription is the same outside the U.S., but write for mailing cost by surface mail. Payment should be made by money order or check payable in U.S. funds. International airmail rates are available and vary; write for specific information. Subscription copies not received will be replaced without charge only if notice of nonreceipt is given by subscribers within six months following publication.

Editorial and business correspondence should be addressed to *Tampa Review*, The University of Tampa, 401 West Kennedy Boulevard, Tampa, Florida 33606-1490. Manuscripts are read only during September, October, November, and December, and must be submitted online through Submission Manager. See guidelines at http://tampareview.ut.edu.

Tampa Review is indexed by *Index of American Periodical Verse* (Metuchen, N.J.: Scarecrow Press), *Annual Bibliography of English Language and Literature* (Cambridge, England: Modern Humanities Research Association), *POEMFINDER* (CD-ROM Poetry Index), *The American Humanities Index* (Albany, N.Y.: Whitston Publishing), and the *MLA International Bibliography*. Member of the Council of Literary Magazines and Presses (CLMP), Council of Editors of Learned Journals (CELJ), and the Florida Literary Arts Coalition (FLAC).

The editors gratefully acknowledge the generous assistance of James Lennon who provided photographs of Maxwell Taylor and his art. Special thanks to Dawn Davies for permission to reproduce some of the extraordinary Bahamian art from her collection. We are also grateful to Dorothy Cowden, Carl Cowden, and Jocelyn Boigenzahn for facilitating inclusion of work from Scarfone/Hartley Gallery and Studio-f and to Therese and Maxwell Taylor for their generous assistance.

Typography and design by Richard Mathews

Printed on acid free paper ∞

Manufactured in the United States of America

For additional information visit *Tampa Review* at
tampareview.ut.edu or tampareview.org

Editor

Richard Mathews

Fiction Editors

Shane Hinton
Yuly Restrepo

Nonfiction Editor

Daniel Dooghan

Poetry Editors

Geoffrey Bouvier
Elizabeth Winston

Editorial Assistants

Sean Donnelly
Joshua Steward

Staff Assistants

Josie Bready
Noah Menendez
Laura Stewart
Megan C. Wiedeman

Contributing & Consulting Editors

Kendra Frorup
James Michael Lennon

Published by the

University of Tampa Press

Tampa Review 55/56

ON THE COVER: *Green Dress* by Maxwell Taylor. 2016. Silkscreen on paper. 22 x 30 inches. Photo by J. M. Lennon.

One of a series of prints created and individually embellished by the artist during a residency at the University of Tampa's Studio-f, *Green Dress* expresses flowing playfulness and affection. Layered profiles seem to ground and support as well as embrace the central woman, whose green dress exudes comfort, grace, and flowing rhythms.

The woman is alone but not alone. Her eyes with lowered lids give her a sense of self-sufficiency. She seems to hug herself, while being embraced by figures and patterns that tie her to cultural and natural continuities. There are flowing forms in the patterns of the dress—curved lines that create rhythms in the composition—complemented by the rhythms of straight lines and strokes at the upper left and lower right that hint at different rhythms: a suggestion of piano keys, but also the geometric repetitions of a fabric pattern that enfolds and links a history of strong, graceful, multi-layered, and enduring female presences.

Tampa Review 55/56

Contents (continued)

Maxwell Taylor. *The Struggle*. 2002. Woodcut. 31 x 51 inches.

Maxwell Taylor. *Moonshine*. 1965. Oil on canvas. 24 x 24 inches. Courtesy of The Dawn Davies Collection.

Night Moves

If ghosts were possible
birds would walk only at twilight,

at the god hour
which descends like a plausible sun

traveling in the wrong direction.

–Michael Burkard, "At the God Hour"

It was the summer I turned eighteen that Trudy's father found work for me as a deckhand on a southbound towboat. At first, the barge seemed to have a strange weight to it, foreign, like I'd grown an extra limb. The water went quiet around us and the sky flattened at the horizon, as if we were about to punch right through the backdrop of a school play. And that's how we moved too—with a caution that seemed to expect we would run up against the edge of things at any moment.

In September, after the job was done, we had a month's leave. I didn't go back home then, but stayed with our second mate, Bud, and his girlfriend in New Orleans. The first night we were there, we got drunk in some soggy little Bywater bar that I was never able to find again, walking around all that month trying to see through windowpanes fogged with grease and asking, "Was it there? Was it in there that I gave up on the idea of going home?"

That night, I followed Bud back to his narrow shotgun apartment, the interior so close and contained it was like a spine you could move through, as if all these houses were reaching front-to-back for something, built in imitation of the river's creaking throat. His girlfriend had set two glasses on the coffee table next to a bottle of some kind of fancy bourbon I didn't recognize. When she saw me in the doorway with him, she went to get another glass without saying anything, but she smiled when she poured and I felt weak with warm feeling for her steady slim wrist, a charm bracelet tinkling there like very small music. One of the charms was a steamboat with a little paddle wheel that turned, and I

remember how watching it made my eye ache, as if it were too tiny to look at.

When she handed the glass to me she said, "My god, Bud, look at him. He's just a boy."

And I'd said, "I'm eighteen," defensively. Bud had laughed and said vaguely, "Dan's old enough to know what's what." But I'd felt alone in my age, as if the world had suddenly emptied of eighteen-year-olds.

The night moved, with us inside it like cargo. We drank the bottle down halfway and Bud had asked sluggishly, "Has the little girl been leaving you alone, Val?"

I startled at this slightly, the ice in my glass like teeth chattering.

And Val said, "Oh we've been getting along well enough. She goes her way and I go mine."

Drunk, my voice seemed to dangle just outside of me like fruit on a branch. I said, "Bud, you didn't tell me you had a little girl," looking around me as if expecting her to appear in some doorway, nightgowned and rubbing her eyes cartoonishly.

Bud laughed like my father used to laugh when he knew something you didn't and was excited to tell you about it, lingering in that instant when the knowledge was all on his side, sitting inside him looking out, like some small creature caught in cupped hands.

"We don't have a daughter," he said. "Val's talking about her little ghost friend," then leaning across the gap between us to say in a half-whisper, "I guess I didn't tell you this place is haunted."

Val said quickly, "Oh don't scare him, Bud," though I'd shown no sign of fear, not so much as the flick of an eyelid.

Bud said, "Dan's not scared of ghosts, are you Dan?" and I felt like a little kid, shaking my head and saying, "Nope," dutifully.

Val began to tell me about her. Val had moved into that apartment a few months before she'd met Bud. Around Christmastime, she'd unlocked the door and seen the glow of her little Christmas tree sort of waver in the corner, like pages of heat above a blacktop in summertime. She said she'd felt a presence on her skin so heavy it was like being touched everywhere at once, all over the surface of her skin, by some huge hand. "Or maybe many small hands," she said shivering a little and taking a swallow from her glass.

"I knew someone was in the apartment with me. Like how you know when you come home if the house is empty or not. You don't have to look upstairs to know your brother'll be there on his bed reading comic books. The house just has a different feel to it."

I nodded at her, tried to show I believed her story, but she was looking at Bud. Bud and the dog in the corner stretched and yawned at the exact same instant, and it felt somehow lonely that I'd missed being a part of their twinned movements, as if my body itched to be in sync with theirs.

"Well that was the start of it," Val was saying. "A few days later, I saw her. Hair in braids, a pale, kind of colorless dress. But you only really see her for seconds at a time, moving at the edges of the room. I hear her sometimes, she hums something, not very well, but I'd know the tune if I heard it anywhere else. Oh and she doesn't like me to leave faucets running. She turns them off."

Bud got up to wind the clocks, muttering about how he was the only one to ever wind a clock around here, and how difficult was it to keep a fucking clock wound.

We didn't talk anymore about Val's ghost. We talked about other things that I don't remember. We laughed when Bud trapped a roach under a hat, asked me if I wanted a pet, even plucked a hair from Val's head to tie around it like a little leash, but when Bud lifted the hat again, peered inside it like a confused magician, the roach had scuttled off somewhere.

Late, late into the night, I was drunk on all fours feeling around the floor for an earring Val had lost, and they told me later that they'd watched me just sort of drop my head like a tired donkey and crawl into the big dog bed in the corner where Bud's lab was curled neatly, and I slept there. All night.

When I woke, light was spilling in, smooth and silver as a spoon, making the lab's fur take on shimmer like rainbows in an oil spill. His breathing pressed into me, a rhythm that spun sleep like a spider web, a rise and fall that was similar to the night shush of wake stirring behind the barge, when you'd lie awake in your bunk and feel the river part beneath you like a crease in a tablecloth.

I think I must've been dreaming about Trudy. I could almost smell her when I woke—the oils of her scalp and the ripe smack of her chewing gum—as if she were the ghost in the room rather than that little girl Val had been talking about. The smell in the room was the smell of my truck the night before I left for the river; the smell of my hands after I touched her, the only time I touched her like that.

And it's true that sometimes the living make easier, more convincing ghosts than the dead. Their absence is more like the itch of a phantom limb, that space you cannot scratch.

I tried to sleep again, in the warmth of the dog bed with the lab's breath knocking against my ribs. The light outside was just beginning to turn gold like the plumage of a bird changing with season, morning frothing up into the room like the head of a beer. And eventually, Val shuffled out into the kitchen, her robe loose and shimmering about her like light on moving water. She made coffee, and seeing my shape curled next to the dog, crossed the room toward me, offering a mug.

"You still here?" she asked, but not unkindly.

They never asked me to leave, and so I stayed. They made up a place for me on the couch, Val tucking the sheets taut around the cushions like a hospital bed. These things felt clean, like new coins: the cups she wiped out for me with a pink rag, the oval of soap she unwrapped and placed in a pale dish, the plain white comforter that had no weight to it, just a vague warmth that kept me separate from the room while I slept.

But some nights I still slept in the dog bed, putting my hand on the lab's head before crawling in with him as if granting a blessing, something my father used to do when he put my sister and me to bed as kids. A little veil of sweat would form between his palm and our foreheads and he would say the words with a voice that trembled with such gentleness that the gentleness was almost frightening: *The Lord bless you and keep you. The Lord make his face to shine upon you, and be gracious to you. The Lord lift up his countenance upon you, and give you peace.* I thought of that word "countenance" as I touched my hand to the lab's face, a word that had made me think of windows as a child.

The lab's name was Bo, and he smelled like the pelt of an otter.

I liked at night when we all sat in a circle around the coffee table, as if we were a halo cast by the drinks that clustered there, golden and beaded with liquid crystal. The outside heat pressed up against the windowpanes like a poor orphan in a story, trying to get a glimpse of riches. I liked the shortness of our names, how each of us could be described in a single breath, a syllable that filled the whole room for the half-second it was said, so that each in turn possessed that space briefly. *Bud, Val, Bo, Dan*—moving to the center of that circle to pluck a drink from the glass-topped table, touch the source of the light before moving back to its edges.

I only once heard Bud call the lab by his full name, shouting "Bodaggit!" when the dog got into the bathroom trash one night. It had surprised me, all those extra syllables like streetlights coming on suddenly that you didn't know were there. I stood in the open doorway, laughing and spilling a little whiskey. "His name is *Bodaggit*?" I said.

Bud looked at me, his face harsh with drink, and said, "You know what a bodaggit is, don't you?"

He pushed the dog's face into the scattering of bloody tissues that were spread across the floor. I saw then that he had chewed up what looked like a used tampon, and I turned away, feeling that I was witness to something that should be private.

"A bodaggit is when a dog's turd gets matted up in the hair around his asshole. And that's exactly what this fucker is—a turd covered in fur."

I turned to look at Val, seated primly in the living room. Her eyes were lowered, and she was cleaning dirt from beneath her fingernails.

Bud let go of the dog's collar and I felt a deep pull of shame, as if I were the one being reprimanded. But I felt ashamed on Bud's behalf as well. He was like a god to this animal and had named his only supplicant something cruel.

The nights grew together, tightly braided so that we couldn't tell one strand from the next. We had already found our places, like constellations: Val on the floor with her legs long in front of her, me on the couch with an arm behind my head and a drink on my knee, and Bud in a rocking chair that he never rocked, sliding forward on the seat and leaning to rest his elbows on his knees, as if the back-and-forth movement of the chair was beneath his dignity.

There were moments when our arrangement felt like a balancing act, felt so fragile that just a passerby looking in the window at us would unravel the braid, scatter the strands, knock our constellation spinning. And so I asked Val if I could lower the blinds at night, and she said, "Oh sure do what you want. The little girl likes them open, but I doubt she'll pitch much of a fit when we have company."

I was "company." It was a good word, a word that I could sit inside of blissfully like a fly trapped in a jar of honey.

Before bed, sometimes Bud would stand up abruptly and go to the kitchen to get the last can of beer. "Who wants it?"

We'd shake our heads and he'd say something corny like, "Well a man's gotta do what a man's gotta do," and then we'd follow him out into the little yard behind their place where he'd punch a hole in the side of the beer with the end of a key and drain it in one smooth and foamy swallow. He'd whoop and throw his hands up over his head, and we'd clap like he'd just performed some elaborate trick, and then we'd all fall quiet at once. We'd just stand with a tired sort of reverence, letting the mosquitos eat freely from the soft flesh behind our knees and straining our eyes to see what stars were seeable.

The stars always stayed small, like the beady eyes of rodents. Their light would crumble into dawn like the battery going dead in a flashlight, that slow fade as you smack the bulb against your palm, hoping to force the brightness back.

"You can't really see stars here," I'd complained one night.

"Well, whaddya call those?" Bud had said, pointing upward with the pierced husk of a High Life in his hand.

"You know what I mean, Bud," I said almost whining. "It looks like a whole different sky out on the river."

He didn't acknowledge this, but I knew he understood. On the towboat, there were nights when the stars seemed to take over, and you felt the world and everyone in it had just surrendered, let all those cold, fierce fires win. And that somehow we'd been overlooked, forgotten—that we'd just drift down the river's black spine toward nothing, looking up at the stars pitching forward across huge distances in arcs of white flame, somehow drawing nearer, somehow dipping to touch us and end us at last.

"Don't go down that road, kid," Bud said finally.

"What road?"

"The road where when you're on the boat you just wanna get off it and when you're on shore you just wanna be back on the river. It'll make you sick."

I realized then we'd said almost nothing about the towboat in the week that I'd been there. Val had her head cocked, birdlike, and trilled out, "You like the work, Dan? Bud said this was your first job."

I opened my mouth to answer her but Bud turned, still holding the withered beer can, to go back inside. "Well you two can stand out here jawing until the mosquitos drain your blood, but I'm going to bed."

Val sort of rolled her eyes and shook her head, but followed him inside. I stood a little longer, watching the stars flicker toward their early morning silence, and feeling the thin pinch of the mosquitos getting drunk on me. I watched two lightning bugs mating above the hedge by the backdoor—their bodies linked invisibly, their lights just barely separate but still distinct like a chord of music. They moved in the air, sparks caught in a flue, carried along by each other somehow, a dance in which it was decided centuries beforehand who leads and who follows.

❖ ❖ ❖

All that month I felt loose, like the sky after a night of snow. It felt like a sort of Christmas there—so many strings of lights dripping from front porches and the low moan of neon in dark windows, the long shimmer of beads hanging from tree branches. I felt I was visiting distant relatives, the shapes of our relations to one another shifting so that Bud and Val came gradually closer, like the orbits of planets aligning. One day they'd seem like a brother and a sister to me, then finally, mother and father—just as kind, just as cruel. We dipped in and out of our roles like costume changes.

I felt we were always on the verge of something, the way you feel when a holiday is approaching, the perpetual eve of a celebration that would not come—that would, perhaps be the act of our eventual departure—returning to the river and heading back north to leave Bo and Val and the little girl in an incomplete circle of one another's company.

The ghost had become a shadow that each of us cast differently, moving like spilled water. Val began to speak of her more and more as the month went on: "She's looking for something in the corner, bent over and feeling around on the ground," or "She's humming a Christmas carol. It's the one that goes . . ." and she'd hum a few bars of "Good King Wenceslas" for us.

Sometimes Bud would play along; if something wasn't where he'd left it, he might call from room to room, "Val! Talk to your little ghost-friend about not hiding the can opener." Even sometimes addressing the ghost directly, making his voice high-pitched and syrupy: "Where'd you put it, honey?" But just as often, he would sulk when Val talked about the little girl, sometimes even breaking into a flutter of rage and shouting, "Will you forget about that goddamn ghost for a second?"

At first, I kept my toothbrush separate from theirs, made a corner of the fridge where I kept my own things: a mesh bag of oranges, a jar of pickles, pre-sliced cheese, and braunshweiger. At night when they made love, I'd go out on the front stoop to smoke or sometimes grab Bo's leash from its hook and we'd walk down the little curl of street a ways. But after the first week had gone by, the toothbrush somehow ended up in the cup with theirs; the pickle jar and the oranges had shifted to a different shelf, were no longer mine but *ours*; and instead of going outside, I'd lie on the couch with my arms behind my head listening to Val's small noises, the creaking of their bodies pushing together, the weighted drift of it like the fireflies trying to pull themselves to some height, coupled, and each only understanding the other body as an extension of its own, almost as if it had grown an extra wing or leg.

When they finished, Val would come out of the bedroom with a hand in her hair, deep in the thicket of it as if feeling for something she'd lost in there. Her other hand held her robe closed, and she'd go into the bathroom that way, run the faucet. Sometimes the pipes would make a noise like a mechanical birth, like the whole house was about to give way to an underground flood. The noise sounded somehow more intimate than the moans and breathings I overheard as they coupled just on the other side of the frosted glass doors. Then, the toilet would flush and Val would come back out into the narrow hall, her hair quieted, both hands clutching her robe. Sometimes I'd catch a sliver of her face in the inward slant of the streetlight through the window. Her face looked emptied—bluish and closed like the faces of sleepwalkers. She once caught my gaze in this moment, our eyes falling together and she startled, brushed hard against the doorframe, the edge of her robe catching on a ragged bit of the jamb.

"Dan, can't you sleep?" she said. I wanted her to come lay a hand on my forehead as if feeling for fever. She looked silver in the shard of outside light, with a faint sheen of sweat coating her face and neck.

"I was asleep a minute ago," I said, wanting to somehow reassure her that I hadn't heard them.

"Did I wake you?" She came closer. Bud was already asleep in the next room. His snores were lilting, high and musical like whalesong. I shook my head at her question, but couldn't tell in the darkness where her eyes were looking so I said, "No. I mean, yeah, but it's okay."

She sat on the far end of the couch. I had to pull up my legs to make room for her. She made her voice very low. "Has the ghost been bothering you at all?" I could barely hear her. I moved my head so both ears were free of the pillow.

"What?" I said, even though I'd heard.

"The ghost," she said, her voice the scarcest brush of a whisper. "Sometimes she keeps me awake."

I felt my heart stir and quicken. "She . . . what does she do?"

"She sobs. Or she sings. Bud never hears it, he sleeps through anything. Sometimes I feel a weight on my chest, like she's sitting there.

Right *here*," she reached to touch my breastbone through the blanket. "She just sits there, and it doesn't hurt or anything, just feels . . . heavy."

I waited, the silence prickling inside my ears, a weight gathering somewhere above us, looking for a place to land, waiting for Val to go back into her room so that it could settle on my chest.

"God," she said, her voice rising almost to normal volume. "You must think I'm fucking crazy."

"No," I said, trembling a little. "I believe you." I suddenly didn't want her to go, wanted her to stretch out there beside me or just sit up all night on her end of the couch until the light swept in to reveal her eyes, patient and watchful, when I woke.

"Don't just say that, Dan. Don't say it if you don't mean it," her voice rose and fell, a strange and desperate lilt to it. She leaned over me, bringing her face closer to mine.

"I mean it," I said, solemnly, meeting the darkness of her eyes and trying to keep my gaze very still.

She suddenly bent to kiss my forehead, so quick it almost seemed like an accident. Her robe fell open a little and I could smell the faint ripeness of Bud's cologne and the shampoo we all used, and underneath it was her own smell, a tang of nutmeg and lavender. I hadn't known her smell before then.

"You really are a darling," she said, her voice back to a low whisper. And then: "You must be freezing, hon, you're shivering." She moved soundlessly to the closet to get another blanket, and began arranging the quilt around me, like a mother tucking in a child.

"You know what I do when I can't sleep?" she said, her hands measuring the outline of me. I shook my head.

"I'll tell you but you can't laugh."

I promised.

"I had a dream once that I was a tightrope walker. Like at the circus. But there was no one there watching. It was just me up on the wire. I think that might be my favorite dream. And when I can't sleep I just try to picture it: the height, the colors of the tent, the balancing of my arms. And sometimes, I'll just sort of fall right into the dream."

She stood over me and there was a long moment of silence when I think she was waiting for me to respond but I didn't know what to say.

"Maybe," she said finally, "you have a dream you love. A good dream that you can practice with."

She patted my knee. "Try it," she said, and went back into the bedroom.

❖ ❖ ❖

It was maybe two nights later that I first felt the ghost.

Val had asked to tell my fortune with a new deck of playing cards. She unwrapped the cellophane carefully, and the clear paper crackled in her hands, this radio static that she talked over. She spoke as she shuffled the fresh deck, sitting on the floor looking girlish in an oversized t-shirt.

"Okay, here's how it works . . ." she lined up the four queens in a tidy row along one floorboard. Her bracelet moved and chimed as she flicked the cards easily into place. "Each queen represents one of your four possible futures, Dan." She eyed me. "So now you have to pick your ladies."

"Ladies?" I watched Bud shuffle in from the kitchen with his fist full of beers. His eyes fell to the cards and he sort of sneered but said nothing, sitting down heavily in an armchair and opening each beer in turn—stutters and gurgles at the lip of each bottle.

"Yes, so this one," Val pointed to the queen of hearts, "represents someone you love . . . and this one," she moved her finger to the queen of diamonds, "is someone that you like a lot. The queen of spades is a close friend and clubs is someone you hate."

"Someone I hate . . ." I echoed slowly

"That's right. It's supposed to help you decide who you should marry. I'll deal out all the cards and they'll tell you which queen will lead you to the most happiness and wealth and all that stuff."

"You really gotta torture him with your girl-scout camp bullshit?" Bud said, passing the beers around. "I swear," he turned to me, "she's gonna have us braiding each other's hair next."

Val punched him playfully on the arm and winked at me, gesturing at the cards spread out on the floor. "Give us some names," she said. "Some of those small town hearts you've broken."

The cards looked tiny and very far away, little stained glass windows staring up from the floor. There was a bowl of ice cream beside Val,

loosening in the indoor warmth. Bud had tried to pour bourbon over it earlier, saying "Come on, lemme liven that up for you, babe," and she'd laughed and pushed his hand away and the bourbon had spilled down the front of her shirt. Val had looked at me, her face a frightened apology, while Bud had pushed his face between her breasts to suck the liquor from the fabric. She pushed him away, saying, "You're drunk," and he had brayed in response and did a little backward shuffle like a football player celebrating a touchdown.

I was watching the gloss of the four cards, their shimmer as the turn of the ceiling fan chopped at the light on the faces of the queens. These women were scarcely women at all, merely shapes pooled from reds and blacks, their unfeminine mouths curling strangely.

Bud's eyes had grown flat like the eyes on the cards. "Don't you have a girl back home, Dan?"

Something in me shrank down, an inward pull of muscles, like swimmer's cramp. I tried to move in some acknowledgement of the question. It came out as a shrug.

"What does *this* mean?" Bud imitated my shrug. "You're not even gonna tell us her name?"

I lowered my head as I had that night when I'd crawled, drunk, into Bo's bed for the first time. I felt a tired heat behind my face, and I knew I couldn't say her name out loud—the soft and open first syllable "tru" and the clip of the "dee" after, quick like the clop of a hoof. I couldn't bring her into the room that way when we'd so carefully measured our places, the corners we each occupied—Bud and Bo and Val and I. There just wasn't room in this space for her. I looked at the cards and didn't even know where she would land. These words: *love* and *like* and *friend* and *hate*. These, also, too small. I couldn't assign her a card. Each possible future was meant to have a different woman, a separate outcome, but I felt Trudy in all of them, saw the line of her face echoed in each of theirs as my eyes darted between them.

"Come on," Bud said, playfully, reaching to slap my knee. "Tell us about your little girlfriend."

I faltered, almost on the verge of speaking her name, trying to shape my mouth around it. But it was too heavy, unwieldy—an excess building, saliva, all her wet hair hanging out the truck's open window as we drove during summer months, drying and tangling in the gusts of heat that tugged the strands in every direction, like some sort of living weathervane. My hand later in that hair, pulling, pulling so her throat rose, thin and white to meet my mouth.

"What's her name, Romeo?" Bud pressed. "Val's little game isn't gonna work if you don't name your queens. Isn't that right, Val?"

Val said nothing. I was looking at my hands but felt their eyes measuring me. Bud creaked forward in his rocking chair, but Val said sharply, "Leave him alone, Bud."

There was a lengthy note of silence and then Bud growled, "Put those fucking cards away, Val. This isn't some third grade slumber party."

Val gathered up the queens somberly, tucked them back in their box. She placed the bowl of ice cream in her lap and began stirring at the white soup of it without eating.

I took one of the open beers from the center of the table and lay on my back on the couch, watching the ceiling fan keep time with its rattling spin. I listened to the clink of Val's spoon against the porcelain, my heart quick as I drank the beer down in four swallows. There was something like movement at the edges of the room, as if I was at the center of a slow spinning, though I wasn't nearly drunk enough for that, and suddenly I felt a vague pressure on my chest just like Val had described—the ghost of that little girl breathing against me like the push of Bo's ribs when we curled together in his bed. I don't know if that's really what it was. But there was a weight, and then a sad shiver in my ear, like electricity when it's just on the verge of being heard.

I felt a thick feeling of smallness, like standing in the woods when you're young, looking up into the wide patterns of light and shadow, and realizing with a shudder that you are alone, that the others have moved far off, their voices and the crash of their footfalls growing more and more distant. Val was looking at me. I must've looked afraid, even though I wasn't—caught inside her so suddenly that way, like a fish in a net. I breathed in fast and even thought maybe I glanced a twitch of fabric just at the edge of my sight, thought I could smell, faintly, her chewing gum.

It was just the way Val had said it would be—except it wasn't so much a *presence* as an absence that moved over your skin. Like when you think a spider might be crawling on you

but when you go to brush it away, nothing is there.

I blinked and shuddered a little and Val said, "You okay?"

I looked at Bud who was staring at me, mouth open a little, eyes waterless and small.

"You just felt her, didn't you?" Val said then. "The ghost."

I wavered. "I don't know."

"Oh no," Bud said, taking a swig of his beer and rolling his drunk eyes. "She's got you too, hasn't she?"

I wasn't sure whether "she" meant Val or the little girl. I kept quiet, and eventually the room blurred back into its usual shape.

❖ ❖ ❖

It was that night, sleepless, my stomach making small noises of hunger, that I thought about Val's dream of tightrope walking. I imagined her in the room, above me, crossing the length of it on a taut rope.

They did not make love that night, and the snores of Bo and Bud intertwined through the walls, waves of inhale and exhale, chest and nose and rattle. If Val slept, she slept in silence.

I tried not to think of the little girl's ghost, feeling the weight begin on my chest and then rolling over onto my side to erase it. I tried not to think of Trudy, this girl I'd known my whole life and now could feel her stretching to fill the rest of it. I tried not to think of the river, how I'd come gradually to know the men of the crew by the shapes of their forearms as they worked; tattoos faded to a greenish nickel coloring beneath the wolfish stripes of hair. Outlines of birds in flight, names of women they once loved or still did, crosses and curling snakes, the good luck charms of spades or diamonds—whatever hand it was that won them a nice chunk of cash—a flurry of things they wanted to keep always in their sightline while they worked, as if to say: this is *my* arm, my grip on the rope, my work and weight, my *doing*.

I felt the absence on my own arm, its smallness and nakedness, when I saw the other men all had tattoos. At night before sleep, I'd hold my arm up close above my face, look into the empty span of flesh as if something might appear there. But nothing did, only the raised veins spreading their bluish currents, like a long lengthwise map of the Mississippi River laid wrist to joint. I didn't ask the other men about their tattoos. If they wanted to tell you about them, they'd tell. But you couldn't help but feel that each tattoo was a very private thing being worn out in the open, like a second face.

We moved carefully around each other, breathed each other's smells—the oils of the scalp, the ropy sweat, cheap Missouri cigarettes and the ripe minty smack of gum. Some of the men chewed gum to get the animal musk of the river out of their throats, but most smoked cigarettes, the small flame cleaning out their insides, harbored in lungs like a false safety.

Once, one of the deckhands fell asleep with gum still in his mouth and it fell out onto his pillow, clung in his hair like a tiny tumor, and all morning he worked, the other men laughing to see that little greenish fist above his ear, like a twin that had never developed, never separated. I was the one to finally tell him, "You've got gum in your hair, Lou," and Lou touched the place where it was stuck as if discovering a wound. He'd seemed so frail, reaching for the wad, pulling it away with such careful disgust, as one might remove a leech, and I'd turned away from the long rubbery stretch while the wad clung, reluctant to pull free.

It was six hours of work, then six hours of rest, around the clock for twenty-eight days— a quick turning, like a coin flipping over and over in the air. My sleep started to get strangely stretched, and dreams stopped altogether. I just pushed over some brink into an easy darkness that felt dangerous in its depth, something you could never quite get back from. My hands bled, became a stranger's bleeding hands—always damp from blood or sweat or dew settling overnight on the ropes, river spray on the railings, opening a fist stiffened from long grip to see the moist damage there. The hands were the thing you thought about losing. Bud had told me you could always spot a new hire by the way he'd jerk his fingers back when the rope spun and tightened with a noise like the breaking of a fish's spine; the way they'd shy away from the rail when the tow moved close to a dock to unload, not trusting themselves.

"That fear of losing your hands," he'd said, "you just forget about it at some point. It never really goes away, but I guess the fear just gets built into you so that you don't have to think about it anymore."

Bud wanted to tell me stories about chains pulling men apart, crushing legs to pulp, bones splintering like rotten wood. I listened, nodded, tried to keep my face still, my lip from curling.

"I'm not trying to scare you," he kept saying. "I'm just trying to make you *aware* . . ."

I didn't think I was afraid, but the fresh cuts still itched in my palm, and it was maybe a week later that I swore I saw a severed hand floating in the water alongside us, turning slowly in the wake we turned up.

We were passing through an area where there'd been recent flooding and there were all sorts of things in the water—dead parrots still in their cages, nightgowns sprawled like drowned ghosts, shingles that had blown free and stretched in jagged lines over the surface of the water as if someone had shoddily tried to lay a road there. Looking down in the water, there was something so white it seemed to give off light, and at first I thought it was some kind of strange flower but then I could see the lines of the palm, the wink of the wedding band where the ring finger was bent wrongly. And before I could move or yell, the hand or whatever it was got caught in our wake and pulled into the froth behind the boat. And was gone.

I don't know if it was really a hand I saw. Maybe it was my fear built up from all those times my own hands jerked when the chains went taut; maybe it was my mind still trying to come to grips with the sudden lack of dreams. But I couldn't shake the thought of it—turning that way like a lily dropped into a bowl of water, the fingers stretched and curled into a little chandelier of bone, the palm upraised as if waiting to receive something—some coin or token, reaching through water for anything solid to grip.

I became less and less sure as the days passed that it was really a hand I'd seen, but I thought always in the moments before sleep about the man it had once belonged to, whether he was alive or dead, his hand adrift without him. Maybe he was feeling some phantom itch of dampness, a waterlogged weight where his wrist opened into empty space. Maybe he felt nothing.

I never told Bud about the hand, worried he'd think I was losing it.

This was, I realized, not the good dream I was meant to fall into that Val had spoken of. I didn't know what my good dream was. It seemed, that night, like I'd been awake for a stretch of weeks when Val finally appeared in the bedroom doorway, rubbing her face. She seemed to know I was awake though I didn't move or say anything.

"I can't sleep for the life of me," she said. "It's too goddamn hot in there. Can I come out here with you where it's cool?"

I sat up, making room for her on the couch. She made a soft, weary noise when she sat down.

"I'm sorry about Bud," she said then. "He bullies everyone when he drinks."

"Yeah, even the dog," I said quietly.

"Even that poor dog," she said, chuckling a little.

There was a long moment of breath between us, the darkness moving in to fill all the cracks in the room, when suddenly she spoke again: "Dan, you know we're happy to have you here as long as you wanna stay, but what about your folks? Don't you have people back home that are missing you?"

I wanted to tell her about Trudy but didn't know how to form the words. All the years we'd spent driving up and down Highway 3 in my dad's truck, the nearness of each other. All we found out: Trudy's sixth sense about cops, how she knew all the speedtraps. We'd round a curve and she'd say, "Cop," evenly, almost bored, before the squad car was in sight. I'd slow down as the curve opened and resolved and there would be the state trooper, hood low with frowning headlights switching on then back off again, like a threat. Sometimes, with a reckless flick of her wrist, Trudy would even wave at the officer, as if daring him to give chase. And all the things she'd leave on the floor of my truck: cheap plastic barrettes; shards of her fingernails she'd nip neatly, like a cat cleaning its face, and spit in little half-moon arcs; a cassette tape she'd made of songs recorded from the radio, that song she'd rewind and play over and over until it seemed a constant static beneath us:

Ain't it funny how the night moves
When you just don't have as much to lose?

And how it had all changed, every inch of road, every piece of her that still clung to the floor of the truck, when I'd asked and she'd said yes.

I let out a sigh, like the ghost was lifting from my chest. "Yeah," I said to Val. "I guess I just needed some extra time away."

She looked at me a little strangely. "You know," she said. "I'm worried that one of these days, Bud is gonna decide the same thing." She paused. "But then—maybe that'd be good for both of us."

"How long you been together?"

"A lot of years. Let's see. I was twenty when we met; he was twenty-two. So almost nine years now. A long-ass time."

I waited for her to say more, but she didn't. Looking at her, I saw her eyes were closed and wondered if she slept.

"We used to dance," she said suddenly, making me startle a bit. "All the time. We used to dance until bar close, almost falling asleep against each other on the dance floor. Then we'd wait on the levee for sunrise, and sleep out there, until the dew woke us up. And the barge horns."

She opened her eyes, but didn't look at me, watched the ceiling fan move the air in the room around. "He drank then. We both did. But not like we do now."

"What changed?"

She looked at me then, her eyes full. "Oh you know. I drink when he's away. I drink when he's here. Trying to fill the gaps, then trying to make up for lost time."

She reached for a pack of Winstons on the coffee table. "I'm gonna light a cigarette in here," she said. "You don't mind?"

I shook my head. The flame bloomed and showed her to me, freckles darkening the corners of her mouth. "Something's gotta change," she said, exhaling. "You gotta go home eventually, you know that. And maybe Bud's gotta stay away eventually. Or maybe I gotta . . ." she trailed off. "But either way, somethings gotta change."

I spoke cautiously, "You want me to leave?"

She ashed into an empty beer bottle. "Now you know that's not what I said." She let out a sigh that hung above our heads with her smoke. "If it were up to me you'd stay forever."

I said nothing, but felt warm and good, and sleepy for the first time that night.

"I'm curious," she said slowly. "What you like about him."

"Bud?" She nodded. I told her: "He makes me laugh. Out on the river, I can't even remember now what he'd say, but he could sure crack me up."

Her eyes were closed and she smiled, seeming to sway faintly against the couch. "He used to read the newspapers out to the crew at the breakfast table," I went on. "And he'd do these funny voices. And like, change little things so we wouldn't know what was real and what wasn't."

She laughed and moved closer, propping her chin on my knees. "You know," she said. "He used to dedicate songs to me on the radio. Those call in radio shows. He'd call from the barge and say things like 'there's nothing I wouldn't do for her.' You know that one song about 'I will dig you a garden where your flowers can bloom. I will build you a new life,' or something like that? And the DJ'd say 'this one goes out to Val,' and it gave me such a thrill every time."

I wasn't sure why but hearing this made me very sad—so sad that I wanted to take her face in my hands, not to kiss her just to feel her borders, the way I'd sometimes cup Bo's face—try to make him meet my eyes, see what is there, golden and unhuman, the dog soul that misunderstands us with such complete patience.

She blew smoke toward me and it held her scent at its center. "I can tell you see the good in people," she said, smiling faintly. "You gotta be careful with that though," she let her cigarette butt drop into the beer bottle where it hissed and sent up its last smoke. "And you gotta figure out how to be good to that girl you got back home."

I watched the side of her face. "What if I can't?" I said.

She looked at me then, her eyes dense and clouded. She spoke very firmly. "Then you stay away until you can. Or you find a girl you *can* be good to. You hear me?"

"Yes, ma'am."

She spread herself beside me on the couch, with her head pillowed on my feet and her feet resting just below my chin. They smelled earthy and clean, like washed potatoes. And we slept that way, curled head to toe, through the rest of the night. When Bud woke the next morning, he shuffled out into the living room and saw us nestled like that, but all he said was, "You two cutie-pies sleep well?" a half-smile crooking his mouth, and he kissed Val briefly on the lips when she rose to greet him, and that was all that was said about it.

❖ ❖ ❖

They had a big fight a few nights later when Val brought home a Ouija board.

"Enough is enough," Bud had said when he saw it tucked under her arm. "I've encouraged this bullshit long enough."

"It's just for fun," Val insisted. "I thought it'd be a fun thing we could all do together."

When things got heated, voices pitched like shards of glass, I grabbed Bo's leash, and the pack of Winstons from the coffee table, and the dog and I got lost in the neighborhood together. I sought out that little bar where Bud and I had got drunk together that very first night on shore, but I had no luck finding it. I ended up outside some sagging tavern with its windows covered over with black paper. I sat at one of the dark metal tables with Bo's leash slack in my hands and, realizing I'd brought no money with me, drank the remnants of drinks people had left—the bleeding cling of cheap bourbon, the creeping foam of a beer so pale it somehow reminded me of lakewater, of cream soda at birthday parties, of how, when we were kids, Trudy and I used to dare each other to cup our hands and drink the shimmer of parking lot puddles. I remembered the taste—the grip against the tongue of these things the earth took and stored—the gravel like dry bread, the brownish and open tang of gasoline somehow stripping your mouth of any knowledge of itself, quieting you. It made me almost homesick, thinking of drinking from those puddles— kneeling next to her and the two of us taking in the weird magic of spill together.

When I thought I'd let enough time pass for the argument to run its course, Bo and I went home. Piecing the streets back together and angling out toward the levee to hear the swish of the barges dividing the water—the cockeyed gleam of that one green eye on the starboard side, and port glowing red across the width of its black bulk.

I tiptoed inside, all the lights out. Bud and Val were already in bed, speaking together in hushed tones with their heads close together on their pillows. I lay down in the wavering stillness of the living room, and tried not to listen.

I don't know what happened to the Ouija board. But I never saw it again, and no one mentioned it afterward.

❖ ❖ ❖

There was a night toward the end of the month that Bud and I sat drinking by ourselves on the levee. The night was straining away from us, out to the center of the river where the current moved swiftest, to touch that quick water where the few visible stars blurred into a swerve of light, like a smashed firefly smeared across skin.

Val had gone to some party with a couple that lived down the street. Bud was looking around him for rocks to throw, holding them in his hand for a moment before releasing them, as if weighing the distance as it built up in his palm.

"You know," he said suddenly, "most times I think she just made the whole thing up—the little girl, I mean."

I waited, but he didn't say anything more, so I said, "Why would she do that?"

He shrugged. "Keeps her company when I'm not there, and gives us something to talk about when I get back. Like, which things she picked up and moved, hair pins and cups and such— which doors she likes open and which she likes closed. She always gives me a full report. I get tired of hearing about it."

He rubbed a hand over his hair, as if weighing himself the same way he did the rocks, as if he were about to pitch himself forward over the water, skimming across before plunging into the darkest span.

"Sometimes I think about leaving for good." He said it fast, tossed a stone, and breathed in deeply, the humid air thick and swelling his chest. "But then," slower now, pausing, "whenever I'm away, I think about her all the time, and I'm just . . . I'm just never really away from her. I mean, I miss her, and I know she's down here missing me, and sometimes that feels good." He shook his head hard, as if trying to get water out of his ears. "Doesn't make a lick of sense," he said.

I said, "It does make sense," and was close in that moment to telling him about Trudy. *"I left a girl back home . . ."* but wasn't even sure that it was true. Trudy had said, "You'll figure out what you want when you're away," and I'd said, "I know what I want now," and she'd smiled sadly and said, "No, Dan, you don't," and that's what Bud was talking about, that figuring it out. It seemed it'd never get any easier.

Bud and I lit cigarettes together, our hands moving to our mouths in parallel, though he switched his cigarette hand-to-hand, as if practicing a slow and clumsy trick. I was remembering Trudy as she was the last time I'd seen her,

or even spoken to her. She was rolling up the window of my truck as if sealing us in, cranking that lever with the same air of purpose and industry that the crew had when they coiled rope, or tightened the tow. It had been my last night at home; my last night before getting folded up into the river and the towboat and its crew like a deck of cards being shuffled. We sat very still in the darkness of her driveway, and she kept her hand on that lever. She didn't look at me; she watched the constellations of dead things on the windshield—the fabric of a severed wing, innards spread like the yellow tail of a comet. She'd said softly and evenly, "Don't you disappear on me now." That was the last thing she said to me, and then she'd opened the door, a little sliver of night slipping back in as she left. I watched her go up the concrete steps into her trailer; the words she left there feeling sharp on the backs of my hands where I gripped the wheel, like a quick rap on the knuckles.

And then, inch by inch, hour by hour, I had disappeared.

Trudy and I had been down by the shore that night, sitting in my truck and drinking and none of it was really unusual except for the fact that I'd be leaving in the morning. She was laughing at something I'd said, the laughter filling and running through her, endless, and I'd felt that I was seeing something that no one on the whole earth had yet seen. No one could see Trudy just then in the cab of my truck, and I'd wanted to hold her like a light in my hands, like the last fireflies glowing underfoot while autumn reached, clumsily, to drown them in frost. Like how, as kids, we'd pinched the fireflies' lights between our fingers so we could smear their glow across our forearms, write our names with their bodies, their light becoming the letters that made up our names, as if we owned light itself.

And I was in that truck, with this girl, this girl whose presence was suddenly like a hunger, like the blank space a star leaves after it drifts loose. *This girl.*

"Well?" she'd said, breaking the silence that had crept in, her eyebrow arced like that same star's movement.

I'd leaned across the gap toward her, bringing her face close, and there was this quick moment when she drew in her breath in fast surprise. It was the first time I'd reached for her. I kissed her then, her head dipping back toward the window, her lips a little stiff but loosening. She was still wearing her seatbelt and I felt it against my chest, this thin barrier between us. I felt her hands there too, a pressure building in her palms, but it was gradual enough for me to ignore, until finally she moved her mouth away from mine and said, "Stop," quietly, and I'd stopped.

I drew away, put my hands back on the steering wheel at ten and two like someone being pulled over for a traffic violation. A great loneliness stirred between us, crickets lisping and the leaves touching against each other, and the night closed in around us.

"I don't want to do this unless it can be for real. I don't want this to happen and then for it to mean nothing afterward."

And then I'd asked her. I don't know how or why but it just happened. "Well, why don't we . . ." I stuttered. "When I get back?"

"Do I get a ring?" she'd asked.

"Of course."

I knew her so well, sifting through all the years of growing up alongside each other, until she became the presence constantly with me, like the tattoo on your own arm, like her name written across me with the blood of fireflies.

"If that's what you really want," she'd said, "then yes."

❖ ❖ ❖

Out on the levee with Bud, I batted the thought of her away as if it were a moth, my hand rising to my mouth to settle the cigarette between my lips. I was looking out into something, some place of water and of fear where voices moved like old men in bars talking to themselves. It was cold on the levee, and I clicked my teeth on the edge of chatter. The nearness of Bud's shoulder was no comfort—seemed like a prop, divorced from body or blood or warmth of any kind. I was very afraid that Bud would speak before I was ready for him to—was even more afraid that he wouldn't speak at all. Trudy's words were still ringing somewhere over the water like a curse: *Don't you disappear*, and I felt somehow faded, distant from my own life.

Her voice was everywhere, and it unraveled me. Bud's voice too still fresh in the air beside me, casting doubt over the little girl's ghost, making her grow dim and break apart like stones dropped in water. I thought of what he

would so soon be leaving behind when we returned to the river: Val moving up and down the length of the apartment while he traveled the river's untiring distances, as if her journey were his in miniature. She'd leave her keys out on the counter as a ritual act, later convinced they had moved, as if Bud could be there to move them, to hush the faucets, to hum low as the dishes clinked against each other in the cupboards like they were also seeking touch—like the noise of our shells finding one another, flesh against flesh. It is all a constant haunting.

I stirred and shifted beside Bud. There had been a long moment of silence between us. I breathed smoke, feeling old, feeling the lateness of the hour as if it could be tasted, filtered through the burning at my lips.

"So you've never felt her at all the way that Val has? Never sensed her presence?"

I wanted the little girl to be real for Val's sake—the mercy of a life dropped into the back and forth of her day-to-day movements through that thin apartment, a tunnel where Bud waited at one end and the ghost made by his absence on the other.

Bud startled at my voice, then shook his head. "I don't think I believe in any of that stuff to tell you the truth."

We are cruel in this—in our doubts—cruel either to ourselves or to those that keep close to us, build proximity with daily patience as if it were a raft that could keep us all from drowning. I had been cruel. I had left, and then tried to erase myself with silence. I had pulled Trudy's hair the only time we'd made love. I don't know what it was that had told me to pull—those long hours of drift between us, wanting to feel something tauten, a line stretching from her to me. And afterward, on the river, I kept thinking of whatever it was that hung tight between us, a long, thin hair straining across the miles, and I kept thinking, "It'll snap. It'll break and then things will get easier," but it hadn't snapped, just kept pulling and pulling. And here it was, still pulling, my hand tightening its grip automatically as if still close to her scalp wanting something to come loose.

When I'd pulled her hair she'd made no sound, had only drawn in a quick breath through her teeth, and there'd been a faint hiss as of a cigarette dropped in water.

"Hey, don't tell Val I said any of this," Bud said.

"Of course not," and I felt we'd made some pact, the smoke from our cigarettes meeting above our heads as if shaking hands.

Back at the apartment, Val had returned from her party. There was a sudden late thunderstorm and the power shut off with a fizzy sort of noise, like the opening of a bottle of champagne. Val lit candles, and we sat around the coffee table as if it were the last time any of us would be doing this. A last time among last times.

The ceiling seemed distant in the darkness of the room, and our voices rang against it as if we were alone inside a cathedral. The candles spread their wax, a loosening of their shape on the coffee table. We pressed our fingers into it. We flaked off bits and put them on our tongues like communion wafers, spitting them out again, with little noises like kissing.

Val sat back among the cushions of the couch, patted the empty seat beside her when Bo passed by, but he only looked at her, wagging his tail, then went to his dog bed in the corner.

"You know," Val said, staring at one of the candlesticks. "I heard that when a candle burns blue it means there's a ghost in the room."

I watched the blue around the wick stretch sleepily, like a mouth opening into a yawn.

"Candles always burn blue," Bud said it gently, not scoffing just stating it plainly, his mouth very straight, a thin line pointing across to the boundaries of his face. "At the center— it's always blue like that," and he pointed, his finger almost indecipherably unsteady. There was just the faintest quiver at the tip, like when you're at the movies and the frame jumps for a brief second and you see the edges around the image and remember where you are.

"Well," Val said with a clear softness, a blur around her voice like the light of stars almost too far away to be seen, a glow perched just on the cusp of being able to reach us. "Well then we must always be in the presence of ghosts."

Bud shook his head, watching the way the light licked her throat, until a flash of lightning made us all look transparent, a thin-skinned blue and white with our shadows suddenly pooling around us like separate patches of flood.

❖   ❖   ❖

Steeplejack

A white gull spins past his left ear, heading
inland from the bay, 1000 feet above Manhattan.

Tethered to his spire, the steeplejack prepares to work
but first looks down. Always, the city steals his breath,

its glass eyes catching fire in the sun.
No wonder Kong pounded his chest.

The steeplejack checks his harness, otherwise
he might follow the gulls into their circles, diving

between steel high-rises or the marble pillars
of a church to perch on a cherub's sooty curls.

He has his back towards Ireland, dungeon
of the North Atlantic, sod his father left,

hollow with hunger, that his son might look,
fast and secure, at the tide still coming.

Doug Ramspeck

Parable of Snow

The mean boys believe in an augury of falling snow,

how it drifts from the shadows of the sky,

burying the land. And what they feel for the ones

they brutalize is a kind of plaintive sorrow,

the way a stream accepts the ice of its own body.

Once I saw one sucking a bloodied knuckle like a succulent

morsel of fruit, saw him leaning against the chain-link

fence and closing his eyes into what appeared, in that instant,

like the suturing of two incisions. The mean boys

are as lonely as a breath struggling to form a cloud

that will not hold, as lonely as the hoof prints of the horses

past my father's barn, where he walks this morning

like the mean boy he surely was when he was young.

R. Brent Malone. *Eve with Serpent*. 1998. Acrylic on canvas. 36 x 32 inches. Courtesy of The Dawn Davies Collection.

Bicycles

It was the time, the year, when my father sat in the carport, pieces of his 85-horse Evinrude scattered around his chair. Gaskets, plugs, bearings, gears, they'd been soaking in coffee cans of gasoline for weeks. The motor bogged at high speed. "It can't be electrical," my father had said when he started. "If it's electrical, I'm a dead man." He'd smiled, showing me that even though my mother had gone to live with someone else, there was lots of life remaining. Now, his half-rotted boat hunkered outside on its rusted trailer near his battered black Ford pickup. At the end of the street and beyond the single-story houses around us, the cloud towers of afternoon storms formed in the West. It was just a South Florida day. Mosquitoes whined in the shadows.

"Hey, Dad." I stood bent against my backpack in the muggy air, looking in at his thin form slung across the chair, his pony tail pointing at the concrete floor. He had a Budweiser in his hand and stared bewildered at the beamed roof.

"I'm taking off."

He sat up and looked at me, then pulled his face together. "Don't be running," he said.

I was so glad to be away. "No problemo."

"You're not supposed to run today."

The air pollution alert was red, going on to purple. There had never been a purple designation before, and we were all traveling slowly into the unknown.

"It's too hot to run," I said and grabbed my bike.

"Ride slow!" he shouted behind me.

The still air was thick, pushing against my face. The nearly identical houses painted in pastels passed one by one in a haze of heat. The entire day had felt strange, as if something were happening just out of sight. I looked around at the low hedges of hibiscus, the oil stains in the driveways. In one house, four children pressed themselves against the plate glass window, silent, their hands above their heads, motionless, staring out. I wondered what it meant.

A few blocks later, the subdivision ended and the land opened up. In the distance to the right stood the white geometric shapes and slants of the American Concrete plant and next to that the Armory. A double line of reservists marched along the chain-link fence, shouldering plugged rifles, their work shirts dark with sweat. I waved, but no one waved back. Beyond them stretched the pines, gray in a haze of heated air. I headed out to the left through the scrub, palmettos and red vines tangled, following the deep parallel gullies of what had once been a fire road.

Alfred met me on the railroad tracks. He was leaning against his fender-less, blue mountain bike and staring down at the gravel between the ties. He'd found an Indian arrowhead there once, and where there was one, he said, there had to be more. His gear sat in a black plastic garbage bag at the top of the berm. The rusted steel rails ran off into the distant pines, curved near the horizon, going out into the rest of the country, everywhere I couldn't go.

"Actually saw a snake," Alfred said. An iPod hung clipped to the waistband of his jeans; the headphones forked at his chin and entered his ears.

I knew he probably hadn't.

"My grandpa said that once there were so many snakes around, cars would skid off the road, driving over them."

"Your grandpa's full of shit."

Alfred smiled, his thin lips pulled back, his pale gray eyes narrowed. He was skeletal, with bony arms jutting from his black tee shirt, knobby wrists dangling down. He cut his brown hair close to his scalp, and I was his only known friend.

"Does sound like a lot of snakes," he said.

We walked our bikes along the tracks until we reached the I-4 overpass. In the cool of the shadowed concrete, thirty or forty Hispanic homeless sat among their bundles on the slanted sand. They watched us quietly as we moved through.

We walked for a mile more, then stumbled down the slope and turned onto a road beaten into the dirt by the gravel trucks. Weeds rose higher on both sides of us. Alfred took off his earphones and hung the cord around his neck. "How's it going?" he asked.

I knew he meant my mother. Alfred lived with his grandfather, an unpleasant, overweight half-bald man. His dad ran off years ago; his mother used meth and simply wasn't around. Alfred read too much pain into my own mother's leaving. "It's no big deal," I said, and yet it was. At nights, though she was gone, I'd swear I could hear her through the walls, and often, as I turned a corner or entered a room, for a second I'd think I saw her, her chunky, friendly body sprawled in a chair or standing in the kitchen.

"Life goes on," Alfred said. His lips stretched into his mocking smile. "The hero struggles against overwhelming odds in a world stacked against him."

"You're an idiot."

"Yes." He smiled and punched me gently in the arm.

We followed the road into a copse of pine and to the edge of the quarry. The concrete company had mined limestone from the spot for a few years, then abandoned it to the rain and the vines. Now, the fractures on the steep sides were rounded and covered in green. At the bottom, a few feet of rich turquoise water, looking rather chemical, reflected the late afternoon sky.

Evening came quickly, a brief burst when the sky flamed red, then purple edging through the trees, deepening to black. My mother had always liked the sunsets in Florida, and I wondered where she was, if she'd seen a lovely sky.

Alfred handed me the Off. "It's worth your life, nowadays," he said, putting on the tragic newscaster voice. Some mosquitoes carried the West Nile virus, some the Zika. Two local people had died. I sprayed my arms, the back of my neck, thinking it wasn't going to help. The breeze alone, rising up from the quarry, was on our side.

We searched for wood, built a fire, roasted hot dogs on sticks. Usually, I liked the isolated feelings, hunched around the burning logs, miles from anywhere, no walls protecting you, but now I heard sounds and imagined the birds in the pines around us, maybe infected with West Nile, dropping one by one from the branches, and it seemed merely spooky.

We ate and washed things down with Gatorade. It grew late, and the mosquitoes stayed away. We were silent for a while, staring at the flames.

Then Alfred opened his pants and pulled out his penis.

"Don't do that," I said, thinking he was going to pee on the fire.

"Let me show you something." Alfred looked up at me, smiling, his eyes large, dark and luminous. I knew right away I didn't want to see this. He took out his cell phone. On the screen was a picture of a young, dark-haired girl. She was cute, pert, reclining on a bed, staring at the camera. She was naked, her arms and legs open. The picture was grainy. At the edges, I could see the chassis of Alfred's computer monitor.

He rubbed, and his penis thickened and extended. "My grandfather showed me how."

I didn't understand then. Later, I couldn't get the image out of my mind, his grandfather with his hand on his crotch, doing the inexplicable.

Alfred's hand moved faster and then faster. "Look," he said, his voice sounding strangled. "Look at this."

I stared down. He groaned and something white like pus came out and fell to the ground, and I thought at first he had hurt himself, that some inside tubing had collapsed, vessels had ruptured.

"It feels really good." Alfred wiped himself with a leaf. "Try it."

I saw no reason to do any such thing. Inside, I was backing away. It was as if I no longer knew the human body, couldn't predict what might happen next. "No thanks," I said.

Alfred replaced himself and started talking about other things and, of course, three days later I tried it myself. My dad was at work; it was late afternoon. I stared at the blue bathroom tile and felt something open I hadn't known was closed. It wasn't at all pleasurable, but even so, somehow compelling. Two hours later, as if in a trance, I did it again.

Time shifted, and the world grew strange. I suddenly noticed my breasts were growing. They jutted out, and I had no idea when they would stop. I imagined myself a girlie boy, wearing bras and ridiculed. I grew restless and found myself late at night in darkened rooms pressed against windows, staring at the neighbors' lights. I could be out there, I knew. In the night, and the wind. There was nothing at all stopping me. Two days later, I went.

My dad was out on a date. He didn't call it that. He said he was going to meet up with a friend, but it was pretty obvious from his new sports shoes, his Hawaiian shirt and the red scrunchy holding his pony tail what kind of a friend he was meeting.

"You'll be okay, won't you?" he asked.

Everyone was asking me that.

"I won't be late," he said, his concerned, parental face on.

"Sure," I said. His expression changed, making him seem younger, happier. I was depressed as hell.

I watched the cartoon channel for a while, then turned off the TV. The rooms were empty. The house didn't feel like mine. The bedroom where my mother had slept seemed strangest of all, and I realized the powder smell had gone, replaced by something sour. Two pizza boxes lay on the floor by the unmade bed. The coverlet hung unused over the frame. My mother's pictures still hung on the walls, grouped flowers, a small girl in an eighteenth century dress holding a water pitcher. Apparently, my mother thought these things unimportant. I suspected my father never noticed them.

I searched through the closets. There were secrets there, I knew. Everyone had secrets, private thoughts they never shared until it was too late. I found the condoms in the bedside table. At first, I had no idea what they were. When I read the packaging, the plastic coins lay like weights in my hand. I took one, just in case.

I'd had no warning when my mother left. A short goodbye was all it took. My dad was inside sitting on the couch, watching evening TV, while I stood in my pajamas in the front yard. Her new boyfriend, Robert, sat waiting in his Lexus. Her suitcases were already in his trunk.

"Sweetie," my mom said. Her face twisted. The green eyes were wrong, her red mouth pinched.

"You'll be okay?"

"Sure." What else was there to say?

She leaned forward, gave me a quick hug, a kiss on my left eyebrow, then ran to the car and bumped her head getting in. Robert looked at me once, and I saw myself through his eyes, a sad skinny boy standing in pajamas too young for his age, a comical figure. Then, he calmly drove to the end of the street, stopped at the sign, turned left, and vanished behind a house.

If I'd had a rock, I thought later, a brick, a tire iron. I imagined what I might do.

Now, the condom was in my pocket, and I was, for some reason, running out the door. It was dark. A mist fell and drew bright cones beneath the streetlights. I was on my bike, with only the silent passing houses and the wind in my mind. I fled through the streets, just going, not knowing where, not caring.

I stopped at the Expressway and the cross of Christ, 120 feet of proclamation visible to passing motorists. I'd heard that underneath the white plastic sheathing was a cellphone tower, messages swooping in and out, helping some church pay the bills. I caught my breath. The damp clung to my face and arms, and then I heard the sound of wings. At first, it was a rush, or a rustle, nearly a buzzing, a sound I couldn't place. I looked up at the red light at the top of the cross pulsing in clouds of color. Then the birds appeared like dark arrows through the light.

One flew past my face and smashed into the dirt beside me. Its body lay flattened, still, and I thought for a moment it had aimed for me and missed. I didn't wonder why. If I were a bird, I might have done the same. Then the second came and fell yards away. A third landed on the concrete curb and bounced and shook a few seconds. Then they were everywhere and the sound of their bodies landing was a drumbeat, nearly constant. I covered my head and screamed as they hit my back, my legs. The air in front of me filled with frantic wings and the collisions of birds.

I learned much later that they sometimes cannot fly through a red-lighted mist. They become confused and directionless, often driving full speed into the earth, but all I knew then was that the sky, too, was hostile, and that no one could hear me screaming.

A week later, I was at Alfred's, telling him all about it. We were in his room, sitting on the bed. He had hung model planes, boats, rocks, glassware, dried flowers, old lunch boxes, board games, baseball gloves on strings fastened to the ceiling. They hung at various heights, filled up all the available space, and walking into his room was like pushing your way through a forest of junk, dense, nearly impenetrable.

"What the hell are you doing with all this?" I asked the first time I'd visited.

"Doing?"

I told him about the birds slamming into me, dying. Just above our heads were two high-heeled shoes, a pair of white panties, a Playboy foldout, a model destroyer painted Navy gray, and a length of clear plastic tubing. I showed him a bruise on my back.

"West Nile Virus," Alfred said.

I imagined the sickness spreading, birds dropping everywhere.

"How cool is that?" Alfred asked.

We got up and booted his computer and surfed for porn for a while. It was amazing what you could find, but by now I'd grown used to my guts tightening, the ache spreading. We watched for an hour or so, then his grandfather walked in, ducking and weaving around the hanging junk. He wore slacks and a long-sleeved shirt, but he had brown patches on his scalp, on his hands, and it looked like his skin was camouflaged, like he was about to do serious battle. He kissed Alfred on the cheek, and it seemed tender and sweet, for an old guy.

"I'm going to bed now," he said.

Alfred grabbed his hand and they walked out of the room together, and I just sat there, wondering, what the hell? I knew I could never ask.

Twenty minutes later, we were on our bikes and heading out. The night was clear and warm, and a few stars fought their way through the city's lights. We sped past the darkened trees, the shrouded hedges. I was riding just to be out, but Alfred was leading the way, cutting ahead, pointing with one hand or the other as we approached the turns. The houses grew taller, further back from the road.

"Where the hell are we going?" I shouted at last.

Alfred braked and jutted his arm out to stop me. "Shish," he hissed.

"What do you mean, shish?"

Alfred smiled. "I haven't done this in a while."

"Done what?"

Alfred didn't answer, but walked his bike onto the sidewalk and through an archway. We entered a small park connected to a private hospital. In the near distance, the scattered lights of the cancer wards appeared and disappeared behind the screen of trees, but where we were was dark, shadowed. The grass lay pale gray stretching beneath the banyans to the lake. During the day, I had seen a green statue of Apollo at the lake's center. Otherwise, the park had nothing—just trees, grass, and a lake with a statue.

"What are we doing?" I asked quietly.

"You can find them if you look," Alfred whispered.

We set our bikes down and continued into the park. I wasn't sure what we were searching for. Branches and leaves hung dark over our heads, and the air moved in whispers. Then I saw a light behind a screen of bushes, a glow, really. We crouched lower and crept off to one side, near a gravel walkway, and I realized I was looking at a campground. There was a tent, several, made out of some sort of cloth, and a lantern inside one of them. Dark shapes sat in clusters in front. A baby whined.

"Illegals," Alfred said.

I was thinking, Homeless.

We watched them for a moment. In the silence, between the sounds of frogs and crickets and distant cars passing by, I heard the quiet voices, male, Hispanic, sounding like the creatures, like the wind.

"Watch this," Alfred said, and threw a rock. Nothing happened. "Try it," he whispered.

"Are you crazy?" I imagined the men rising up, animals prodded from a cave.

Alfred threw another stone and the talking stopped.

Oh, God, I thought.

He threw another and another and suddenly the dark shapes leapt into violent motion. The lantern flashed silhouettes, then went black. A child cried. Women questioned plaintively. The night squirmed and roiled. It was horrible. It was wonderful.

"You can pretty much run them wherever you want." Alfred looked at me. "Come on."

I grabbed a handful of rocks and stood, trying for distance. Some, I'm sure, landed among them as they ran. I heard screams, howls. "Damn!" I shouted and punched Alfred in the arm.

"Hey!" he said.

I hit him again, not knowing why. He jumped at me, and we fell to the earth. I smashed him, and again, and again. His face seemed pale, astonished. Blood ran dark across his lips.

I sat on his stomach, while the night was loud around me. Why was I with this guy? I wondered. Didn't I have any better friends?

I stood and walked to my bike, mounted and rode away. Behind me, I heard Alfred scrambling to his feet. "What the hell?" he shouted. "I mean, what the hell?"

After a few minutes, he was riding beside me again.

"Where we goin'?" he asked.

"I'm going home."

He was silent for a few minutes. "Good idea," he said, finally. "My grandpa doesn't like me to stay out too late."

It seemed already too late.

His house was on my way, so we rode silently through the night, ghosting back past darkened houses, the somnolent lives in their curtained boxes. I felt stiff, monumental, as if time inside had stopped.

"Some night, huh?" Alfred said after a while. He slapped a passing mailbox with his hand, rocking it on its post. "My Grandpa says we only live once."

I pedaled faster.

"He says the only important thing is who you're spending your time with."

I'd had enough. I listened, but didn't comment, and eventually he fell silent again.

We both stopped at his house. He propped his bike on its kickstand near the garage, then looked at me. "Later," he said.

"Sure."

"I don't know if I pissed you off . . ." He waited.

I didn't know, either. I didn't understand a thing.

"My Grandpa's probably not sleeping. He can never really get to sleep unless he knows I'm okay."

"Sure," I said, feeling sad for us both and not knowing why.

"Gotta go," Alfred said.

When I got home, I wheeled my bike into the carport, past the cans of engine parts soaking in gasoline, my father's customary outdoor chair, and let myself into the house. "Dad," I called, but I already knew he wasn't home, yet. Maybe wasn't coming home that night.

"Well, shit!" I shouted, and kept shouting it for a while, as I wandered from space to space, until I was back again in my bedroom. There was my bed, with the black and green blanket my mother thought I would like, the hanging shelves on the walls loaded with fossils I had collected, models I had assembled, all of it ne-

glected. Nothing there. Without knowing why, without thinking, I punched a hole in the plaster. My knuckles bled, but there was this hole and lathing splintered and, beyond that, dark hollowness. How totally cool, I thought.

Two weeks later, my mother came back to stay.

I was lying in bed, staring at the TV on the shelf, watching the news as the reservists shipped out for maneuvers. Their eyes were wide, their faces blank. Then she simply walked into my room and stood near the door. "I'm back." Her hair was cut now in bangs over wide, expectant eyes, and for a moment she was just a woman in a short skirt and a tight black top.

Still, she waited. "Aren't you going to give me a hug?"

Here, I thought I'd been missing her. Now, I wasn't sure I wanted her in the house. "How's your boyfriend?"

She tightened her eyes, becoming more the mother I knew. "I'm with your father, now. We've had a talk. We've reached an understanding. Besides, it's none of your damned business."

I thought it might be.

"Aren't you going to give me a hug?"

I swung off the bed and walked over and put my arms around her. I felt hers tight across my back.

"You've grown."

"You've been gone."

"And you've changed."

Nothing stays the same, I thought.

She held me at arm's distance and we stood there for a few minutes. I noticed her eyes were larger, bleary, swimming in fluid, and I wondered what she was thinking. She was like someone I had met long ago, or had never met at all. "Welcome back," I said.

She hung around for another six months, then left again. So how strange is it, how bizarre, that a few minutes ago my father walked up to me in the dining room, where I had my homework spread out on the table? He sat across from me and was silent for a moment. His fingers pushed my analytic geometry text away.

"It wasn't my fault," he said.

I set my pencil down. "What wasn't?"

"Your mom."

I thought a moment. "Okay."

"I just wanted you to know. I didn't want you to hate me."

"No problemo," I said, and looked at the man, his bemused expression, his kind sad eyes, and I spoke the words I knew he wanted to hear. "You're all I've got left," I said. "What would I do without you?" They sounded sadder than I intended.

"Cool," he said, then pushed himself up, and walked slowly out of the room.

❖ ❖ ❖

Robert Rothman

Skunk Drunk

Not on liquor, that weak moonshine, but drawn out
by the thick-furred night silking through the walls
and porous glass, diurnal eyes purblind

as felines at birth, feeling into the dark
strangeness, past the human habitations, beyond
streetlamps, sidewalks, concrete, the familiar dropping

away like a name that suddenly has nothing
to do with you, into an open, a rounded
glass of field where all is seen, the stars

far off and indifferent, you feral and wild
dancing, sleek and supple-bodied, black
magic coursing, with a stripe of moonlight on your back.

Thomas Reiter

Pinned in Place

A bed sheet hung out to dry
became a screen for shadow animals.
But of all laundry days in the neighborhood
the windy ones were best,
the clothespins like little men riding
lines that tried to buck them off.
One at a time we ran down the aisles
between snapping sheets
that wanted to put us in our place.
Timing them, you faked and cut
like famous halfbacks. But if a sheet
tagged you it put you down, pinned
by the whiteness floating
against a sky washed by the bluing
our mothers added to the wash water.
Could anyone make it through those days
untouched? You waited for
your chance, then jumped up and finished
the course, rising if you fell again.
Later, let the sky darken suddenly
and we'd be sent out to empty the lines.
All up and down the block, kids
running with bed sheets in their arms,
running like firemen rescuing children.
All night those sheets lay draped
over furniture, as though we were leaving
and would not return for a long time.

Balsa

On a beach in the Leeward Islands,
this loaf-shaped remnant of a balsa limb
from which the sun has drawn out
the last of the Caribbean Sea.
Without such driftage as this
what would the waves bring to term?
Here comes a boy, thirteen, pulling a wagon
along the tide wrack and gathering
the reef's antlers, castles, and stars.
He hammers that coral till it's powder
he and his grandmother bag
then take by donkey cart to sell.
It goes into mortar for monuments
in Independence Square,
no distance at all from Pinchtown
where he lives with her in a house
he built with the leavings
of last year's hurricane: its frame
mahogany limbs from the tide wrack;
the walls tin signs for soft drinks,
lottery tickets, petrol; the roof sailcloth.
Far from here, airworthy trees
with their absence of annual rings
become kits of scale-model
fighter planes. Suspended above
where a boy lies sleeping, his Flying Tiger
dives out of the sun at a Zero.
Here a boy working the tide wrack
picks up a piece of driftwood
he has no name for, such lightness
as he's never been given to imagine.
The trade wind at his back,
he lofts that balsa into the sea.

Paige Sullivan

The Street of Beautiful Homes

My mother used to warn me that strange men
lurked in the woods, waiting for children to snatch,
and that a ponytail was made for clutching.
But on a street of beautiful homes, it's hard to worry
when lamps glow still and orange in the windows
and you believe in the steeple's point above the trees
even if you don't believe in the altar beneath it.
Standing in my running shorts and sneakers,
I could think of worse things to want than this.
Call it the longing of someone who wants what feels
out of reach, call it the musing of someone who catalogs
rooms in which each thing has a place and rests there,
who watches untrimmed hedges short-circuit with fireflies.
Forgive me for mentioning the fireflies, for any talk of light.

Bill Christophersen

July

Summer shimmies in: cerulean skies;
greenery whose color's meant to last
(unlike April's lime); the silver cast
to the morning light; cobalt dragonflies
patrolling tracts of soporific grass
or treading water in the humid air;
the kids, just shut of school, with time to spare—
eyes glazed, thoughts encased in frosted glass.
Month of torrid afternoons, sweet
protracted dusks and the unexpected rush
of neon plumage darting from a bush—
an indigo bunting knifing through the heat
vectors, sudden as a high-school crush,
then gone the way it came: in a tripped heartbeat.

Antonius Roberts. *Emerging from the Shadows.* 2007. Acrylic on canvas. 46 x 28 inches. Courtesy of The Dawn Davies Collection

Adam Sullivan

In the Shadow of Greatness

doorbell announced my presence in the specialty bike store with a chime, but other than that nobody seemed to notice. I'd just come from a job interview, so I was the only person with buttons on my clothes. The rest of the staff and clientele had poured their taut, tanned bodies into Lycra and Spandex. I was out of place, even while subconsciously sucking in my stomach.

""Hello," I said, and after a moment the lean, bronzed clerk looked up. "I'm here to pick up a bike."

He made his way over to a binder, and flipped through a dozen invoices. "What's the name?"

"Sullivan," I said. "Michael Sullivan. It's for the triathlon tomorrow," I said. He looked me up and down.

"It's for my cousin," I said. At this, he smiled, the way you do when your assumption turns out to be correct.

"Yeah, here it is," he said. "Mike."

What threw me was the air of entitlement. True, he knew more about cycling than I did, but then again he worked in the Goddamn store, so of course he did. Also I didn't care, so I hoped that leveled the playing field.

Cycling is immensely popular in San Diego. Mountain bikes, road bikes, fixed-gears and BMXs were omnipresent, dotting every bike lane, off-road trail, and Subaru in the county, but I'd managed so far to avoid the bug. I owned a bicycle, understood how to put air into the tires, and could pop an occasional wheelie, but that's where the relationship ended.

When he brought the bike around, it was sleek and intimidating, and it weighed no more than a carne asada burrito. "What kind of pedals do you need?" The question surprised me. I'd wrongly assumed that, along with a chain and seat, bicycle pedals were considered fairly standard components, rather than aftermarket options.

"Foot pedals?"

He wasn't amused. *Well, what the hell do you*

expect? I wanted to say. *We've already established that it's not for me.* Instead I just shrugged.

"Well, are they Shimanos? Forte? Are they Speed Play? Garfunkels? Velociraptors?" At this point I think he was actually trying to be helpful, but after he rattled off the fifth name, they stopped sounding like actual words. I shrugged again. "Can't you call your cousin?"

I couldn't, though. He was on an airplane. He was much busier than I was. That's why I was picking up the bicycle.

He sighed, as though this were all part of some master plan to make his life more difficult. To his credit, the guy eventually gave me a bag with three different types of pedals, and a stern lecture about preparation. He actually started to soften and sympathize with me, until I broke his heart by cramming the bicycle, unceremoniously, into the trunk of my Civic.

Mike was in town for less than twenty-four hours, so I'd offered to put him up. He was flying into San Diego to do a triathlon, a race that consisted of unnatural amounts of swimming, cycling, and running. He arrived after midnight, and we caught up for a while in the garage, as he tuned up his bicycle and prepared four separate water bottles, each with its own energy-enhancing concoction. He tried to explain the difference between a road bike and a time trial bike, but it was late, and I was drunk and having a difficult time feigning interest.

The next morning, we were out the door by 4:10 a.m.. The sky was dark and Mike ate his organic oatmeal from a Tupperware he'd brought with him. We made the forty-mile drive in record time, but even so, Mission Bay was already crowded by the time we got there, and we had to park a mile and a half away. Mike wanted to loosen up, so he clicked his bike shoes into his pedals (Shimanos), and started off toward the event. I locked up the car, shouldered my backpack, and began the long hike over the bay bridge.

When I reached the apex of the bridge a

half-hour later, the sun was coming up, and I could make out a sort of shantytown. This was the transitions area, where hundreds of half-dressed athletes buzzed around temporary stations like protein-drinking mosquitos. Men and women of all ages nested in their assigned plots, hanging their bicycles and preparing their shoes for a quick change as soon as they came plodding out of the water. Mike was running an Olympic triathlon, which began with a 1-mile swim, followed by a short twenty-five-mile bicycle ride, and ending with a six-mile jaunt around the bay.

When I got to the end of the bridge, I stopped to catch my breath. Finding my cousin in the hive of activity would be impossible, so I just called his cell. "Hey!" He sounded surprised to hear from me. "Where are you? Where are you at right now, like exactly now?"

We met up by a large palm tree. Since I'd last seen him, he'd gotten significantly more nervous.

"What's wrong with you?"

"Who, me? Nothing. Why? What do you mean?"

"Well, for starters, you're talking like a crackhead."

"Hey, what size shoe do you wear?"

I told him that I was a nine.

"Okay, cool. Cool. Cool. Hey – can I try one on?"

I realized that the look on his face—the stammering, the preoccupation—wasn't pre-race jitters. It was full-fledged panic. He held my sneaker up to his bare foot; it was at least two sizes too small.

"Yeah, I think this might work."

"Mike? Where are your running shoes?"

A pause. "I left them at home."

My first instinct was to laugh, but he was already sweating and probably wouldn't have a sense of humor about it. "You left them in San Francisco?" This, from a man who packed his own meals, as though oatmeal were a rare and exotic dish that would be impossible to find in San Diego.

It didn't matter, he couldn't even hear me. He was in the depths of a full-blown panic attack, underwater before the race even began. His eyes darted back and forth, searching the shore for palm fronds or scraps of discarded tire to wrap around his feet. "I left them in my suitcase."

I opened my mouth to speak, but he continued: "I could run it barefoot."

There was an unrelenting determination in his eye—I really thought he would run it barefoot, and I was tempted to let him.

"Mike—you're going to the airport right after this."

A blank stare.

"Your suitcase is in the car."

Still nothing. I savored the moment.

"Your shoes are in the suitcase. In the car."

The look on his face was that of a person who has just been pulled from a burning building. It's not often that you get to witness that precise moment, even rarer still that you get to take credit for its creation. For a moment, I began to see why people better than myself spend their lives helping others. I was heroic. I brought salvation.

But just as the relief swept over his face, fear washed over mine. I looked at his feet: bare. Then, to mine: comfortable running shoes. I said what we were both thinking. "transitions is closing."

He nodded. I sighed. "How long do I have?"

He looked at his watch. "Twenty-two minutes."

The trouble with the hero business is that, from time to time, it requires a little more than just words. Real heroism requires actual effort, and I remembered why I so rarely get to see that look of elation. I handed him my backpack and started to run. My muscles, fueled only by coffee and beer, cramped up immediately.

Running a mile and a half in twenty-two minutes is a walk in the park for the kind of person who prefers it to walking in the park, but my entire body protested, revolted, and ultimately called for a strike. By the time I reached the car my lungs were on fire, and beads of sweat coated my glasses, giving everything a hazy, dreamlike patina. I grabbed the shoes, allowed myself thirty seconds to gasp like a beached carp, and pushed off the car, back toward race.

I made it back with less than a minute to spare, lobbed the sneakers over the fence, and fell down. I wanted to say "Good luck," but no words would come out. He squeaked over to the shore in his wetsuit like a jittery penguin, and when the buzzer rang out I watched them all scramble into the water, 150 grown men frantically flippering toward the shore, off to dodge dolphins, buoys, and kelp.

I was worried that I wouldn't be able to spot him, but Mike had what he considered to be a fool-proof plan. "I'll be in the red swimming cap," he told me. What he didn't tell me was that although he did have a red cap, so did 150 other people. Each wave of triathletes was identified by cap color, and everyone in Mike's group had exactly the same uniform: black wetsuit, goggles, red cap.

Several minutes later, I watched the red caps clamber out of the water, up onto the beach, jogging through an oversized inflatable donut to get their bicycles. With eyes and hair off the table, everyone looked exactly the same. I felt guilty I couldn't spot him, but how often are you called upon to identify a person by their gait? Certainly some people have telltale affectations, but I'd never seen my cousin storm a beach before.

Watching everyone overcome the swimming challenge inspired equal amounts of admiration and shame. These weren't professional athletes, just regular schmucks like me. Pro athletes were paid, handsomely, to be excellent. These people were not. Here they were, hundreds of people, up at the crack of dawn, ready to test their endurance and physical limitations—voluntarily. They did it not for money; they did it because they wanted to, and that made their journey all the sweeter. But the more people that climbed out of the water, only to bound up the beach—not stopping for a cigarette, a snack, or even just to vomit in the sand—the more I felt a spotlight shining even brighter on myself.

Standing in the same spot for fifteen minutes makes it difficult to sustain one's awe. For the first few minutes it's interesting, but it quickly gives way to tear-inducing boredom. As a spectator, you're forced to stand there, a captive, waiting for that one person you know, that one in a thousand. While you're waiting, there's little to do besides second-guess life decisions you've made. Namely, getting up at 4 a.m. to feel shitty about yourself. I distracted myself by cheering for other people. "You'll probably live to be a hundred!" I'd yell. "That looks like an expensive watch!"

Finally, I got to see someone fall. His red cap popped out of the wake, and he struggled to stand. This rare display of weakness briefly pleased me, as it validated my own sense of failure. *Good*, I thought, until I realized that he couldn't get to his feet because he had none. He swam the whole thing with only his arms, and still managed to come out of the water before most of the others. On the shore, a woman was waiting with what looked like two jai alai cestas. The man quickly toweled off his legs, stuck his stumps into the prostheses, and bounded up the beach like a kangaroo.

Once the last of the red caps had made it to shore, I accepted the fact that I had officially missed my cousin. He had run right past me, so close I could have slapped him, but instead, I was encouraging the guy next to him, telling him how he needn't worry about heart disease, or varicose veins.

Walking back through the crowd, I began to notice the legless man wasn't the only amputee at the event. In fact, dozens of arm- and leg-less men and women were participating. It was as though they took the shit hand life had dealt them and doubled down, racing in spite of their disadvantage. I found myself jealous that they had something to prove.

The cycling was 40k, which was two 20k laps up and down Mission Bay Blvd. And because I'd missed Mike coming out of the water, I'd also missed him in transition, and so had no idea what color his helmet or jersey was. The cyclists would zip past at 20 m.p.h., so I had even less of an opportunity to identify him. I smartly took a piece of the wall just before the turnaround, to catch the cyclists as they slowed. I figured, if I caught him going one way, I could be ready to cheer for him once he made the loop. I took my place on the wall, and mentally awarded myself first place for good ideas.

I wedged myself in between families against a police barricade, and staved off boredom by coming up with a cheer that would make everyone else's pale in comparison. Most of the time you'd hear the generic "Go!" or the slightly more personalized, "You got this!" But I wanted mine to stand out. The woman on my right found her husband and bellowed: "I love you, Daniel!" Which was good, but I knew I could come up with something better. However, time was running out, and I was giving myself whiplash trying to find him as the bicycles zipped past. The pressure mounted when the family on my left brought out signs that read: "Buen Suerte Hector" and "Rapido!"

Mike was much faster than I had calculated

in my mind, and so as he came into view, I let out an awkward holler that sounded like, "Yay-eeeee-ooooo!" The entire process took five seconds, and still I flubbed it.

To make up for it, I ran to the Transitions area to cheer him on as he changed into his running shoes. This was decidedly less action-packed than the cycling or the swimming, and no one else seemed to be showing this degree of support. I imagined other spectators taking notice. "Now that's dedication," they'd murmur. Other athletes, too, would see me and then turn disappointedly to their own bare-minimum families, with their Venti iced coffees and half-hearted hoo-rahs.

Without so much as a pause, Mike threw me a smile and was off to the final leg of his journey.

To accomplish any one of these events in a given day is impressive; to do all three back-to-back is nothing less than extraordinary. What's more, he was having fun.

Perpetuating this fun was a small army of enthusiastic coeds in turquoise jerseys. Their job was to hand out water at aid stations, and in their free time, holler compliments at people they've never met – cat-calling like construction workers in sneakers.

"You guys are sooo amazing!" "You're the best!" I don't say things like that to my own friends and family, so coming from a total stranger it tends to come off as cloying and desperate. After all, any one of these people could be a bank robber or an identity thief; they just happened to be wearing a racing jersey.

There's nothing wrong with a little encouragement, but enthusiasm wears thin, leaving only an undercurrent of supplanted inferiority. Yell "You can do it!" long enough, and eventually all you hear is, "I can't do it!"

After high-fiving him on the first lap, I raced around to the finish line, determined to get a good photo. It was strangely anti-climactic. There were only a few people there—reporters for the local papers, volunteers to hang medals around the athletes' necks, and me. There were no throngs of devoted fans, and again I chalked it up to being a better spectator.

Once he crossed the line, we walked together to an area cordoned off for the athletes. We stood in silence for a while, and I spotted familiar faces. Double amputee guy was eating a banana. The douchebag from the bike shop was nursing a cup of Gatorade. Five hundred dehydrated triathletes, and me. We sat in silence—he drenched with sweat, me wrapped in a sweatshirt, both hearts pounding in our chests.

"So, what did you think?" he asked

"Oh, it was great. Really impressive."

"I get so inspired at these things."

"Yeah, I can see why."

"How about you?"

"Hmm? Oh, yeah. Totally inspired."

"Really?"

"Yeah, really."

"Because there's another race coming up in a couple months . . . "

And in that moment, everything changed. That's how it always happens. Showing your support is dangerously close to showing interest. I'd painted myself into a corner, and very soon I would have to start coming up with excuses for why I hadn't yet bought spandex. What he failed to understand was that, more than a running partner, he needed me as a spectator. I wanted to tell him to open his eyes. That I was the other people, the squires, the ones who bring you your protein drinks and gym shoes.

Instead I said nothing, completing the final hurdle in my own personal gauntlet. Protecting him from the awful truth: that my mediocrity is the very thing that makes him great. I am the control group. The cautionary tale. The "before" photo. I'm the very reason you exist. Without me, you're no different from every other triathlete. Sure, the money you raise by racing may cure cancer, and running may give you the calves of a Greek god, but you can't do it alone. I help you help others. I make you make a difference. You can run for the finish line, but I'm already there, showing off my enduring patience, my rock-solid self-esteem, my devotion, ready to meet you for Gatorade, and bananas, and glory.

❖ ❖ ❖

In the Park

The bonsai trees pose behind the glass
like little girls wearing too much makeup
or old women dressed like children.
Their leaves and spring blossoms
are too large for their branches, disproportionate
their slim trunks gouged and twisted
with memories of inflicted droughts, near-fatal cuts.

The man in charge of the display whispers to the trees
as he works them over with the shears, tells them they're pretty
as he keeps them from growing up. Roots, thick and sinuous,
quietly search for a way out beneath the display
of dry moss and gravel, tap against the glass at night
tell stories so slow they take decades to end.

Blueberry Picking

We choose the ones that seem to pulse
heavy-ripe from hours in full sun,
stretch the fabric of t-shirts taut—
a hammock for collection. Bellies full
of fried scallops, ice cream,

constellations of fresh freckles on our faces.
We know nothing of loss.
Vaguely keeping watch, our aunts
and uncles park in lawn chairs on the porch,
filling glasses with fresh ice, tonic and gin,

overpriced limes from out of town.
We're not allowed to swim to the dock alone,
we need life jackets and bums on seats
when we take out the canoe. Lily's last summer
she'd just turned ten, Aunt Nessa let her

paint her nails bright pink at the lake.
The grown-ups remain hushed
and focused, like they're trying to remember
stage directions. Last time we saw fireworks,
I said they made me think of Lily,

mom's eyes met mine sharp and silent.
Only once I tried to ask what happened—
she studied the horizon. *We move forward.*
It's the only direction God gave us.

Ellen Doré Watson

Mother Going Gone

Year after year you keep on being gone, gone
after years and years of gone, of marginal, mute,
vacant, of breathing, and then, within minutes, a shy
descent, some huffs and stutters, and a hushing
to waxen, no, to stone-gone, finally unloosed
(to our tired, to our relief) to revisit us—gleeful,
earnest, jigging *you*, who I've worn on my left pinky,
on my worn face, all through the fading, the warm
forgettable grief, the still water of it, until my own
tides' tugging, morning's horror-mirror, rude singleton-
time, its skeletal, long view of the hurtling, the way
the body speaks of it, first one syllable then two, and you
still gone, and him here, ancient, healthy, walls of all-
he-is inching inward, leaving him small and dawdling.

John Cox. *Untitled (Young Boy)*. 1995. Acrylic and silkscreen on paper. 41.5 x 29.5 inches. Courtesy of The Dawn Davies Collection.

The Teenager

Something felt unclean to the teenage boy. It was the lack of separation between days, the same jeans that carried him onward. He took a bar of Irish Spring to his mouth, scrubbed at the red wine stain, a thread between his inner and outer lips. The Florida sun rose, canvasing the previous sleepless night. All the people in their box houses were waking up in air-conditioned rooms. He inspected his teeth at different angles in the medicine cabinet mirror, catching fragments of the girl moving in the bedroom behind him.

Everyone in the neighborhood grew up Catholic, and whether they were confirmed or went absent in the presence of God, they held that essence inside. The boy lived in the current of sin and penitence. His mother owned a construction business. He didn't know exactly what his father did, but it involved the word "sales" and no one seemed to mind that it required for him to be away for weeks at a time. His father always flew first-class and talked of *stewardesses* and *football stadiums* whenever he returned home. The teenage boy lived unchaperoned, preferring to find guidance in his one friend. The teenage girl wore too much eyeliner and made decisions for them both. They were of the same stock. They got each other, and it's this understanding that propelled such grief between them. This existence of credit card and gated community allowed him to feel violenced as they moved back into the inebriated day.

"Are you almost done? I need to do my hair," the girl said into the reflection. He combed his hair with his fingernails around the plastic frame of sunglasses.

"Yes," he said.

"I didn't do my biology homework," she said.

"You'll find time," the boy said.

❖ ❖ ❖

The girl lived in a house covered in coquina shells—a sterile, coastline castle that her mother won in a settlement. Her father was from Cuba, owned a tile company. Her mother slept a lot. When she was awake she moved through the house as if her body were made of syrup—ignoring her daughter's empty wine bottles as she made the way to the fridge for some cold-pressed juice.

There were tiny straws scattered on the glass coffee table. The boy scooped them into his jacket pocket and thought about extinct animals, although he wasn't sure why. He was zombied and fogged by sleeplessness. The dodo was the only one he was sure of, and maybe a carrier pigeon or something that looked like a zebra. Its name was hidden in a place he could not access at the moment, despite the intrusive thoughts. He felt that if he rubbed his tongue along the roof of his mouth long enough, at least one of these elusive insights would return. The girl tried to put her hands in the boy's pocket and he swatted her away. She shuffled around in a small black make-up bag, stained with light powders and red blotches of something. She pulled out a smaller white bag. She pulled out a ring of keys saying, "I bought it, so I can do it when I want."

One of her key chains was half of a metallic heart with the word *BEST* on it. The boy possessed the other half, which read *FRIENDS*. She gave the boy this piece of tchotchke as a sign of ownership rather than sentimentality. He kept his half in a pocket in his backpack with Wite-Out and a half-eaten pack of Lance sandwich crackers. There was something mathematical to the girl's actions, the way everything had a purpose, the way her hands moved in the air like an invisible audience was always watching. She dipped her car key into the white bag. The crystal flakes refracted light. "Meet my good friend Bumper McKey," she said to no one. The powder disappeared. She repeated the steps—replacing her face with the boy's. He rubbed his tongue around his mouth and thought, "Vanishments. Tasmanian wolves. Somnambulisms. Nice to meet you, Bumper McKey."

"Wait here," she said, "I need to wake Mom up and get lunch money."
"Is she awake?" he asked.
"I don't know," she said.
"Will you eat lunch?" he asked.
"I don't know," she said, walking away.

He put on chapstick and wore his sunglasses and could taste the bitter herb dripping in the back of his throat, mixing with old tannins. He loved the directions, the instructions, the way the girl ordered him and provided movement. Static electricity galloped in the back of his throat. He thought of the Virgin Mary, tried to remember her prayer in Latin. The girl came back through the door. She slipped the bag of powder into his jacket pocket saying, "If it's on me I'll do it all before we get to school," in a voice that he found untrustworthy yet agreeable.

❖ ❖ ❖

On the interstate, there was a powerful clarity in the upper hemisphere of the boy's body. There was that thought surfacing again: the extension between one day and the other being severed and the breadth between virtue and hubris becoming blurred. Day, night, everything felt controllable and protected. Intense recall—those extinct zebras—they were called quaggas. He sang words in his head until they annoyed him. The music on the radio reminded him of light bulbs dropped against a linoleum floor. He desired to listen to only one song, but did not know its title or lyrics, only a little bit of the melody. The boy felt like a chauffeur, felt like he was always driving someone around, although he didn't have a license. Legalities felt optional.

The girl had a notebook in her lap and didn't pick up her pen between words. She tried to miss as many classes as possible, but homework somehow felt necessary and guilt-inducing, which might have been the Catholic in her too. The boy saw a sign for Starbucks from an exit, thought about breakfast, remembered eating like it was a good friend who rarely visited. He thought of school, of chemistry class. He

only enjoyed the lessons on titrations: the buret which resembled some part of an IV–and the pH balance–that concentration turning pink. Orange juice: acid. Whole milk: base. Coffee... acid? Maybe a base if you add milk? The girl screamed and kicked her foot into the phantom brake of the glove box, and the boy slammed his foot down until there was no more movement or noise, just a faint smell of something burnt, or burning. The boy hadn't noticed the contrast between the speeding cars and traffic halted up ahead, which was not ahead, but where the car sat at that current moment. No damage had been done, but the cars in the other lane felt personified to the boy, the headlights of the sedan behind him like giant pupil-less gaze.

"I've only had this for two months and my mom would kill me if it got dented," the girl said. She was sitting with her arms crossed, an empress of leather throne. Her knuckles were white, gripping a pen in her shaking hand. The boy didn't say anything. He couldn't imagine the girl's mother lucid enough to get angry, let alone *kill* anyone, but he kept his mouth shut because the girl's face had gone crimson.
"Let's go the other way to school," the girl said, "I hate the interstate."
He signaled and went down the off-ramp and felt relieved, calmer with the distance from that one spot, where he imagined everyone was still talking about him, the screeching tires, the asshole who didn't watch the road, and how everyone almost died, or worse, ruined a good paint job.

❖ ❖ ❖

At lunch, he bought a piece of pizza from the cafeteria and the cheese fell off onto his tray in one plop, leaving a red triangle behind. He bit into the clump of cheese and slipped the rest into a trashcan. He wanted a salad, or something covered in dirt, and he wondered if that meant he needed more zinc. There were facts somewhere in his head, he knew them, where did they go? Maybe it was iron? This thing that he needed. The girl called him. His ringtone was a popular song, but it sounded a little off and his friends thought it was from some beeping video game of the past. He picked up the phone and a woman, some teacher he had never seen before said, "No cellphones on school grounds." She repeated it with her arm extended. "You, with the cellphone. Hey, hey you!" The boy walked into the men's bathroom and locked himself in a stall that smelled like tikka masala or else some type of lasagna.

"What was that about?" the girl said.

"A teacher. She was yelling about my phone," he said.

"Tell her to fuck off. I called into the office and signed you out for a doctor's appointment."

"What kind of appointment?" he said.

"Does it matter?"

"I want to know—in case they ask."

"Fine. Ear appointment."

"Did you say 'ear appointment' when you called into the office or did you just make that up right now when we were talking? I just want to make sure."

The girl hung up.

The bell rang and he walked out into a sea of bodies. He could see the teacher somewhere behind him, standing, darting her eyes around, looking. He felt sorry for her, but mostly because her head reminded him of a toothpaste cap, and he thought that was no way to live.

❖ ❖ ❖

"Where are we going?" the boy asked.

"I don't know. Let's just drive around," the girl said.

"I don't want to drive," the boy said.

"Okay, I'll drive," the girl said.

She cut a nugget of weed with safety scissors whenever they stalled at a red light, the green bits falling onto an old *Introduction to Wicca* book she kept in her car. The boy focused at the cover's esoteric sigils until those designs made him dizzy in his daydreams of casting spells. He turned his focus to the rapid motion of the scissors slicing. The scissors' handle was pink and it reminded the boy of titrations, and he regretted something, but he couldn't find the word in his head to match the feeling. All the buildings they passed seemed the same to him: strip mall after strip mall of Burger King, Publix, Smoothie King, Vitamin World, Steinmart. They parked in a K-Mart lot and smoked a pipe until the air felt thicker and crawling and it pushed them out into the balmy, afternoon sunlight. The boy asked if K-Mart had a popcorn machine. The girl said that's gross, and she doesn't remember.

The boy looked at his shoes and said he needed a new pair, and the girl replied with, "Yes, always," as if everything physical was a variable to be manipulated and obtained.

They walked between the aisles of scuffed linoleum, and the girl put things into her purse that the boy knew she didn't need. The boy found a new pair of shoes like the ones he was wearing. He brought them into a dressing room and put the old shoes in the new box and the new shoes on his old feet. The whites of the rubber soles were fluorescent. He felt holy. *Et benedictus. . . Et benedictus . . .* He whistled hymns as he looked down the deserted aisles.

He found the girl and she said she felt nervous, like someone was watching her. He said they should leave from the garden exit because it was less crowded, and who would want to steal a plant anyway? They wandered outside and walked beside bags of mulch and something that smelled chemical. He thought of his father dragging fertilizer on the tomato garden his mother planted when he was younger. Nothing ever sprouted, and they never tried again. The boy saw a Venus fly trap and put his finger between its soft teeth. It lazily closed its mouth. He asked the girl if she could get it for him, and she said no, and what did she just say, and she doesn't want dirt spilled in her purse.

There was a tall man with a buzzed head and bodybuilder arms by the store exit. The boy remembered a movie where a hero walked through a gate of Sphinxes and they shot laser beams out of their eyes. That part frightened him as a child, and he felt frightened now as he walked between the parallel security gates. He expected the high pitch of an alarm, as if red lights would go off and spin around everywhere like a nightmarish game show. He felt relieved when nothing happened, until the tall man said, "Excuse me, you two there, excuse me."

The girl took off running in the direction towards her car before another word came out of his mouth. The man changed his passive stance and moved toward the boy saying, "Excuse me, son, I need you to empty out your pockets." The boy ducked around the man and took off running in a different direction from the girl. Was this instinct? The tall man was right behind him, grabbing onto the boy's jacket, but the boy flew out of it like a shell, a different skin. He kept running and looked back—the man had somehow tripped. He was on the ground and trying to get up and the boy could hear an adrenaline voice in his own throat throbbing *yes yes yes yes yes* and he kept running around the side of the parking lot and there were trees in the back and he didn't stop and flew himself past the branches and one scratched his face and he kept running and his shoes slid through mud and he tumbled over into a tree and hit the ground.

His face was hot, mouth gasping for air. He didn't want to be heard, so he bit his lip shut and pushed air heavily in and out of his nostrils. He tasted metal, dirt, maybe zinc. His boxed ears only hearing something rising and compressing inside his body. He thought about the tall man, the girl, the police. He thought of his mother, his father, his favorite jacket, and then the little bag of blow in the jacket, and he wasn't sure which one he missed the most. Was this the body's chemistry? Muted pop music cheeped from his jeans' pocket. He ripped the battery out the back of his phone. He feared noise and wondered if anyone heard it. Someone might have. He stood up, feigning quietness, and walked further into the moist terrain.

Was this nature? For the first time he wondered why people settled in Florida. Who would want to live in a bog of insects and steaming air? He understood why people would want to build over it though, suffocate it by casting it all into asphalt and limestone. Mosquitoes buzzed and bit and he kept rubbing the back of his hand on his face. He was getting lines of blood and dirt all over himself. The new shoes already looked like his old ones now, wet and slobbering and filthy. There was some sort of pride to all this however—the feeling of not being caught, of going into the confession booth and just sitting quietly, smiling.

The boy walked into a camp of sorts. There was an orange traffic cone nailed to a tree and splotches of red spray paint on another. There was a broken folding chair and layers of blankets on the ground, sheltered only by blue tarps nailed between trees. There were crushed aluminum cans covering some magazine with a naked woman on the cover. He leaned against

a tree for a long time, focusing on the sweat and the ache of his body as if it was the only thing left that was his. After his legs grew tired and he convinced himself that no one was coming to look for him, no one was going to trigger his feet to run again, he sank to the ground. How long had this camp been here? What kind of person would live here? He thought of the homeless people he saw sleeping at the foot of the Sacred Heart church downtown, and how he would have liked that better, if he were homeless. Cold stone and concrete. No trees. Less insects. He took the shoes off and laid down at the edge of the blanket. He watched the shoes intently, as if they held some mystic gift to call out and fix everything.

❖ ❖ ❖

The sun set into a full moon; the light was still adjusting itself—a confusion of orange and stars. The boy wondered what happened to the girl. How many times did she try to call? Which amount was enough? Did she tell her mother? His mother? Was anyone looking for him? What punishment was headed his way? This was an afterlife of sorts, he thought. The phrase "the moral of the story is" repeated itself inside him, but there was only white space after the verb. The trees rustled.

A man came through, carrying a piece of plywood like a staff. In the dull light the boy could see a broken bottle of beer tied to the top. He was wearing a dirty shirt with a map of Florida on it that said ASK ME ABOUT MY GRANDKIDS. His face was begrimed and his beard was frazzled—an electrocuted cartoon character. The boy wasn't sure what a shaman looked like, but it sounded like the correct word for this stranger.

"Who the hell are you?" the man asked in a low growl. The boy imagined the broken glass being dragged across his neck. The late night news and all the JonBenét Ramseys of the world made him fear something that he couldn't put a finger on until now. He said nothing.

The boy was bewildered and wanted to laugh or maybe cry, but staying completely still seemed to be the most non-threatening action. "What, you deaf? Get the hell out! Get the hell out of my home!" the man shouted. He realized he was lying on the blanket and the blanket was under the tarp and that was probably a home by some sense of the word, so he stood up and stepped to the side. He may not value the shaman, but he valued himself, some part of self he could preserve to not end up like the man who stood before him.

The man leaned on his staff and closed his eyes, as if an intense focus was needed to summon his thoughts. The boy thought about pushing him over and running, as he was currently unarmed. Homeless people are probably easy to kill, he thought. Was this instinct? He thought about glass, quaggas, prayers, and still he did nothing.

"Why are you here?" the man asked impatiently.

"I'm hiding," the boy replied, surprised at his own honesty. The man laughed, but it was more like a howl, which turned into something more like a cough, and then spit.

"Good boy, good boy," the shaman repeated. Then he licked his lips and frowned. The boy stepped back a little. The shaman said, "Do you think I'm going to hurt you?" The boy said, "Do you think I'm going to let you hurt me?" and neither of them said anything for a long time.

"What did you do?" the shaman asked.

He had been so good at lies before: fictitious friends and coffee shops, a spreadsheet of alibis, touching himself under a blanket that God couldn't see through. What could he say? The powders and smoke, the pockets and purses. Guilt was genetics, it was conditioning. Silence was preferred in the company of strangers.

"What did you *do*?" the shaman asked again, approaching. Which sin to confess? Does the word "parable" only appear in religious texts? Was everything else a fable, a fairytale, a myth?

"I stole," he said, pointing down to the caked shoes near his bare feet, which throbbed with mosquito bites. It was a safe choice, a tangible sin. A little truth. The shaman put his hand on the boy's shoulder, finger sliding under the collarline of his t-shirt. *Et benedictus fructus ventris tui.*

"Do you think I had a son? Do you think he looked like you?"

Was this a non-sequitur? He couldn't imagine this man with a son, a family, anything besides this tarp and traffic cone. He thought, for the first time, how someone ends up living behind a strip mall in the suburbs. This felt like a lesson. *The moral of the story is.* Be rich. Grow up. Be white. Be tall. Be a man. Be blameless. Only fuck up in when no one is watching. Or fuck up in public if you hold the power. *Who holds the power?*

"I don't know." The boy said, "You look like a shaman," into the confessional booth of the night. In all the books he read in school, the hermits were wise. The people who disappeared were wise. The evasive were wise. What story was he projecting on this man? The man rubbed the boy's collarbone with dry, dirty fingers. What was "sheer madness"? Why did people say that? He thought of safety scissors slicing weed. Shears. *Introduction to Wicca.* Why were some rituals privileged while others entered margins? Magic laughed at and prayers held sacred. *Ora pro nobis peccatoribus.* The teen boy's mind connected in synaptic tempests. One thought, then the next: pops of power and toxins and blood and spit. He knew why the shaman inquired, why he knew the boy would not have come into this camp of his own volition. Cause and effect. There, too, was a heat lightning occurring inside him and anything could happen at any second and his entirety was reduced to a stranger's fingers. Quaggas, quaggas, quaggas.

They stood there, quiet, only connected by an uncomfortable touch. The boy thought of things to say, escape routes, conversational resurrections. He thought he should have empathy for this man, but he possessed so little that even that concept of understanding a stranger's pain felt as unknowable as a shaman. There was nothing but this moment when all things could get better or worse like all things do and could and the man rubbed the boy's pulse point, worked his way to his Adam's apple, palm held steady. The boy moved his smaller, cleaner hands to his own shoulder, let it sit there—then, over to the stranger's fingers. First, gentle. Then he squeezed. His grip was weak, but he enclosed the man's hand with all of his strength, old bones cracking beneath his urgency to demonstrate violence. The man let go, pulled back, shaking.

The moon settled and nothing danced. Palmetto bugs shifted under the swamp grass, or else, everywhere. The broken glass sheened. They both stood there, listening. Cannibalisic images flashed in the teenager's head. His body splayed out, pinned to the tree like the orange cone.

Then, "Go home." That's what the man said. That was it. "Go home." The shaman turned away, the boy unaware of what knowledge lurked behind that squalid face with no present eyes to meet his own. His voice was neutral. He was talking from somewhere else, looking into another landscape. The boy crouched, moved out of a distance where the shaman's fingers could reconnect. The boy reached down to pick up the shoes he had set by the blanket.

"No, the shoes stay here," the man said, eyes focusing on him, seeing him again in the now. "I own them now. Leave before I own you too."

How could he get home without shoes? What would his mother say? What would he say when he saw her? The only path he knew was shoes. Every day he wore shoes, and he could not leave without shoes. This was survival. The boy grabbed onto the shoes and with a quick movement the shaman prodded the boy's arm with the glass-staff. The boy didn't mean to cry out as loud as he did. He was bleeding from his forearm. He felt this pool of id inside him, wanted to sink his teeth into the man's neck and mimic the same wound. It felt animal, biblical. He hesitated, adding up the math of blood, this thirst for destruction for himself and all others. He would murder him and every homeless man who looked like him. *This is power*, the one he was unable to relinquish. The man beckoned, a smile like snakemilk. What is the nature of prey? The moment of blood hitting air stretched into the humid, filthy darkness. The longer the boy stood and stared, waiting for himself to move, the slower his heart beat. Suddenly, he felt a sadness. A pity. Something. The rage felt like it was flushing down his legs, moving from his bare feet into the wet earth.

Why were his legs still in this spot? Why was he?

The boy decided to turn away, run in the direction that felt right. The man was cackling, speaking to a son-figure that was no longer there. A child. An object. The boy slowed down when the nightlights of the parking lot glowed through the palmettos and oaks. He walked out from the wooded area, twigs pushing up under the arch of his foot. What world had he fallen into for the evening? It was like he fell into the spells from that book in the girl's car, entered a world outside the rules he knew how to manipulate, control.

The parking lot looked alien now. He felt the texture of concrete as he stepped back onto the edge of the lot, switching over to a different geography. Although the sun had set, the ground was still emitting warmth. When did the sun set again? Was it really that late? He walked the perimeter of the garden section of K-Mart—all the customers were gone, the sidewalk plants moved back inside, the gate closed. Some lights were emitting from the main store, but whatever people were inside were from another world too, just there to put things on shelves. The parking lot was empty except for a few cars scattered like a concluding game of chess. Stock boys and backseat sex. The boy wondered where that bodybuilder man went, what happened to him. Did he go home, angrily sitting in an arm chair, throwing back a beer, still thinking of that teenage boy, the one who got away? The boy who had ran into the swamp had come back, back into the stillness of the suburbs, where he was moving around inside the same body. Almost the same. There was a new wound, but he would force it to heal.

The teenage boy walked, feeling as if his entire body was burning with a shameful secret. Being barefoot had its remoteness. He thought of his feet in the sand at Fort Desoto beach, and his feet pushed into the long grass of his grandparent's backyard, his own failed childhood garden where the tomato seeds did nothing. He thought of his feet in his shoes and tried to not think about his feet as they were right now. Urban legends of needles on the ground and the things kept inside them and how those things entered toes and crept. He was not the type of person who was supposed to walk these grounds in these unprotected feet.

A stale scent of French fries carried through the breeze; the McDonalds at the far corner of the plaza was the only other store left with its lights on, although it looked empty. He walked to the end of the lot where the main road stretched on for miles. He wondered where the steady flow of cars was headed to, now that everything was closed. Where did these people have to be? Wasn't it late? Didn't they have families? He stepped out into the road and looked up at the traffic light, and the light down the road, and the next one: a distant firefly. All the lights were blinking in unison, a steady caution of yellow, the pulsation: on and off and on again.

He stuck his thumb into the air and felt cinematic. Is this how the girl felt, with all those invisible people watching? Where had she gone? Who had she told? Would the two of them ever be the same again? *BEST / FRIENDS*. Would he go to juvi tomorrow? Could he hide his gash, his feet? He felt like such a child. How could he get home without the girl? What could he say that wouldn't ruin everything? The moral of the story was . . . . A red car pulled over to the side of the road, first slow, then slower, and then the emergency blinkers came on. A woman with curled gray hair rolled her window down. She looked welcoming, yet suspicious. "What are you doing out here? What happened? Do your parents know?" All he could say was, "Some friends played a mean prank on me, and I need to get home." This was the language he knew best, the words dark, darkening. His age was quelled: he was a child and this woman was his mother and she was so sad and sympathetic and said, "Get in, get in, I will take you home. What did they do to you? Where do you live? You poor baby, you poor, poor baby," and all he could say was, "I'm sorry, I'm so, so sorry." She touched his shoulder after he got inside her car. Her pointer finger grazed his bare neck, goose bumps erupting in Braille from that spot where he had been touched in many tactile languages before. He made sure he held the arm up at the right angle, so she saw it, saw what had happened to him in the distorted light of her sedan. He wanted a witness before he went on to change the story, to erase, to make things right again with himself situated in the spot that felt like his.

He pulled down the visor and looked at his face in the mirror. There was a scratch on each side of his face, resembling war paint. Somehow, blood had gotten between his inner and outer lip. He licked his dirty finger, covered it in saliva and started scrubbing again.

Erin Hoover

What Kind of Deal Are We Going to Make?

As a teenager, I found the remains of a fetus
in a plastic bag by the road. I wanted
to take it to the police, but my boyfriend
wouldn't let me put the bag in his car,
though every day I allowed him
to undress me in his parents' basement
in between rounds of World of Warcraft
and Doom, afternoons bursting the skulls
of his adversaries open with a semiautomatic.
It's dead, he said. *What are we supposed
to do about it?* We drove away. Of course
we did. What wouldn't I have traded then
for the balm of male affection, its
half-heart? Now I live on a bald scab
of grass, a swingset's chains twisting
figure eights, where I'll hide out until
I am the last woman standing. Once,
I followed a guy to a bar bathroom. Cutting
out lines on the counter, he said: *What kind
of deal are we going to make?* I pushed away
his hand heavy on my belly, his eyes
mugging my breasts. Running down
the hierarchy of flesh, he asked me to lift
my skirt, and I did, pulled it to the bloom
of my upper thigh. It's what a girl's days
are made of: What body part, this time?
And what will I get for it? I'm not sure
there's anything left of me, that palm-treed
oasis of okay I imagine for other people
always out of my reach. No inch
unclaimed, except I did what I thought
I wanted, and the reckoning that brought.

Planter's Moon

Light enthralled
by layers of darkness, white moths
swarming at nightfall.

I sit in the garden
counting seeds: stock, portulaca, marigold,
campion, thyme, sidalcea.

Time baits its invisible clock.
A seed stirs in earth,
or it dies. By day the sun lifts

its mandibles high, now the moon's
a white bird flying
against the walls of fortress sky.

Crack of birth, first leaf unfurling
spindly, straw-colored light.
Imagine the first

insinuation of flower, the delirium
of multiple branchings
while white stars flower

under the raven wing of the sky.

Gian Lorenzo Bernini. *Bust of Constanza Bonarelli (Detail)*. c. 1636-1638. Museo del Bargello, Florence, Italy. Photo by Nicola Quirico.

Bernini's Busts

Bernini believed the subject's true expression
was revealed just before or just after speaking.

The sculptor was unconcerned with what was
said. The words, marble dust. He looked only

for how the forming of the thought, of feeling,
rendered the face. Listened for the expressive

stone silence just before or after it was broken.
His lover's lips, just parted. Her artless tongue.

Maxwell Taylor at the University of Tampa's Scarfone/Hartley Gallery. One of his woodcuts, "Love and Responsibility," can be seen behind him. Photo by J. M. Lennon.

A Conversation with Maxwell Taylor

Maxwell Taylor was born in the Bahamas and first studied art there with Don Russell at his Nassau Academy of Fine Arts. He later worked as apprentice with the renowned Chelsea Pottery and was employed as a ceramic designer there during the late 1950s and '60s. In 1968 he moved to New York City, where he studied at the Art Students League, later learning photo silkscreen at the Pratt Graphic Center in 1972 and printmaking at Bob Blackburn's Printmaking Workshop from 1969-1977. During this period he was strongly influenced by African American and European artists, and he sharpened his own commitment to social realism and activism. He spent fourteen years in New York and also traveled to Europe, continuing to create new ceramics, paintings, and prints. His work was exhibited at the 1968 Olympic Games in Mexico, at The International Printmaking Exhibition, 1971 in Santiago, Chile, and in 1977 as part of the exhibition Bahamian Art Today at Brent Malone's Matinee Gallery. He held a one-man show in 1979 in Nassau and in 1983 was part of the group of ten artists selected to celebrate the Tenth Anniversary of Bahamian independence. In 1991, he joined B.-C.A.U.S.E. (Bahamian Creative Artists United for Serious Expression), with Brent Malone, Antonius Roberts, Stan Burnside, Jackson Burnside, and John Beadle. He has presented numerous solo exhibitions, and his work is in distinguished private collections, including those of the late Nat King Cole, Sir Harold Christie, and Dawn Davies.

Taylor was a visiting artist at the University of Tampa in February 2016, when he introduced an exhibit of his work at the Scarfone/Hartley Gallery and created a series of silk screen monoprints, individually embellished by the artist, with UT Master Printer Carl Cowden. While working on the series, Taylor came to the Tampa Book Arts Studio with Kendra Frorup, a friend and fellow Bahamian artist on the UT faculty, for a conversation with Joshua Steward, a printmaker and editorial assistant at UT Press, and Richard Mathews, UT Dana Professor of English and Editor of *Tampa Review*. We had recently completed a limited letterpress first edition of *The Rich Mouse*, a previously unpublished work by the American woodcut artist J. J. Lankes, whose Washington hand press is a centerpiece in the Studio. Lankes, best known for his woodcuts for the poetry books of Robert Frost, is credited with helping to inspire a modern interest in woodcut art, and our conversation naturally turned to woodcuts.

Mathews: Thank you for taking time out from your work in Studio-f to sit down with us for a few minutes to talk about your work. You are a fascinating artist and printmaker from all kinds of standpoints. But I was surprised yesterday when you told students that you spent more time in the U.S. than in the Bahamas.

Taylor: Yeah, I spent most of my life in the States, more than in the Bahamas. I would just go back and forth. I spent twenty years in South Carolina. I spent about fourteen years in New York. And then I have spent some time in Florida . . . well, I have been in West Palm Beach about six years, something like that.

Mathews: Yes, I understand you're living in West Palm Beach now, but you were also in South Carolina for quite a while . . .

Taylor: Oh yes. I still go back and forth. The house there belongs to my kids, not me. They inherited that. But they don't particularly care to live in the bush anymore. I love the bush, you know. It's a place where it's nice and qui-et. If I want to get nude I can run all around. [*Laughter.*]

Mathews: How did you wind up in South Carolina in the first place?

Taylor: My first wife was from South Carolina. She was an artist also. But she died many years ago. I ended up getting married again.

Mathews: What first drew you to New York City—and when was that?

Taylor: When I was a boy in Nassau, I used to take trips from Nassau to Miami, right? And after getting from Nassau to Miami, I used to take a bus from Miami and head straight to New York to see the museums. And then I fell in love with New York . . . the cloudy, sort of dull-looking atmosphere of the place. That still attracts me.

Mathews: What a contrast to Nassau!

Taylor: I certainly loved the atmosphere of the place.

Mathews: When it comes to that, I guess that Florida's more like the Bahamas.

Maxwell Taylor. *Dusk in New York*. 1973. Linocut reduction on paper. 14 x 27.5 inches. Courtesy of The Dawn Davies Collection.

Taylor: When it gets dull, you know, and artistic-like, I love it there, I get inspired when it gets sort of dull and cloudy. I don't like it when it's bright. You know—maybe I'm not a *bright* person . . .

Mathews: Well you do have bright colors in some of your work. Your color palette in some of the silkscreen prints you are working on now is quite vibrant and saturated.

Taylor: Yeah. That is work I'm doing here in Tampa, in Florida. But, New York, I *still* like it. I was just up there for the last couple of months to take a course in lithography—and I was right at home.

Mathews: Great. And what first led you to the Art Students League in New York?

Taylor: Because I couldn't get a scholarship during that time. [At the Art Students League, if you were accepted, tuition was low.] In the Bahamas, in those days, the only people to get scholarships were elite and well-known folks, and stuff like that. A street boy, growing up in the Bahamas, I couldn't get a scholarship.

Frorup: It wasn't until the 1970s and 1980s when students in the Bahamas really started going off to school. Students took advantage of new opportunities to be able to go off and study. And so the '60s and '70s is when it started to change. It was not only for the elite any more. And a lot of the students who went away, didn't go back.

Taylor: And not only that. If you were going to school in the United States at that particu-

lar time, you had to show the American consul that you had sufficient funds to support yourself. And then you had to take blood tests and all kinds of other things. That's how it was. I wasn't sure about going to the Art Students League. I had sent them some paintings, and they sent me a letter that said, "We'd be glad to have you." Matter of fact, when I heard from them I was destined to go into the United States Army. I had gone to the American Consul at that time and I told him I'd like to join the United States Army, because there wasn't anything in Nassau for me to do. Nothing.

Mathews: How old were you when this was happening?

Taylor: Let's just say I was in my teens. Let's say that.

Mathews: You had made up your mind that you really just had to get out into the world.

Taylor: There wasn't anything in Nassau for me really, you know. I was hired by Dupuch Publications . . .

Frorup: It's a big publishing company. It still exists.

Taylor: Yeah. And I worked down there for a while. But I couldn't stand just sitting around, waiting for them to give me something to do. I said, "Nah, this ain't for me," and I left.

So it turned out not to be the Army. And when I went to New York I felt right at home. This was during the African-American Civil Rights movement—when they were finding their identity. There were riots and Malcolm X and Stokely Carmichael, so it was an exciting place for me.

Frorup: Did that influence your work at the time?

Taylor: A little, but I think what really influenced my work the most was looking at a lot of books. That started in the Bahamas. We had a very good bookstore called Moseley's Bookstore in Bank Lane. Most of the books were on European artists. I used to get books on Rembrandt. I used to get a lot of books on Francisco Goya. Books on English painters, Mallord William Turner and all those guys. I used to just look at them and read and draw from them, you know. I started to think about what I was seeing, and I said, "Man, I gotta get out of here." Mind you, a lot of my contemporaries during that period went to Vietnam—they went to the Army. But a lot of them, when they came back, weren't really good anymore.

Mathews: Maybe you're lucky that you didn't wind up in the Army.

Taylor: Yeah, could be. As sort of the coward that I was, I probably wouldn't have survived overseas. The first shot I heard, I'd have probably run, or something like that, you know. But, yeah, I was destined to go into the Army.

Mathews: Had you started out thinking of doing woodcuts and prints as an artist, or were you mostly painting?

Taylor: I had thought about prints, but I was mostly painting. I was working for Chelsea Pottery.* *[See the image on the following page.]* That closed down. After that closed, everybody went their own way. Brent Malone, he went to England. Kendal went to New York.

Frorup: Was that Kendal Hannah?

Taylor: Yeah. Kendal went to New York . . . and he overstayed his time!

Frorup: Yeah, he was stuck.

Taylor: And what Kendal did after he overstayed his time, and I don't know if they were looking for him or not, but Kendal turned himself into the police station and they sent him back home.

Frorup: He was deported. As an international visitor . . . You know, coming from the Bahamas—you're allowed about six months. I'm not sure what the exact time allowed was back then. So you get something like a six-month stamp, and if you stay beyond that, then you've pretty much ruined any chance of being able to come back again.

Taylor: Yeah, I think it was three months.

Frorup: Was it only three months then?

Mathews: Was that true for students, too?

Taylor: No, students were a year. One year, then you had to renew. But as a visitor, you got a visa for three months, then if you wanted to stay longer, you had to go back to the consul or immigration office and they'd give you a longer stay. Even if you wanted to work, you had to get permission from immigration to work.

I remember when I was in New York, I didn't work for a whole year because . . . Well, I was always *honest*. I didn't work until I had permission. When I was at the Art Students League, I had met Japanese students . . . A lot of them were there, you know. And what I noticed about them is that they were really veterans in terms of their craft. . . . It's amazing—they were so disciplined. But you know what they came for? They came to *study*. A lot of them also worked without documentation—that was quite common. But me? I was scared! I told you I'm a coward, and I wouldn't work unless I got permission from immigration.

* The Chelsea Pottery (1952-1997) was established in 1952 by David and Mary Rawnsley at Radnor Walk, London, taking a name and location that echoed the most famous pottery of the British Arts and Crafts Movement, the Chelsea Art Pottery of William DeMorgan. David Rawnsley had trained as an architect and had been an art director with major British films when he was in his twenties. After World War II, he went to Paris. There he opened his first pottery studio and met fabric designer Joyce Morgan. When he returned to London and started the Chelsea Pottery with his wife Mary, they invited Morgan to become their principal instructor and designer in what was at first an Open Studio, where anyone could work and learn. However, soon they became known for their highly decorated earthenware, using inlay and overlay painting and vivid colored glazes. In 1959, the Rawnsleys left the London studio to be run by an associate, Brian Hubbard, while they relocated to the Bahamas and opened Chelsea Pottery's Nassau studio in a large eighteenth-century town house. Morgan had come with them, but she returned to London within half a year. The Rawnsleys remained to develop the Nassau pottery, with a flair of its own. After about two years, Mary and children returned to London, but David went on to establish a pottery in Mexico. Meanwhile, the decorative Chelsea Pottery style won international fame, with orders from throughout the world including the exclusive U.S. department store chains of Lord & Taylor and Nieman Marcus, and famous individual customers, most notably The Beatles. The Chelsea Pottery created an annual Christmas mug for Paul McCartney for about twenty years. For a more complete account, see the Chelsea Pottery history at www.studiopottery.com.

Chelsea Pottery. *Rooster*, c. 1958. Earthenware. Glazed by Maxwell Taylor. 20 inches h. Courtesy of The Dawn Davies Collection.

Mathews: When did you begin to do the printmaking? The woodcuts? Did you begin with wood, or did you begin with linoleum?

Taylor: Let me tell you something. When I was in the Bahamas, as I said, I used to get a lot of books, and I used to read up on woodcuts and printmaking. I couldn't get tools in Nassau . . . I would read about V-gouges being used, and I didn't even know what they meant, you know. But I gave it a try. In fact, I've given a print to the gallery. *[Can we get a title for the print he is talking about? When and where was it made?]* I've always saved that print. I had just gotten some old chisels, and the regular carpentry tools. I got some of those old things and found a piece of wood. And I cut the wood up with that, you know. And then I got a brush. I'd draw the thing out, and I got a brush. And I said I didn't know what the brayer was either, the roller. So I got a brush and I'd paint each line separately with the ink. The ink I used to get there was from printers—it's just like the ink you've got here [in the Tampa Book Arts Studio] because we had a printing shop. I'd put the paper over it and I got a bottle and rolled it over the surface [to take an impression]. Since then, I've been printing, you know.

From the time when I saw the prints of guys like, specifically, Rembrandt. And I didn't know what aquatint, engraving, and stuff like that was, but I saw the prints of Rembrandt and Francisco Goya, and other artists, and I just wanted to make prints like that.

One of the most fascinating things was when I took that trip to New York—from Miami to New York—I remember when I went to Miami, I still had to go in the back to get a ticket; I still saw signs of "white-" and "colored-only"— that's what they used to term it, that term. But it didn't bother me really, you know. I had an uncle who lived in Harlem, and when I went there, I lived with him. I said, "I've gotta go to the museum," and I walked almost thirty blocks, or something like that, to get to the museum. And guess what? They had just bought a painting called *Aristotle Contemplating the Bust of Homer.* [Note: The Metropolitan Museum of Art bought the painting in 1961.] Then at the same time, they had an exhibit of Francisco Goya. It blew my mind. Even right now today I'm trying to see if I can get my aquatints to look more like Francisco Goya, because he's a fantastic artist and printmaker or etcher.

And I was taken aback by woodcuts when I saw the work of [Ernst Ludwig] Kirchner, one of the German Expressionists and Emil Nolde, who was a fantastic printmaker. I didn't really know anything about woodcuts until I went to the Art Students League.

Frorup: Is that where you got your formal training?

Taylor: Yes, the Art Students League. You know what? That's why I tell the kids, when I was in Nassau in school I always got hits on my back—you know, they'd take the switch and—*fow! fow!*—you know, because I wasn't learning anything in school. My mind wasn't on school at all. If I was in school, I was looking underneath the desk at those girls and stuff. So, you know, that's just how we were at that time. We used to be up to mischief. We used to get a broken piece of glass and if you were sitting down, we'd take it and slide it underneath you. We used to do things like that in school. But I had no interest in school at all. I never had an interest in school. Always fighting and getting beaten up.

Frorup: You just wanted to be an artist.

Taylor: But . . . I just liked *drawing*—It's true, I started drawing in school. But mind you, a lot of others, my contemporaries at that particular time, they were better. They were very good. I know a guy by the name of Ben Walks—that guy could draw anything. He drew his own comics. Beautiful. Wonderful talent. But I think there was nothing for him to do. I think he became a tinsmith. He lived in Freeport. But I always had the ability to draw. As I told Kendra, I really didn't see any hope for me being an artist because I probably was going to be a carpenter or something like that. There was nothing else for me to plan for there.

Mathews: But then I guess if you thought about being a carpenter, that's a little like using a chisel for a woodcut or shaping wood as a sculptor. At least you were working with wood.

Frorup: Of course there is nothing wrong with working with your hands as a carpenter, but it is usually an anonymous and routine kind of work. There's not much chance to express your creativity. But did you study woodcuts at the Art Students League?

Taylor: It wasn't really formal. At that time, not many students were learning about woodcuts, but I had a very good teacher—Roberto De Lamonica—and he introduced me to woodcuts. That was the medium I stuck to. I loved lithography also, but the woodcut was a simple technique that I could even do when I was home. So I concentrated on that. When I was living in New York, I had a closet in the apartment where I would do all the work on my woodcuts. Some days I would work six days a week, but every chance I got I was working on woodcuts. And in a sense that's how I got to perfect the technique of it.

Frorup: Max has really been able to do this, to find his own way to express himself as an artist. If you ask *any* Bahamian artist, or any artist from the Caribbean, to name five Caribbean artists today, Max Taylor is going to be among the five that inspire them. But, Max, who inspires Max Taylor, from the Caribbean?

Taylor: From the Caribbean?

Frorup: Or the Bahamas, yeah.

Taylor: Nobody particularly.

Frorup: [*Laughter.*] Well, I suppose that shows how much you turned outward for your inspiration and influences, but your work still seems Bahamian to me. [*To Mathews and Steward.*] He's very big. He's modest. He's huge!

Taylor: You know who I thought was really good was Brent Malone. He was also a very dedicated artist and really helped a lot of people.

Frorup: Max Taylor and Brent Malone—Kendal Hannah—made the world start to look at Bahamian art in a different way, beyond the straw market or the folk crafts or the traditional Island beach scene. And so, they are the pioneers. They made the world look at us differently.

Mathews: Well, this might be part of the effect of your getting out to see more of the world. It seems as if you stretched yourself and experienced larger influences. You got your hands on some new tools. But now your name is also identified immediately with Bahamian art. In a way, it seems you also brought Bahamian art to that larger world.

There are a couple of things that fascinate me about your prints, and I want to be sure we talk about them before we let you get back to work. One of them is the *scale* of your printmaking. Because, I mean most of us have come to appreciate woodcuts through books and prints on a smaller, page-sized scale. Wood engraver J. J. Lankes, for example, who is one of our strong influences here, has some prints that are relatively large—larger than an ordinary book page, say 16 by 18 inches. But you have taken

woodcuts to a completely different scale. You are talking about measuring your work in multiples of *feet* instead of inches. And I was saying to our studio associate, Joshua Steward, who also cuts and prints wood and linoleum on a larger scale, it's hard for me to even believe that you're cutting these blocks using the ordinary small tools. There is so much physical work to carry out cutting on that large a scale. How did your move to work at such a large-scale happen?

Taylor: Do you know the work of M. C. Escher?*

Steward: Yes. And Escher has those unexpectedly large sizes with his wood engravings, sometimes ten or twelve feet long, or more.

Taylor: Yeah, because he was what, a mathematician? He was partciularly interested in scale.

Steward: That's right. He built his work using mathematical concepts like infinity, symmetry, tesselations, and such.

Taylor: You know, it's just amazing how he works—how he's able to design things that make us look with fresh eyes at elements like scale and perspective. I'm always so fascinated by his work, you know. So he is one of the influences, I would say.

But I think woodcuts as well as engravings take a considerable amount of *discipline*. Especially the wood engravings. It's surprising how much your tools relate to this . . . because you have to *master* those tools. But I think to me what is so fascinating is—woodcuts or linocuts—I look at it as something that always consists of *drama*, no matter if it's, you know, a scene or whatever. The large size can add to the *drama*. And then, with a print, you know it's always maybe fifty percent white and thirty percent black. A dramatic contrast. And I love photography, also; I love black and white photography, which I also get a lot of ideas from, in terms of a tonal value system: medium, light, dark. That's why, as I told you, I'm still fascinated with the works of Gustave Doré. You know—I study their prints. And then, again, you look at the work of Käthe Kollwitz—I don't know if you know her . . . fantastic artist!*

* M. C. Escher (1898-1972) was a Dutch artist who became known for his intellectual constructions of "impossible objects" frequently using geometrical and mathematical construction techniques and playing with abstraction, contradiction, and optical illusion.

. . . because Käthe Kollwitz will have just about *that* much cutting, and then all around there is nothing but *black*, you see. It's amazing how she can do that. *Dramatic.*

Frorup: The scale of your work is almost life-size. And so it puts you *in it*, you know? It's dramatic.

Mathews: You can see that dramatic flair in the way you're approaching it very much.

Taylor: Well, you know, in my studio, I have a table. It's about eight or ten feet. I put my whole block on the table, and I get on the table *with* it . . . and I'll be sitting right in the center of the block. I'll sit right there and cut until my legs get tired, then I come down and rest them.

Frorup: How often do you get down to look at it? To sort of step back and look at it?

Taylor: You know, that's very important. I find that that's very important because there are a lot of mistakes I make. And when I say mistakes . . . because there are many times that I really don't have the space to take the block and put it up to stay off it about ten feet, just to view it. And I don't have the space to, really see the effect . . . but that's important in doing blocks of that size, or even a painting of that size—stand back and look at the dimensions, see what's happening.

I'll give you a story. You know when I used to paint, right? When I was painting, and I'd finish a painting, I could take that painting, stand it upright about eight feet or ten feet from me. And I could stand up and look underneath my leg, and I could tell whether that painting was in balance or not. Now I can't do it! I don't understand it; I can't do it! I used to take that painting, and look under my leg, this way and that way, and I could tell. But now I don't know what happened—that's gone.

Mathews: You can't see it the same way.

Taylor: Yeah, I don't know. But I always could've done that, put that painting up and *correct* it. Correct it for "this is going *that* way," but now I can't do it. I lost it.

Mathews: When did you lose it, do you think?

Taylor: I don't know.

Mathews: One day you just realized it wasn't there.

---

* Käthe Kollwitz (1867-1945) was a German-born artist known for emotionally charged prints and wood engravings in the Expressionist tradition, particularly focused on human suffering and social injustice.

Taylor: Maybe. But, you know, with the woodcuts, really, I think I enjoy it more than anything, even more than painting. I did a lot of paintings in Nassau because I didn't have the equipment in Nassau to do a woodcut—to print it and stuff like that. And so I began to paint for quite some time.

Mathews: Well the other thing that I mentioned, the scale of your work fascinates me. Also the way your *hand* is so clearly visible in it. The *handcraft* aspect of it is just part of the full effect in a context where I think a lot of contemporary printmakers have worked hard to look more technically polished, mechanically perfect, or something like that. In your work, you still see the hand.

Frorup: The stroke—you can *feel* that.

Mathews: Yes, you can feel the stroke of your hand in the work and it comes through so strongly. I think it comes through in your woodcutting especially. And I think that's a really appealing quality, apart from the images themselves. The images are wonderful, and they pull me in, but the sense of your hands being there, and your having *made that* is just so strong. Machines do so much of our work for us now, we don't see that handcrafted aspect as much, in my opinion, even in people who are doing crafts. They look slicker. Or there's something that makes their hand disappear.

Taylor: But now I think there's a new technique called laser cutting—

Frorup: Yeah.

Taylor: —on wood, but you can always tell the difference because of the clean cut. In a natural woodcutting you'll always see the . . .

Frorup: . . . the end of that stroke.

Taylor: Yeah. You always see a little primitivism that exists inside it, you know. A little sort of awkwardness that exists inside it using the tools and so forth.

Mathews: I think that's very appealing in your prints. It gives them more *feeling* . . . and impact.

Taylor: Well, thanks a lot—I appreciate that very much. But sometimes it's not easy because my hands cramp up on me, you know, and I have to stop.

Frorup: It's funny you said that. Even in the silk screenings, you know, the series of monoprints you are working on now, I was curious as to how you keep that *hand* in it. Now that they're starting to really get pulled together,

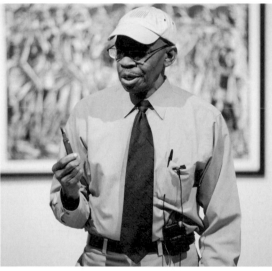

Maxwell Taylor shows students some of the tools he uses.

you can still *feel* it—the overlap of color, the strokes—it's still there, and that's nice. That's what's so refreshing about it.

Do you think you might experiment with some of the laser cutting and engraving? Does that appeal to you?

Taylor: Not really. It really doesn't appeal to me. But, right now I would really like to, you know, do some more silkscreens—

Frorup: You're hooked . . .

Taylor: And when I say "do silkscreens," what I told my students the other day is that the silkscreens that I'm doing . . . those silkscreens are not really the way that I want to do silkscreens. I tell my students that when I do those drawings that I made for the silkscreens, you know what they consist of? They consist of my *hands* controlling my mind, you see. When I do the woodcuts, it's my *mind* controlling my hand. Now how do you put that in the right perspective? I put that in the right perspective because every woodcut I do, I have to do a series of drawings. When I do those silkscreens, you give me one big flat wall, right? And I can just go like that [*waves his hand with quick gestures*], just like that. Quick and spontaneous. It's a whole different personality, a whole different technique, you know. I don't know if you understand that . . .

Frorup: I do understand. But you know what? It doesn't convey that way in the woodcut works. They're so fluid and so, you know—the lines aren't static. I mean, they're smooth lines that have, you know, this sort of emotion. And it doesn't feel like it's your *mind* controlling your hand in the woodcuts.

Mathews: Yes, I agree.

Frorup: You know, in fact, it's the opposite. It looks like the opposite.

Taylor: Yeah, but I have to . . . every woodcut I do, I sketch. I have to sit down and sketch and sketch and sketch until I get it the way I want it. Then I'll prepare my block. I take my block and I put gesso all over it. Sand it down and everything. Then I get some acrylic and a fine-point brush, and I mark it out. I'm going to send you one of my woodcuts because these new woodcuts I do, you might see the difference because I get a dry brush. I use a dry-brush technique on these woodcuts, and I put in the dark spots and then I rake it, *grind* it like. And then you see all these little fine lines in the dry-brush technique. So that's what I'm trying to see if that's going to have an effect.

Steward: That's informing the mark-making with the tools?

Taylor: Yeah.

Frorup: Okay.

Taylor: It's very interesting. You know, I say *man*, I like these lines. See all I need now is a tool that . . . [*He gestures with a raking motion.*]

Mathews: Well it's great to know you are holding onto such an open, experimental attitude as you approach your woodcuts—and that you are discovering some new and different ways of working.

Taylor: Yeah, I'm going to send you one. It's about four feet by four feet . . . It's *big*.

Frorup: And his studio, if you go in, I mean, the prints seem *massive* in the studio. Not so much in the gallery space. They don't look as massive because the space is so much bigger.

Mathews: See, this is a Lankes cut that we just printed. [*A cut of two mice playing checkers, approx. 3x4 inches; see below.*] And then this is the scale of Lankes that we're working with. [*A plate from the Lankes miniature book.*] He also did a lot of little miniature woodcuts.

 "Scratching Dog," by J. J. Lankes. 1940. Shown here at actual size.

That's a little dog, and if you flip through the pages, you'll see some of his other tiny cuts.

But this is a book that we just finished. [Shows him *The Rich Mouse*]. Lankes wrote and illustrated this book. And there are some charming woodcuts . . . *for children of all ages*, as they say.

Taylor: Yeah it *is* charming, because . . . you

"Checkers" by J. J. Lankes, from *The Rich Mouse*.

know, that's why I say I keep *looking at* woodcuts. Because I really like the way you can *see* what is happening . . . how *disciplined* this is in terms of how he cut his wood.

Frorup: Controlled line, repetitive line—yeah.

Taylor: I'm not afraid to admit that there is a lot of primitiveness in my work, and in the cutting process compared to this, you see. I'm not afraid to admit that. But, yet at the same time, between my work and this, it's still in a sense effective, you know. With these guys, I always admire their vision, in terms of the cutting, in terms of how they . . . I would say like how he did this table right there (pointing; see engraving below left). And what he did *in* that table— look at how he did the legs. This one—nice . . . But then, as he comes up with the side of the table, he made a medium gesture with the tool, see? Now, I don't know what kind of tools he used to get that, you know.

Mathews: He was using the ones that he shows in his book, *A Woodcut Manual*. It's just the basic hand tools.

Taylor: You know, telling me that, he's the sort that he really would give . . . what's that now? What do they call that now, those little prints? I forgot. Not thumbnail.

Frorup: Miniatures.

Taylor: Miniature prints, yeah. Yeah.

Mathews: These are the tools he used.

Taylor: Yeah, these are . . . I know these tools. I know them. I have a couple of them, but I don't use them, you know. But yeah, these tools, I think they use . . . they are very good tools—they still sell them; they're very popular. They're not Lyons [E.C. Lyons, manufacturer of printmaking tools.] Lyons have a . . . I think their tools are not like this. I think I have . . . no I don't have any in my book at all.

Mathews: Well, in any case, when we were working on this book, Josh took some elements of the Lankes designs and made a block to print decorative paper, which we printed letterpress and used to bind the book.

Taylor: Yeah, I can see that's his wood grain.

Mathews: Basically, Josh took the background from one of Lankes's images . . .

Steward: . . . in one of the Lankes woodcuts, and made it work, yeah.

Taylor: That's fantastic. Now, you know— see, the wonderful thing with his [Lankes's] cut-

Maxwell Taylor's large woodcut, "The Immigrants (Come on)," 2004, 31 x 51 inches, shows the effects the artist achieves with a small hand tool. "My interest is in strong subjects, especially the downtrodden, and human survival," Taylor says.

ting . . . Let me see if I can show you what I mean here . . . Okay, you see how he did the skies?

Mathews: Oh, the sky with clouds. Yes.

Taylor: Right. Now you see my large wood-cuts? As I tell my students, I have to use a little tool and I have to cut and cut and cut until I get the texture that I really wanted. And not every-body's going to do that. Now, as I told you, I also have an electric woodcutting tool.

Mathews: A Dremel?

Taylor: No, it's a . . . I got it from . . . I forgot the name of the company. The company I got it from is right here in Florida. But what I don't like with that is, I tried to get the effects—mind you, you can get some very straight lines with it. But, when I do this here [*indicates strokes in a woodcut*], I'm doing this, you see? [*Makes a motion with his hand, as if holding a tool.*] Flicking and flicking like that—with the electric tool that I have, I don't get that kind of effect with it at all, you know. Mind you, it's pretty good for some things, but it doesn't really work for me.

Frorup: So the finished prints look different?

Taylor: When I send you one of the prints, I just want you to look at it and see if you rec-ognize the difference in cutting. I want you to

recognize that some areas I cut with it, and I couldn't understand it, so I had to go right back to those same tools—those same little v-gouge tools—to get what I really want, you know. That's what I have to do with every single one. I just have to cut and cut.

Mathews: So you're still doing your work by hand, using those same small tools?

Taylor: I'm using small tools, yeah. Because now I'm getting to the point where I'm trying to get my *left* hand involved, you know. (*Laughter.*)

Mathews: Can you do it?

Taylor: No—it takes a lot of *discipline*. The minute I start doing this (*makes a cutting motion with his left hand*) I start to think too much. But it takes a lot of different brainpower to use it—your left hand—to get it trained to do that.

Frorup: It would be nice if you *could* use both.

Taylor: Yeah, if it comes to that—if I live long enough, if I *cut* long enough, you see . . .

Mathews: I expect we will find you cutting with tools in *both* hands—maybe starting to do woodcuts with your feet or even your teeth as well, one of these days.

Thanks for talking with us. I think we'd bet-ter let you get back to work!

❖ ❖ ❖

Shawna Ervin

Knowing

I know this poem.
This line. A word.
Superfluous, conundrum, break.

I know right here, now,
the not quite yet, always not yet,
what I can't unknow.

I'd like to know
wisdom resting in silence,
the space between your fingers and mine.

John Cox. *Self-Portrait with Two Rabbits*. c. 1996. Silkscreen on canvas. 18 x 18 inches. Courtesy of The Dawn Davies Collection.

Lesser Escape Artists

1.

There's blood in the end. I'm not going to toy with your emotions by keeping you in the dark about that. He was, after all, an unusual rabbit. (Don't worry, an assistant meat man said, that critter could talk his way out of anything.)

There we stood: she, possibly pregnant, rabbit in hand; butcher, cleaver dangling, hand on skinned haunch (nanny or billy not clear); me, distracted by movement in a back shop corner.

It was your standard butcher shop: glass case, filigreed walls, wood chopping block (waist-high, double-wide), the small stage where the Pips would later perform. The metallic tang of raw meat. Behind the counter, shelves reached to the ceiling, packed with jars and cans (kidney pies, pickled pig parts). We failed to see the goat lurking in the shadows.

What I learned: what you escape *to* is as important as what you escape *from*.

But first, the rabbit. We knew nothing of breeds. Suspected we might be breeders ourselves (what got us into this). Five-and-a-half pounds, deep red coat, wild ears, muscular flank, well-rounded hind quarters. We didn't appreciate what we had, even apart from his ability to wax philosophical. ("Desire fractures us all," said the rabbit, about to go on the chopping block.)

2.

Not even the butcher wanted a blind rabbit.

"What am I supposed to do with *that*?" he asked, cleaver in hand. Tall and thin, he wore a white apron over a crisp white shirt. That mesmerizing knife (wood handle, double rivets, angled blade). "Hasenpfeffer?" he spat. "Pot pie?"

We stood before the meat case. A chalked sign on top announced the day's special. She held the rabbit by its ears.

"Blind taste test?" she offered. He missed the humor.

We heard music coming from the thermostat, the heating vent.

"How do I know where that's been." The meat man made a face, fussy. The cleaver caught his reflection. "Besides, I've got my fingers in other pies right now."

He was no ordinary butcher. Logged thirty-plus years in theoretical physics. String theory (Einstein's violin, etc.). The last twenty of those working with the knowledge the theory didn't hold up. He told us: "You work on it even though you know it's not the real thing, because it's as close as you know how to get."

"Word," she said in solidarity. Her fingers touched my arm.

"Meanwhile," said the butcher, gaze softening as he reconsidered her, "the company is charming and the food is good."[1]

From the next room, a man muttered something about mung bean stew.

On the shop stage, a string quartet set up and played. Two male, two female. Blood-stained white dinner jackets. The viola looked suspiciously like a loin of beef. They butchered Mahler.

An assistant meat man hovered, awaiting instructions. Overhead hung a string of geese, their necks impossibly long.

She was looking for a way out. Eight days earlier had come home with a cleaver of her own: "This us isn't working."

Me: (Flummoxed, flabbergasted).

She: "Hasn't been for a while. You see it too."

I didn't. Besides, I said, in a world this crazy we need something to count on, however imperfect.

Not so, she said. "What you call stability, I call stasis. It's stifling."

I got her to give it a fortnight. Sure she'd come around. We'd shake it up. A phase—lunar cycles, etc. Then, panic. Her period, already late, took a pass.

Step 1: To make a delicious rabbit stew, first catch you a rabbit.[2]

---

1. *The Trouble with Physics*, Lee Smolin.

2. *Mrs. Beeton's Book of Household Management.*

BRIDGE

Dorothy Dietrich was the first escapologist to perfect the bullet catch, taking a .22 in the teeth. A trick even Houdini never attempted—too much risk.

3.

The special that day was fainting goat.

The case contained the usual items: black pudding, head cheese, sheep's stomach, sundry sausages. The cellist sawed at his instrument. We needed to string together a convincing story to get rid of the rabbit.

I told a tale: young boy borrows gun, goes hunting; hare scared sightless. The butcher didn't bite. Went about his work. Cleaver sang against chopping block. In the shadows, the goat flinched, nearly fainted.

She (to me, incredulous): "Why lie?"

It was true I'd fudged our facts: I'd thought a kid would bring us closer. She was skeptical. Still, we'd always said if we did do it, we'd go old school. Home birth. Midwife. Doula. So naturally, I thought, the old rabbit test to prove pregnancy or no.

"What is *this*?" she'd said when I brought him home. She unveiled his privates. "The rabbit has to have girl parts. That's the whole point." On top of that, he was blind. She was unhappy with me. She'd been reading Mailer—*The Fight, Executioner's Song*. "There's something to be said for brutal honesty," she said.

So: what to do about the furry fellow with the wrong parts.

"We take him to the woods," I said. "Turn him loose."

"He's BLIND," she shouted. "You might as well kill him yourself." I suggested a search for an adoptive home. She was adamant: rabbit disposal; drugstore pregnancy test.

Back at the meat counter, she explained our true circumstances.

"You know that test is long debunked," the meat man said. "No science to it."

She looked daggers at me (eyes aflame with butchered Mahler).

"Science also shows us that all orbits are elliptical," the rabbit offered.

Me: (There's truthiness here. I could learn from this fellow.)

To which the butcher replied, "Your pickle is of a different nature." The meat man spoke of the failings of theory (string and otherwise).

Once a firm believer in parallel worlds, "Now I tend to trust what's in front of me." He arranged chicken hearts in a corner of the display case.

"Trust this," she said, proffering the rabbit. "Please." Her pause pregnant. "We need to settle our situation—once and for all." Looking back, you could say I was blind to certain signs.

Step 2: Remove lungs heart liver kidneys.

The butcher smiled. Sweet on her, but a man of principle. He took three yellow pills from an apron pocket, mouthed and swallowed them.

On the counter, pig's trotters. Sow's ears.

He pointed the knife skyward. "Monogamy is counterproductive," he said. He had a full hermeneutic for human relationship modeled above him in sausage and string. "Besides," said the butcher, "why bring a child into such a world?" Cleaver whacked meat, wood. "Particles flying everywhere. No strings connect."

Bits of bone clipped our clothing.

"Abstractions," she said. "Here we are in front of you." She batted her eyelids. "What's one rabbit more or less?"

Me (waffling): "How can we do this to a sentient being?"

"A fair point," said the rabbit. "Why make me your scapegoat."

She lowered him, as if out of earshot. To me: "His plight is not your problem. For you," she said, "two things matter only: sympathetic story; dip stick urine test."

Fine. I phoned a pharmacy, discreet. They'd deliver. From the next room, a meat man requested the Moroccan workers' remix.

The quartet stopped playing. Slunk away in shame.

The sausages suspected a link.

Me (to her): "He doesn't want the rabbit."

She: "Convince him."

Somewhere a gun had gone off (a .22), a bullet raced toward me, and I remained (mostly) unaware. Distracted by the goat in back, now furtive in tan raincoat and porkpie hat. Unsteadily biped. Scruffy chin hair. It saw me see it behind sunglasses. Its legs stiffened; wobbled. I sensed forces at play. I watched the animal—rubber hands attached haphazard to sleeves—handle a can. Remove it from a shelf clutched between hooves: two pounds of Spotted Dick.

"Do us all a favor," the butcher said. "Take your rabbit and go home."

The rabbit's ears twitched. "Given half a

chance," he told the butcher, "You and I could get along."

The meat man wrapped two brown paper packages. Tied them with string.

"Today's special," he told us. "On the house."

He reclaimed his cleaver. The packages quaked, toppled over.

The goat in back dropped the can, clattering, to the floor.

BRIDGE

Turned out the rabbit was something of an expert in legerdemain. He'd learned from the best: "For Houdini," he told anyone who would listen, "identity was something you escaped *into* from your past, leaving behind lovers, limitations—whatever bound you."[3]

She: "I want someone I'm willing to stick my neck out for."

Mahler: (crescendo)

Mailer: "A cleaver is the only knife designed to be swung like a hammer."[4]

Me: I like Mahler more than Mailer (much).

Rabbit (dangling): "What Houdini's audience came to see him escape from was shame."[5] He paused. "Oh, and death," he added. "Let's not forget death."[6]

4.

He didn't look like a butcher. Long head and wire-frame glasses, he looked like the kindly pharmacist in a nostalgic television drama. Behind the counter, he wrestled thrashing hoofs. He had the goat spread-eagled on the chopping block. Stacked neatly beside: 1 raincoat, 1 porkpie hat, 1 pair folded Ray-Bans.

The can of Spotted Dick lay abandoned on the floor.

I felt faint. "I'm not comfortable with where this is headed."

"It's too much," she told the butcher. "What we swallow to have someone to hold." The rabbit wiggled in her grasp.

Me: "It's the cost of companionship."

She: "It can't be." Desperation in her voice. "Why settle for so little?"

In the thinking fortnight, there'd been little discussion—little dissension. I'd read this as progress. Now, before the meat case, the

rabbit dangled between us like a foregone conclusion.

"Come on," she urged the meat man. "Sometimes humans have to help each other."

He seemed to soften. But then:

Clad in rabbit-fur coats and Ray-Bans, three goats (bipedal) took the small stage. Two carried Fender Stratocaster guitars with some urgency. The third held a boom box, the chalked *Special* sign tucked under his wing.

The rabbit: "Tell me we're having goat for dinner."

An assistant meat man bleated in the corner, a handful of string cheese.

I felt culpable. I liked quantifiable solids. Stable trajectories.

Hooves scratched against chopping block. The butcher stayed the squirming with an expert hand. Tightened his grip on the cleaver.

Onstage, the disguised goats started to sing:

It's poetry in motion
She turned her tender eyes to me

Guitars jangled. A boom box behind them kept the beat.

Spheres are in commotion
Elements in harmony

The butcher sharpened his blade on a long steel. I felt my innards go fluid.

Step 3: Joint the rabbit into back legs, front legs, saddle. Cut the saddle in two.

The stage goats executed a wobbly shuffle step.

The butcher tested the blade's bite. "I'm a meat man. Not some second-hand shop to ditch undesirables."

She: "Think of it as mercy. This us is over. The string's played out." She turned to me. Tenderness in her eyes. "Sorry, but someone had to cut the cord."

I took the bullet in the teeth—it shattered them and kept going.

The stage goats executed a wobbly shuffle step:

She blinded me with science
Failed me in biology

The butcher raised his cleaver in the air.

The rabbit. "What lesser escape artists fail to learn: getting free is the adventure, not being free."[7]

---

3. *Houdini's Box*, Adam Phillips (Butchered Edition).
4. *Mr. Mailer's Big Book of Husbandry.*
5. *Houdini's Box*, Adam Phillips.

6. *The Rabbit's Guide to Escape Artistry* (Wild Hare Edition).
7. *Houdini's Box*, Adam Phillips (Open Door Edition).

BRIDGE

Houdini's binary: paralysis = failure; mobility = success.

Mailer: "There is nothing theoretical about a punch in the face."[8]

Mahler: "I want it to fall like an axe."[9]

Step 4: Turn up the heat in a heavy-base fry pan.

5.

Cleaver poised in mid-air, goat on the block, the head man attempted to place it all in terms of the cosmological constant: "There's a counter-energy required to keep the universe in static equilibrium."

Until then, I'd never thought of myself as a repulsive force.

He brought the cleaver down.

The goats, adjusting Ray-Bans for maximum coverage, gave it all they had:

Blinded me with science
SCIENCE! SCIENCE!

That was when things took a turn—goat hindquarters now divided into equal loins. With a clatter of hooves, the band's lead goat keeled over.

My life flashed. Safe. Small. The bullet clipped my jaw, veered south.

A trio of meat inspectors—each wearing amber-tinted alchemist goggles—arrived to investigate.

The butcher (blood-spattered) raised an eyebrow.

The rabbit hung perfectly still in her grip. She watched the door, intent on a different arrival.

The butcher pressed a button under the counter. Cat's cradles emerged on tabletop displays. A web of string filled the air. I brushed some off my face. Felt her bullet lodge in my back. Painful, but I'd live.

A synthesized fanfare, and the assistant meat men burst through swinging doors, moving to the back beat and singing the background parts.

Sci-ence! Sci-ence!

Onstage, the two unfainted goats—stunned, saddened—did their best to carry on. Slashing guitars. The boom box played a keyboard fill. The meat cutters moved as one. A half-dozen, a chorus line in blinding white butcher coats. Their choreography impeccable. Shuffle step on the downbeat. A flourish of arms. They were Pips: supreme. They wore splatter shields. Half-turns and hip flourishes, proto-Motown moves. Bodies in profile, they turned their heads to us:

When she's dancing close to me
I can smell the chemicals

Full turn. Hand clap. They sliced the air with synced cleavers. We wiped blood from our brows.

Step 5: Sear the rabbit joints in the hot pan.

The rabbit listened close, sniffing for opportunity. I, too, strained to see.

The lead goat struggled to his back feet. Rejoined the band and brought the tune to a close. The meat inspectors discovered the chalked Special sign. Regarded the cleaved goat. On stage, the band eyed the exit. Elaborate string structures obscured the way. I spied her across the room, as already at a great distance.

The inspectors huddled, goggle-eyed. One typed into a handheld device that then spat out a paper. He handed it to the butcher.

Meat man: "What's this?"

"Restraining order." The inspector fingered the Special sign. "Til we decide if it's a protected species."

Rabbit: "Are any of us really protected?"

I caught his blind eye. Determined to help him how I could.

The goats, rejuvenated, kicked off a deep groove.

The butcher, now meatless, began to see the rabbit in a new light.

BRIDGE

A partial list of things to escape from: handcuffs, straitjackets, cages, coffins, small boys, large guns, steel boxes, a firm grip on your ears, barrels, bags (cloth), dead relationships, burning buildings, string quartets that butcher Mahler.

6.

In the end, of course, none of us escape the blade.

The rabbit saw it coming.

The butcher grabbed a marker and a blood-stained chunk of poster board. *Today's special,* he scribbled. *Blind rabbit.*

---

8. *Mr. Mailer's Book of Bluster* (Blockbuster Edition).

9. Score Notes, *Symphony #6 in A Minor,* Gustav Mahler.

By now, cat's cradles connected everything in the shop. The butcher waved his cleaver to slice free a space for the sign.

The music got festive. The goats shed their coats and became a horn section, swinging side to side to Motown ("Ain't Too Proud to Beg"). The lead goat did the Funky Chicken.

I watched for an opening.

Rabbit: ears cocked.

Behind us, the door opened and the pharmacy lackey strolled in.

In a fine bit of choreography of her own, she tossed rabbit to butcher, grabbed drugstore package. Tore it open.

The meat man held the hare. Laid its head on the chopping block.

The rabbit, remarkably calm: "Historically, butchers did not serve on juries because their work was thought to harden their hearts."[10]

The meat man raised his cleaver high. "Nothing against you," he said. "It's the way the world works."

"Here goes," she said. Stuck the pee stick between her legs.

We all waited. Butcher, blade raised. Me, eyeing rabbit escape routes. Lackey looking for a tip. Inspectors, goggle-eyed.

Rabbit: "All history is the history of unintended consequence."

"Pink," she pronounced. "I'm free." Pecked my cheek and left.

The band kicked into a Memphis groove. The lackey left behind her (leaving the door open). Inspectors and meat men cheered. Even I felt happy for her.

In the melee, the rabbit wiggled free. I saw the way, clear. Tossed a coin to signal him. It bounced on the cutting board. He executed an elegant backflip, landed on all fours. Hightailed it for the open door.

It happened so fast: Hare hops into street. Blind to oncoming meat truck (oh bitter irony). You can imagine the rest. Me, I closed my eyes. There are two theories about what happened next. The prevailing one is simple: blood; traces of fur smeared a considerable distance. Critter crawls off to die. That's the official story. Even a body, found later. I almost bought it. Then, a few weeks after, I got a package in the mail— a manila envelope containing only a blood-stained coin.

Real? Some assistant meat man's cruel joke? What do you think?

In a world this chaotic, I choose to believe.

❖   ❖   ❖

---

10. *Emile, or On Education*, Jean-Jacques Rousseau (Approximated).

John Beadle. *Fragile Crossing—No. 20 of Sixty-five*. 2005. 28.5 x 24 inches. Courtesy of The Dawn Davies Collection.

Alicia Fuhrman

Salvage

"You can't unsee them once you know how to look," Wes tells me, strides ahead, but I don't rush. It's early, hunting hours, and in the felty darkness of barely morning I'd be lost anywhere else.

His fast steps go quiet. Only then do I pick up my heels and follow. The ground's got a hard freeze, but two months ago I'd be trailing dust, when this path was split by windrows and glowed at night like grass-blades kept the sun in.

Far off the crooked barn shows up navy blue and the main road black as a river. I try to look through the half-dark and time, before last season's flood and they laid asphalt down, and the land was worn but without traces I recognized. But haven't these miles always run smooth? I recall Mom saying once that the whole Virginia Blue Ridge was cut by the moon. Gravity pulled the ground apart, pushed it back together. I've walked all over these fields and hills and still can't see it.

I catch up to Wes. He's straight-backed with his goose gun on one shoulder, looking sort of military but also like waiting for a bus.

"You're lucky Aldy's late," he says. "Always late, but drives fast," and grins.

I don't know Aldy up close. He's just my brother's hunting friend and our neighbor over the summer. Mornings they went shooting for crows and coyotes, I'd hear his truck rattle down the uneven crop roads. And forgot how easily I knew the sound until yesterday, when the cool air shook and I knew immediately why. Wes says he's got reasons to come and go, but I'm not sure what.

I spot white headlights on the rise. They flash and vanish between the hills. After a few seconds that motor drone fades in, then Aldy's truck pulls up. Wes goes to load his gear in the cargo bed and I'm standing there with the ground buzzing when the passenger door swings open. There's Aldy with an arm reached across the front seats and close enough to touch, looking as if I've known him my whole life—sun-beat in November, like wherever he's gone since couldn't take the summer flush from his face; somehow windswept in the idle air; bright and pale and startlingly awake—an imprint of the months I love here most. When the copper burn of a harvest moon makes the nights seem less.

"You as good of a shot as your brother?" It's the first thing Aldy says to me.

"Hey," is all I say back at first. Then: "Maybe, I don't know yet. Maybe Wes just gets lucky."

Aldy laughs easy and too quick. "Maybe you're right."

I can't think of what comes next; Aldy switches the radio between off and static—no station's playing this early—and our last minute as strangers goes like that until Wes comes around again, all business.

"I've scouted out a spot for today," he states. "Near this feeder stream by the mill. Lots of straggler birds."

It's a little late for migration, but the past few years have warmed up some, thrown the great flight off.

"Well, get in," Aldy says, looking right at me. I doubt Wes notices.

We drive off. After a while the landscape turns red; you don't wonder why the light bleeds, just stare. And listen to their talk like white noise.

"Up North this sun means a storm coming," Aldy says. "Red sky at morning, sailor's warning."

"Take a left here—"

"Red sky at night, sailor's delight." He laughs short again, but Wes doesn't; I think how he's always kept quiet, even facing the worst.

"—then another left, and you can park in the dirt."

"Is that true about the storms?" I ask, or don't because none of us really hears. We're slowing to a stop when Wes jumps out and the half-shut door is left stuttering until Aldy kills the engine. Outside looks like any rundown corn-field, all rotted crop and no grass. I get out and stumble over this weird patch in the ground, sort of plastic and square. I scan the rest of the field. The shadow of a baseball diamond shows beneath the dead earth, and I realize I've just tripped over second base.

"Hey," Aldy says, "here." And tosses me a shotgun. "Unloaded," he grins, "but nice catch."

Wes is across the field, skirting the line where the trees begin. He moves quick and unpredictable, like a sniffer dog. From any distance I'd recognize him in a beat. I look down again at the base, scuff it—wonder how long since a game's been played here and why they left. I recollect what I told Mom on one of those nights it was just us: "Nowhere else can be better than here." I didn't want her afraid of ending up alone, but she stayed quiet, with that lipstick smile like she knew better. I never could stare her down. I look up again to see Wes waving my way and Aldy already walk-ing. I remember the empty gun and how I'm supposed to see things different after today. Because we've come to hunt, and I've only ever shot targets and clay.

The light changes within the woods. Most of the leaves are fallen but enough branches still make shade. I have to remind myself it's the same day we were just driving and the view was red for miles. Now I can't even tell where we're walking, but I still keep pace. Some-where close I hear the shush of the mill creek, wonder if it'll be running in a year. After the flood came the drought, but I know the town's been going at the land too. I think of that black stripe again. More roads.

"Let's split," Wes says. "Water starts there," and points. I strain to make out where the ground falls into a bank.

Aldy's whistling softly through his teeth, the same line over again. I plan to ask him where it's from, but he's facing off towards the creek.

"I'll track ahead a little more," Wes contin-ues. He shakes a little box from his shirt pocket, and for a second I think he's offering me a ciga-rette, but it's just shells.

I click in the safety with my thumb, load up. Enough little metal pieces to explode an ani-mal. Above the trees, the sun shifts, and white streaks suddenly pattern the duff where we're standing, and I imagine I can feel a differ-ence on my skin. Those dapples glitter, fade.

Then just as quick clouds turn everywhere dull again. But none of us is worrying about a storm.

Aldy quits whistling and says, "Well, you coming?"

He's asking me, but I'm watching my broth-er. How many times Wes disappeared from the house, only to show up hours later with arm-fuls of whatever he killed, and turn away while Mom smiled over the haul—I know he's at his best alone. And won't fight me letting him go.

"Just don't blink," he calls back, "don't blink before the shot," then disappears into the trees.

Me and Aldy stick close to the bank, keep quiet. Below the water surface has frozen but the stream beneath is strong enough to cut a path through. What's left is a crust. I listen to the current move, but soon the water gets shal-low and the reed-grass thick. Then Aldy throws an arm out and stops me.

"Here," he whispers. We crouch and stare, but I can't see what he does. "One shot'll flush the rest."

"The rest?"

He takes my hand, traces an outline in the reed bed with our fingers. "Try and squint them out," he says. "Look for the bright dots—those are the eyes."

And then I find bright dots. Two grey geese, feathers like tree bark, are masked low within the growth. I know Aldy's betting on a few more hidden. He lets my hand go: "I'll fire, you fire."

The air cracks open so hard I expect it to bleed, but only the sound echoes back at me. I shoot steady at a flying blur, watch it drop. But something is off. I haven't killed the thing, just broken it. While Aldy's goose lies flopped dead in the rill, mine's flapping crazy with one wing, the hit wing, dragging it from flight.

Aldy jumps forward, makes a sort of tackle. I watch him in one motion pin the bird with his knee then snap its neck.

"Bright dots," is all I can think to say. He looks at me different. Through gunpowder and floating down. The last few feathers sway, settle. I picture him on a sailboat somewhere with wintry sun on the Atlantic making him squint. We will always know this light the same way.

I hear Wes coming. He's not trying for stealth. "Well," he says, "well, well." Nothing like a hunt gets him talking as fast. Aldy stands with a goose in each hand.

"One of those yours?" Wes asks me.

"Yep," Aldy answers fast. "Textbook killshot on her first go."

I say nothing, and Wes looks proud. Only briefly but it's enough: I forget for a second that back home Mom isn't waiting. Three days she's been gone, and Wes keeps saying to give her a week. I don't worry about back home. Until some hours later, Aldy gone, and it's just me and Wes stringing geese up in the yard to drain; he reminds me.

"Give her a week," he says, "another few days."

His voice is quiet and sort of shakes. I check each of our clothesline birds, afraid to find my traitor shot through a wing and nowhere else— so then, how did it die? But I realize Aldy must have kept that one. I touch a dark spot on the neck of another. It's only a soft scab and my finger comes up damp. All across the farm fields looks still, but I'll see anything coming. I don't want to blink. I wait for Wes to ask again, tell him I'll wait up.

Sometimes

Sometimes it doesn't matter what you say,
      sometimes it matters where you are,
under the magnolia tree, for instance,
   the pink blossoms
      looking like giant startled eyes

and somehow there's no need for saying
      anything about the pleasure you feel
  hearing the sound of rain on a barn roof
     or a jazzy minor 7th lifting softly from a piano.

And what is it about holding the hand
      of your best girl and feeling at 14
  nothing of the past or future
just the desire of a boy
      who's lost all his marbles
somewhere between a touch and a kiss?

Sometimes the language of pleasure
     needs no syntax or parsing
  to make you feel everything's in sync.

And here is the crepuscular night
      making you want to connect all the stars
  with your finger in one continuous line
as if you could do it and whatever seems
      furthest from you is nearest.

Sometimes it's how a moment pans out
      into gold maybe, a small shining to hold
  in your hand for luck or mystery.
Sometimes even nothing you can say
     will keep it there.

Ghost Dog

I dream she comes to me when it's cold
and the windows are ice-crackled and hard
and she snuffles at the linen sheets
and licks the bedposts for the salt.

I can almost smell the odor of wet fur,
feel her breath along my fingertips.

But she must be a shadow now in the moonlit field
or traveling an unwinding road
and all the rivers are one river for her,
and all the woods without demarcation.

Still, I've put out paper lanterns
by the roadside, whispered her name
into the bordering trees.

Is there ever a *goodbye* that echoes back an answer?
I stand at the window tracing a line of ice
as if it were a frozen river
anyone might cross.

Goodnight, old ghost. Goodnight
to all that isn't here. And all that is.

In every bark I hear, I hear her bark.
In every gust of wind, the sound
of something passing on its way,
unleashed and masterless.

the cedar chest

our entry hall holds a cedar chest / we sit on to tug on boots / a chest filled not with linens or off-season clothes / but with the childhood art of our two boys

we know / with our sons now grown / that it's time to cull the stock / and as apartment dwellers / we could use the storage space / we even attempted the task once / but found it overwhelming / for the art stalled us with memories / of course / of our boys in all their balky stages / but it also sidelined us / with memories of our own balky / trainee-parent selves

we had to learn / for example / that when confronted with a page of crayon scribbles / to say not *what's that* / which deflated them / but to say *tell me about it* / then listen / and watch / their scribble world / rise sensibly alive

then came their first self-portraits / made of big circle heads / stuck with arms and legs / their bodies not yet visualized / though the needs of those bodies came to consume our own / teaching us to tackle child care / work / extended family / and chores / while sleepless / forgetful / edgy / and dulled / ourselves reduced to big circle heads stuck with arms and legs

next appeared the mixed media of sand and beads and glitter glued onto paper / of clay figures / cut paper / and photo collages / artwork that sprawled all over the apartment / coating what little remained of our battered adult stuff / especially when a boyball of friends descended / and we found ourselves taking a crash course in hair-splitting / balance of power diplomacy / our skills and patience / abraded and upgraded / by tugs of war between these ostensible allies / in their battles of fantastical fabrication

then suddenly / true representation flourished / striking sketches of family and friends / and self-portraits that now had full bodies / and deft expressions / art that taught us the close aesthetic analysis we applied to discern the artists' inner lives / as they strayed further and further from home / and from casual confidences / an analysis that became our lifeline / to their unfolding / autonomous selves

then the art cache ended / for what they produced they kept for themselves / or discarded before we could corral it / a seemingly sudden loss / we had to learn to make hard / grudging / peace with

so when we revisited the artwork / that one time / and found so many growing pains / both the boys' and ours / hauled up / and exposed / we loaded it all back in / dropped down the top and / challenged / as our final lesson / to appreciate the completion of our own long / collaborative / interactive project / proceeded to sit / side by side / happy and happily / on it

Daniel Gabriel

Book Hunting on Skid Row

As a child, I was a voracious reader. It took me years to stop reading every single billboard, every single street sign, every scrap of printed paper I came across. I burned through my school library, my town library, and the handful of Chip Hilton and Hardy Boys books stocked by our local five-and-dime and liberated by me without need for any pesky cash register transactions.

Given the parlous state of our family finances, this might well have been the limit of my acquisitions. But there was one further source of literary access: the used bookstore run by the Salvation Army down on Skid Row, which was confined (unsuccessfully) to the middle of the Mississippi River, on Nicollet Island in Minneapolis. All the stores on the Row featured used goods, except for the bars, and even there one could hardly be certain of the provenance of any given tipple.

The Salvation Army bookstore was a musty, dark place, with never-dusted shelves and a cantankerous proprietor who dozed behind a small desk. From time to time he would blink awake with a snort, glare around him as if to blame whomever else might be in the shop, and then resettle himself back in his dreaming-chair, until such time as the making of change might be required.

There were rarely other patrons in the store, but when there were they tended to be freight riders or bindle stiffs who had wandered in out of the weather, looking for a place to sleep, or piss. Sometimes both objects were achieved along the darker back aisles. Once my search for oversized picture books about knights and castles drew me along the far shelves near the cloth-hung doorway that led to the back storeroom, where my wanderings ended abruptly when I came upon a grizzled figure in a torn army greatcoat who had managed to fall asleep upright, propped on an overflow shelf of paperback romances. From the smells coming off him I could deduce that he had both imbibed

a large quantity of liquor and successfully relieved himself in his pants.

I never revisited that particular back aisle—but then I never told anybody about the incident either. I knew it was all too likely that our bookstore expeditions would end, and that would be a catastrophe I could never endorse.

The first few times we went there—a gaggle of mop-haired word-hungry siblings ranging from babes in arms to my eleven years—we were escorted by Grandmom, a former school teacher from the West Virginia hills who took back talk from nobody. Ever since Granddad had retired, he and Grandmom spent half the year traveling North America in their pop-up van, Itchyfoot. (This was in the early sixties, well before a younger generation began filling the roads with live-in vans.) Each summer they'd pull into our driveway and I'd dash out to inspect the latest additions to their rolling home. We always got two shopping trips out of their visits. One was to buy shoes for each of us five children. The other was a journey to that fabled Sally Army store, where we were each allowed to select as many books as we could carry. (Since they cost 5¢ apiece, Grandmom knew we couldn't empty her purse.)

In those early days, my attention was on completing my collection of Hardy Boys and John R. Tunis adventures, along with the occasional book on pirates, or baseball, or whatnot. I began to learn about first editions, and failed continuity across a series, and the collector's struggle to find that last final rarity that so often is a justifiably-forgotten side remnant of some author's *oeuvre*.

As I grew into my teens, I began making my way to the Salvation Army store on my own, without waiting for Grandmom's annual visit. Now I was free to look for any old thing I pleased, with no concerns that my stack of books would be studied for "appropriateness" by any of the significant adults in my life. If I wanted to peruse *The Last Days of Al Capone*, or

"The Bikini and Who Can Wear It," such was my choice. One day I found *The Autobiography of Malcolm X*. Another time it was a slim Ace Books volume called simply *Junkie*, by some guy named William Burroughs. I couldn't believe that anybody would willingly display their addiction in such a manner—or that a publisher would print it.

By the time I was deep into high school, I was an expert at mining the shelves for hidden gems. This is where I first encountered James T. Farrell, via *The Young Manhood of Studs Lonigan*. Soon I was back for the other volumes in the Studs Lonigan trilogy. I concocted a high school research paper on the dissonance of modern youth as evidenced in the rise of motorcycle gangs thanks to stumbling on a paperback named *Hell's Angels*, by one Hunter S. Thompson. On an unpainted green wooden shelf labeled "Music/Art/Movies" one day I picked up a book by an author completely unknown to me—Mezz Mezzrow—simply because of the title: *Really the Blues*. I was deep into discovering the blues, and bought it at once, though Mezz's book was all about jazz, and reefer ("the mighty mezz") and a million scenes on the bandstands and stage doors of the American night.

In time, the city condemned Skid Row and both sides of the street were leveled to make way for the brand new Hennepin Avenue bridge. Life on Nicollet Island continues—there's a small neighborhood of converted boardinghouses, a classic old inn, and the imposing brickwork of DeLaSalle High School. But the island's real treasures—those innumerable five-cent books with their hinted promise of bold, nefarious deeds—are lost to the winds of time. Except for the rescued ones that still populate my shelves at home, reminders of younger days.

❖ ❖ ❖

Charles Harper Webb

Where the Cat Can Sleep

For years, Jim hauls around Dad's warning
like an old sea-locker: *fleas, ticks, lice,*
rabies, toxoplasmosis, cat-scratch fever . . .

Then, one cold day, Chloe pounces on his bed.
His hand, raised to stop her, floats
down to her head. His blood-pressure floats

down, too. No wonder stroke patients
do better with a cat: the way she settles
like a hen into a nest; the way her eyes squint

and smile, claws moving out and in, warmth
flowing into his cold skin. Her purr
motors him back to when people first

stored grain. Rats and mice gathered
to feast. Wild cats crept in to feast on them.
Kids found mewing kittens, loved

their tumbling furriness, ignored
their fleas, and brought them home to Mom
(a soft touch, even then), and Dad—

harder, but not impervious. "Can we
keep them?" the kids cried in their long-lost
languages. "Pretty please . . ."

Lover, the Lord Has Left Us

I.

On the third night in the bowels of the boat, so long
that the mice have stopped being startled of us,

the ship halts and heaves like a heart wrecking
itself. So sudden the stop, we fall flat like dominoes with nothing
       to fall against. We hit a baby whale.

Ropes whip themselves against the mast, and the sound of brass

chisels at my teeth. In unclean waters, whales can forget
their directions, the young sometimes won't

eat enough and their hearts freeze
in the Atlantic, the captain says. A sailor who doesn't speak English
lays his chest flat against the deck, feeling

      the vibrations of the calf's moan so piercing

it makes the boat planks rattle and tickle into the smallest bones
of our toes.

II.

Whale, noun. A very large marine mammal.
     See tailfin   see sixty-six thousand pounds   see
the closest you can come to touching God.

Wail, noun. A prolonged cry of pain or grief.
     See scream   see sob   see the sailor
face-down on the deck. The first mate

tells me that man belongs to an indigenous tribe that believes
humpbacks are the oldest gods. Their song the force that spins the planet.

We name the whale Samson. After our boat's name, *Delilah*.

III.

The thirteen of us stand around, still—each of us the eyes of our own storm.
The cook swears it must have been our numbers
that vexed us. I watch the water measure the sunset from honeygold
      to blackblue and every color for loss in between.
We trade the candle flame
for its smoke   and walk away from the lamps learning
nothing of alchemy. What takes eventually gives,

whether wood floats until it soaks enough to sink
or massive gods shatter into single cells, into phytoplankton.

When the ocean outside of you merges with the ocean
inside of you, we call it drowning. When body and barrier are no longer
synonyms. When we need to name a shipwreck,
      we call it a man

still sobbing face-down on the deck, three hours later. Rain
      mimicking the shape of his grief. Alone and useless

as an oar left out to dry. An exclamation point that fell over,
forgot its reason to stand. Look—this is only one kind of drowning.

Look how blind the body is with only its hands to hold on.
The captain says Sailor
      know that when the water lifts you it also lifts bodies

      from their graves when cemeteries flood. Know
      it can't tell the difference.

John Beadle. *Ring Play—Study*. 2003. Acrylic on aluminum. 25.5 x 19.75 inches. Courtesy of The Dawn Davies Collection.

Katherine Schaefer

Ring

Norman's ring is too big for me. It twists and spins, a heavy weight on the middle finger of my left hand. The gold band is a quarter-inch wide, and thick like a piece of pipe. I'm used to it being there now, most of the time. It crashes into my own ring, on my fourth finger just to the left. Mine is a delicate, thin piece of gold, the top of it shaped to match the engagement ring I seldom wear anymore. Our two wedding rings, then, side by side, on my hand for the past six weeks, ever since the transplant.

"It's a go," the charge nurse had told us just before his pager beeped and he hurried out of the hospital room. Norman and I looked at each other, wide-eyed, dumbstruck. It was the news we'd been hoping for ever since the middle-of-the-night phone call summoned us to the hospital, nearly twenty-four hours before. The news we'd been preparing for during the past five months while Norman's name had moved up the waiting list. The news we'd been dreading for the last ten years, when he was first diagnosed with primary sclerosing cholangitis—PSC for short—a rare autoimmune liver disease. Were we ready? We had to be: the transplant was a go.

Another nurse came in, wearing purple scrubs. "I got the good word," she said. "They'll come get you soon. You need to take off any jewelry—you can give it to her for safekeeping." She tilted her head in my direction.

"There's just my wedding ring," Norman said, "and that doesn't come off. I haven't taken it off since the day she put it there thirty-one years ago."

The nurse raised her eyebrows. "Well, you have to take it off *now*," she said. "They won't let you keep it on during surgery."

"But I can't," he said. "It won't fit over my knuckle." To demonstrate, he tugged the ring upward from the base of his finger until it hit the middle joint. Anyone could see it wouldn't go any farther.

"Not even with soap?" she said.

"Nothing," he said. "When I had hernia surgery they let me keep it on. They just put some tape over it."

The nurse looked skeptical. "I'll just check with the surgeon," she said, and left the room. Minutes later, on my way to the restroom, I passed a mini-conference of nurses being held at the charge desk. Nurse Purple Pants stood in the middle of the circle, her arms folded across her chest.

"Dr. K. says it *has* to come off, but the patient says it *won't*."

"Maybe you should tell him what can happen during a twelve-hour surgery, when he starts to *swell up*." This delivered in an ominous tone.

"You know what we did when I was over in cardiac? We had this one guy . . ."

Uh-oh, I thought, as I moved out of earshot. They were going to make him take it off; maybe they'd have to use a saw. How did they *do* that, anyway? And why hadn't we thought to go to a jeweler and have it resized? But even three days ago, we'd never imagined ourselves here so soon.

When Norman was listed for transplant, we were told he'd probably have to wait at least a year before a liver was available. The waiting time was unpredictable, though. It's not the way I used to think transplant lists worked, back before I ever dreamed I'd have to know about stuff like this. The wait time for livers doesn't go by how long you've been listed; it's not first-come, first-served, like waiting for a restaurant table. Once you're on the list, you're given what's called a MELD score, which stands for Model for End-Stage Liver Disease. Since nobody wants to say that phrase out loud, people just say, "What's your MELD score?" or "Where's your MELD at?" It's a combination of three different blood tests, and it basically measures how sick you are, how soon you are likely to die. So when Norman's weekly bloodwork jumped dramatically, indicating the rapid on-set of liver failure, his name moved to the top of the list.

"Do you think it'll be soon?" I'd heard him ask Richard, one of the transplant coordinators, on the phone. As soon as we heard that Norman's MELD score was up to twenty-six, we started worrying. Norman had a big sculpture commission he was working on under dead-line, and we both had so many preparations to make before the transplant. Having his wedding ring resized was the least of it; the thought hadn't even crossed my mind.

"What'd Richard say?" I asked when Norman hung up.

"He couldn't say one way or the other—said it could be tomorrow, could be a year from now," Norman told me. "But then he said, 'I wouldn't go out of town if I were you.'"

The next night, at three a.m., the phone rang.

I woke with the certain knowledge that this was it—not a prankster, not a wrong number, but the summons we'd been waiting for, the one we were dreading. When I answered, I heard the unfamiliar, accented voice of a doctor whose name I didn't recognize, asking for Norman. I felt completely awake, energized as if a cold, blue electrical spark had jolted through my head, my eyes wide open, limbs shaking as I stood by the side of the bed. I passed the extension phone over to Norman, while strug-gling to untangle its curly cord from the legs of the nightstand. Only the day before I'd dug this old phone out of a drawer and plugged it into the unused landline jack by the bed, wanting to always have an extension everywhere within reach. The hot-pink plastic receiver felt so light and insubstantial in my hand. Its ring echoed in my ears: high, cheap, tinny. Such a piece-of-crap phone with which to receive this weighty news.

Beside me, lying in bed and hiked up on one elbow, Norman answered questions into the phone. "Yes," he said. "About 120 pounds . . . . No, no fever, no infections . . . . Yes, O positive. I believe so; that sounds right . . . . Wait—what was your name again? Can I get your num-ber?" These were questions and answers we'd been instructed about when we went through our mandatory training class months before.

Norman hung up the phone and looked at me. Our two cats had been sleeping near us, one at the foot of the bed, the other on the win-dow seat. They were awake now, too, their eyes wide and wondering at us, the ringing phone in the middle of the night, the oddly strained sound of our voices. "He's going to call back," Norman said. "But it sounds like this is it. A match."

They try to prepare you for this moment, but it's nearly impossible to wrap your mind around all the feelings you have when the call comes. You know that someone has died, that there are people somewhere out there who are in the most agonizing shock and grief. You know that this generous person who died was an organ donor, and that a match has been made, blood type and body size being the most important criteria for matching a liver between donor and recipient. And because you know all this, even though you also know that this mo-ment will save your husband's life, it's impos-sible to rejoice. Joy, if and when it comes, will have to wait for later.

Besides all that, you're just so damned afraid.

By the time I got back to Norman's room, the verdict had been rendered: the ring must come off. Either Norman would have to manage it or they'd remove it some other way. Nobody said just what that way would be. Norman went into the bathroom and shut the door. There was the sound of water running in the sink. I pic-tured him squeezing liquid soap on his finger, yanking at the gold band, trying to force it past the boulder-like knuckle, an obstacle to every-thing that lay ahead of us.

The nurse in purple reentered the room with the charge nurse and a short, swarthy man wearing scrubs, a surgical mask dangling from his neck. "We borrowed this guy from cardiol-ogy," she told me. "He has this really good trick for getting rings off—says it works every time."

"I got it!" Norman burst out of the bathroom, holding the ring up like a Cracker Jack prize. "But it wasn't easy. I don't know how I did it."

Desperation, I thought. Pure panic.

The cardiologist turned around without a word and was gone. I wondered what his trick was—I wanted to see it. Norman handed me the ring. "Here, keep it for me until you can put it back on my finger."

"Are you sure you've never taken it off since our wedding day?" I said. "You must have, at least once." I slipped my ring off every so often, usually to soak it in a cup of sudsy dishwater with my engagement ring, without a second thought.

"Never," he said.

I reached for the ring but then stopped. "Wait—how about this? Put it on my finger and I'll wear it for you until you can wear it again yourself." I held out my left hand and he slipped it onto my middle finger, next to my own wedding band. The ring was too big, but it felt like my knuckle was already swelling, growing larger to keep it in place.

"It's the best we can do," I said. "Don't worry, hon—we're still married. It's OK that you had to take it off. It doesn't mean anything." But I could tell he felt a little sad about it, disappointed somehow, like he'd held a Guinness world record for thirty-one years and now that record had been broken.

After spending the whole day and half the night in the hospital waiting for the transplant to begin, when they finally came to take Norman into surgery it seemed so abrupt, all those long hours collapsed into mere minutes, seconds, a single moment. Two anesthesiologists, a man and a woman in surgical scrubs and caps, came to take him to the OR. One of them pushed him down the hall in a wheelchair, moving fast, while the other trotted alongside with a clipboard, peppering Norman with questions. I trudged behind, carrying a white plastic bag stuffed with his belongings. In the elevator, the numbers lit up as we descended from six to five, four, three. When the doors slid open, I followed after them, thinking I would be allowed to go along into pre-op and wait with Norman until he went into surgery. But no, the male anesthetist told me, frowning, this was it, as far as I could go. They were taking him directly to the OR. Everything was happening so fast.

"You go that way, turn right, end of the hall," he said, impatient to get on with things.

"Someone will call you with an update," the woman said, sounding nicer.

"OK, hon, this is it," I leaned over and held my face close to Norman's. "Good luck, sweetie. I love you. See you when it's over." We kissed quickly and then they turned and wheeled him through the swinging doors, out of sight. I turned away and headed for the waiting room. The entire night stretched before me, empty. I curled the fingers of my left hand into a loose fist, and heard his wedding ring click against mine as the two bumped together.

Throughout the next several weeks, while I went back and forth from the hospital every day to sit beside Norman's bed as he slept, or while he spent two hours at a time trying to consume a meal, I wore his wedding ring next to my own. While doctors and students clustered around him, asking questions and scrutinizing lab results before hustling away, while RNs changed shifts and I wished he could still have the last nurse—the nice one, not this new, stern one—or yesterday's nurse, or the day before's, I wore the ring. While he vomited dark blood, while he was wheeled away for tests and scans and more tests, while he walked the hallways with physical therapists or with me, stopping to look at every painting on the wall and check out every window with a view of the Mississippi River, I wore the ring. I wore the ring at home while I fed the cats and changed their litter, while I paid the bills and took out the trash, while I stared numbly at the TV or a book, while I slept and woke, showered and dressed.

Sometimes I sat and gazed at the ring, that small chunk of gold occupying my middle finger like a squatter. It didn't look right on my hand. I couldn't get used to it, its clunky weight, its dull sheen. But I also felt as if I could wear it forever, as if I wanted to never take it off, just as he had never taken it off up until the transplant. It seemed like some sort of symbol—not just of the two of us, our long marriage—but of capability, control. For those weeks when I wore it, I felt like I was both of us at once, husband and wife combined, solely in charge of everything we had once done jointly. And I wasn't sure if I ever wanted to give it up, whether I would be willing to take the ring off and give it back to him when he asked.

By the time Norman came home from the hospital for good, a month had passed, and I readied myself to cede his husbandly role back to him and return to our mutual effort of being married. It had never been a matter of one or the other of us being in charge, or having precedence over the other. We had always been a team, and we were still. But when he had needed taking care of, when I was called on to shoulder our responsibilities so he could put everything he had into healing, I had been up to the task and had carried it out, and I would do it again if necessary, gladly. But I didn't have to do it forever. I wanted my husband back, our team marriage back. I was ready to be a wife, and a wife only, once again.

Now, six weeks after the transplant, we call the jeweler who made our rings for us over thirty years ago. Back then, he ran a small, stylish shop in a newly-renovated warehouse in the artsy part of downtown Minneapolis, an area dotted with art galleries and French bistros and offices of architects and designers. I remember the goldsmith as a fat, surly man, who from his appearance you might have expected to belong to an underground biker club, riding a Harley on weekends with his pals in leather vests and sleeveless jean jackets, cryptic patches displayed across their broad backs. His early shop had halogen bulbs hanging from track lighting and when he pulled out my diamond solitaire and presented it to me across the counter, it sparkled blinding white with flashes of pink and blue and yellow. "It's a headlight," he said to Norman and me, and his employee looked over as if to verify it. "Yep, it sure is," he confirmed. And I had smiled, imagining a motorcycle headlight shining forth on my finger.

The goldsmith is still in business all these years later, amazing in a way, but then, Norman and I are still married, too, so which fact is more amazing? We found him listed in the phone book. His shop has moved into a renovated White Castle building, one of those enameled metal structures with a tiny fake turret and crenellated battlements that once sold small, square hamburgers with fried onions on soft steamed buns, in a gleaming steel interior meant to look reassuringly sanitary in the 1930s. The building was disassembled and moved to its present location, on a commercial street south of downtown in a much less chichi neighborhood, although still an interesting one. Similarly, the goldsmith's business is more interesting than it was before, since his main concern now is running an accordion shop and giving accordion lessons on the side. He still makes jewelry, too, but maybe just for people like us, former customers from back in the day who seek him out, maybe for repairs on their old rings, to reset a loose stone or stretch a gold

band to accommodate a finger grown arthritic or fat.

On a snowy day in early December, I wedge my car into the only empty parking space next to the former White Castle. It's early afternoon, and the small building appears to be crammed full of people, but Norman and I still have to buzz at the locked door to gain entry. Whether the security is meant to protect jewelry or accordions, I don't know, although when we enter there is no jewelry in sight. A tall, white-bearded man grudgingly opens the door and looms over us, glaring through his half-rimmed glasses. He is the same surly man I remember from three decades back, but he is no longer fat, and he was never jolly: the anti-Santa. When we state our purpose, he leads us to an office area tucked into a back corner and takes a seat behind an impossibly cluttered desk. "Hey, would ya help those folks while I take care of this?" he says to a younger employee, nodding toward a middle-aged couple who are transfixed by the walls of the front room, hung with accordions of all sizes and colors—red, blue, silver, ivory, black—their fanciful names inlaid with cursive letters spelled out in rhinestones or mother-of-pearl. *Weltmeister. La Divina. Excelsior.*

Norman and I perch on the edges of dusty office chairs with sprung upholstery, seats nearly covered with papers and small metal parts: rivets, buckles, screws. We tell the goldsmith he made our rings for us over thirty years ago, thrusting them under his nose for inspection, as if he might somehow remember and welcome them back after all this time. We tell him our story of the too-small ring, how it had never once been removed until this past October, and the reason why it had to suddenly come off. There is a bit of business while he measures the size of the ring, and then the size of Norman's finger, before declaring that this particular ring could never have fit on that finger at all, that it could never have come off. "Impossible," he says.

"Well, it did fit and it did come off," Norman says.

"By some miracle," I add.

Meanwhile, the accordion shoppers are taking one instrument after the other down from the wall for inspection. The woman slips the straps of a little red one over her shoulders to assess its size and weight. From the snippets of conversation I overhear, I gather they are shopping for a Christmas gift, looking for something small, not too heavy, not too pricey, maybe for their grandchild. It seems the woman played accordion herself years ago, and now wants to give one to this special child who may have expressed an interest in passing. The conversation veers off to the woman's own fond memories of accordion-playing as a girl, the lessons she took, the recitals she gave. I wonder if the grandchild for whom this small, red squeezebox is being purchased has any inkling of what is coming her way on Christmas morning, whether she will be as enthusiastic about the gift as the grandmother is about bestowing it. Not to mention the recipient's parents, who will have to suffer through it, as well.

The goldsmith and Norman discuss whether the ring can be stretched enough to fit over his knuckle, or whether a new piece of gold will have to be added to make it bigger. The band is a thick piece of metal, not too delicate or flimsy to bear stretching. Norman tells the goldsmith how he once made custom jewelry himself, years ago, and how if he still had his equipment he would put the ring on the mandrel and pound it down to stretch it. He believes it can be done without breaking the ring. The goldsmith's deepening scowl suggests that this is the exact wrong thing to say, that he wants to reply with something along the lines of "Well, why don't you just do it yourself then, hotshot, since you're so smart?" But he bites his tongue, which for this stubborn, oppositional man is no small thing. I can see something of myself in him, how much I hate being told what to do.

The woman decides to take the red accordion hanging on her chest for a spin, and the maddeningly cheerful strains of "You Are My Sunshine" suddenly fill the shop with overwhelming noise. The reedy tones bounce off every surface in the steel-walled building, so loud I can't hear myself think.

You are my sunshine, my only sunshine.
You make me happy when skies are gray.
You'll never know dear, how much I love you.
Please don't take my sunshine away.

❖ ❖ ❖

The jeweler says he will first try to stretch the ring enough to fit, which will cost such-and-such amount, and if it doesn't work—which

he believes it won't—he will cut the ring and put in a new piece to make it large enough, which will cost somewhat more. "I'll join it and smooth it out and you'll never even know it's there," he says. Although Norman is frugal to a fault, I know it's not the extra cost of adding a new section of gold he objects to. He doesn't want the ring to be cut through, doesn't want a new piece added to the original. He wants the gold band to remain as it has been for the past three decades: uncut, intact.

"It's OK, honey," I say. "Whatever he needs to do." Cutting into something, putting in a new part if necessary—we have to get over our fears and superstitions about all that, I think. Isn't that why we were there, after all? But maybe that's why Norman is so attached to the idea of the uncut ring: something still pure and untouched by all this change that's been thrust upon us. Something old and original to our marriage.

The jeweler drops the ring into a small Ziploc bag and starts making out a receipt. "It'll be ready by the end of the week," he says, not looking up as he writes. Norman glances at me, this time knowing not to protest, for fear we'll both be kicked out of the shop for being difficult customers.

Accordion music leaps into the air again, a different instrument being tried out for comparison to the first.

The other night dear, when I was sleeping,
I dreamed I held you in my arms.
When I awoke, dear, I was mistaken,
And I held my head and cried.

❖ ❖ ❖

I suddenly feel like screaming at her to stop. I can barely hear myself think. Although just what it is that I'm thinking, what internal thoughts I need to hear, I don't exactly know. If she would only stop playing—allow me some peace, a quiet, empty space inside my mind—maybe I could find the words I'm looking for, access the emotions I've been tamping down for weeks. Months.

Norman hands me the receipt and I put it in my bag before we turn away, leaving the ring behind. We thread past the accordion shoppers and salesman as the goldsmith rejoins them, already brightening at the prospect of dealing with what I can see is his real love, accordions, happy to put the old goldsmithing business aside.

We step outside into what now seems a quiet intersection filled only with the noise of passing vehicles, their tires hissing on the slushy street. As we walk past the Castle façade to the parking lot, I hear the accordion's shriek rattling the glass windows and vibrating through the metal walls. *Please don't take my sunshine away.* I never realized what a sad song lurked in those cheerful major key chords before. Hadn't I ever paid attention to the lyrics?

"I was hoping he could try pounding it down while we waited," Norman says. "It wouldn't have taken all that long. I didn't want to part with it."

"I know, hon. Me, too," I say. "But it'll be OK. We'll get it back soon." How many times have I reassured him like this in the past two months—the past two years, even, as he grew more and more ill—telling him that this or that thing, whether little or big, would be OK? When I had no knowledge of whether everything really would, in fact, be OK.

A week later, we get a voicemail: the ring is ready. The White Castle is uncrowded and quiet when we arrive, and the goldsmith is a bit friendlier, almost expansive. We wait while he retrieves the ring, then sits down at his desk before shaking the gold band out of its plastic bag. Delicately, he holds it up between his meaty thumb and forefinger for us to see. It looks like new, with thirty years' worth of scuffs and scratches polished away to reveal its original shiny gold surface. He hands it to Norman, who begins to slip it onto his finger, then stops. "You have to do it," he says, turning to me, holding the ring out.

"OK," I say, a little embarrassed, but willing. The ring slides on easily, passing over the knuckle with barely a hesitation.

"I was able to stretch it," the goldsmith says. "Didn't have to add a piece after all." He doesn't say, *like you thought I could,* and Norman doesn't say, *I told you so,* although the unspoken exchange hangs in the air. "It's a perfect fit," Norman says instead.

"I still can't believe it ever came off in the first place," the man says. "That ring should've never even fit you at all." He leans back in his swivel chair while Norman writes out a check.

"So you had a liver transplant?" the goldsmith says, as if now that our business has been concluded, he feels like having a chat. "How long ago now?"

"Two months," we both say at once.

"Well, you're lookin' good, man," he says. "Best of luck to you."

When we leave the shop, I drive north on Lyndale Avenue instead of turning east toward home. "Where are we going?" Norman asks. "You'll see," I say. Fifteen blocks along, the tall spire of the church where we were married comes into view. "Our church," he says. We always call it "our church," although we have rarely set foot in it since our wedding day. I have an idea that we might stand on the front steps outside the double wooden doors, where I can put the ring on Norman's finger again properly. I park the car and we walk up the stairs, where Norman pulls on the front doors to see if we can get inside. They're locked, but there's a sign posted saying to enter through the side doors. I'm fine with standing outside, but Norman wants to go in, so we walk around to the side, tugging at each locked door we come to, until we find a big new glassy entrance off the parking lot that must have been added on sometime in the last decade. Even these doors are locked, but a receptionist inside buzzes us in and tells us it's all right to go into the sanctuary.

When we reach the threshold, the church interior is dark except for a light behind the altar, where an organist is practicing at the console, his back to us while he pulls out one stop and then another, trying to find just the right combination for a festive version of "Good King Wenceslas." As he plows through the carol in fits and starts, we tiptoe up to the top step before the altar where we stood side by side on our wedding day, our feet silent on the thick maroon carpet.

"Wait," Norman whispers. "Aren't you supposed to be on this side?" We switch, me on the right, him on the left.

"No, the other way," I say. "We had it right the first time." Giggling, we change sides again, then, facing one another, we grow serious. I take off my ring and hand it to Norman, and he hands me his in turn.

"With this ring, I thee wed," he whispers, sliding my ring back onto my finger. Then I take his hand and put his ring back onto his finger—"With this ring, I thee wed"—and we kiss, and hug, and kiss again. We tiptoe back down the steps then, so the organist can practice in peace, although I'm not sure he is even aware of our presence.

Back outside the church, a cold winter wind in our faces, we walk to the car in our down jackets and jeans, no beaded gown or rented tuxedo this time, no friends and family throwing rice. We get into my Honda and drive across the freeway bridge, taking the back way toward home. No afternoon in May, no fancy reception with cake and champagne. We aren't twenty-somethings anymore, but fifty-somethings, and one of us has a new liver stitched up inside him, functioning as it should be, keeping him alive. Keeping us married.

Thomas A. West Jr.

Music Box

On R. & R. in Ginza Mart
I found her a music box
  for Christmas. It played
"China Night", and I heard
that when Mother listened
    to the plaintive notes
she wept, perhaps for my
absence, perhaps for her
not knowing where I was,
when I'd return, or,
            if.
Until she died she kept the box
hidden, silent as an unmarked grave
in a neglected plot. Once I asked her
why. Her lips like old scars paled.
She said I had betrayed her by going off
        to God Knows What,
while she was left alone with her
  imagination and her fears.

Decades later the blackly lacquered box
is on my desk. I open it and see
a loaded carbine aimed at my gut
a hill erupting quietly before the burst
that deafens   that withers reason
an almost endless string of bunkered nights,
a sleepless catalogue of ghosts creeping up
        the ridges of my dreams.
A legless girl begs, a starved orphan cowers
        in a garbage dump.
I close the lid. It won't shut all the way.

Moira Linehan

Mr. and Mrs. I. N. Phelps Stokes

John Singer Sargent, 1897

Here, the art of the line where she's paused
for the moment, paused just for a moment
for she's on the move, she's on her way out
in her heavily starched white linen skirt,
front panel with crisply pressed pleats down each side,

the sheen of the skirt so shiny it seems
this part of the painting has just been cleaned.
The new art of dressing to be on the move,
no longer yards and yards of trailing fabric.
Now a distinct A-line skirt, though still floor-length,

Sargent's long vertical brush strokes following
the form, this skirt half the length of the canvas,
though for the moment her brisk energy's held
in check. Yet she has had time to angle
her left arm, place its hand on her hip

to display her rings, she the newly married
Mrs. Phelps Stokes. The art of the vertical
line repeated in her pale gray striped blouse,
then the balance of the horizontal:
the wide, heavily-padded puffed shoulders

of her dark blue serge jacket and impossible
leg-of-mutton sleeves. The width of those shoulders,
the width of the skirt's hemline. So here the art
of composition: a triangle inverted
atop an isosceles, those two shapes held

in place by her wide belt. And Mr. Phelps Stokes
proves the point as he stands in shadow behind
his new wife: his long long legs, slightly spread
as one more triangle. The art of the line,
arranging him as background fixture.

Tell Me

Tell me it's not too late to be made
sensible, to start listening to real adults,

even my mother, by giving up the foolish dreams
of childhood I've carried like a heart

murmur—close to the chest, detectable only
when an ear is pressed against the body.

At what point exactly is the switch flipped?
I'm twenty-five and still waiting

to be activated by some force, some thing
that will come for me in the middle of the night,

split open skin, reach in somewhere below
the ribs to press on some secret lever, as a lover

would, and turn me on. Some people I know
are switching professions—hanging up

butcher and palette knives, hammers and wrenches,
for a white coat and stethoscope, believing they'll find

God or validation, residing in the body
like a tumor in the gallbladder they can extract,

cup in sterile hands, study under stark fluorescence.
But despite all this, here I am, still floundering,

and I don't know about the future or what I believe,
but I do know this: there is a pen in my left pocket

and my body is a sheet of paper I press against,
promising not to change no matter how much time passes.

Ceridwen Hall

Immaculate Hemostasis

the surgeon wrote. A medical term, my mother translated: almost no blood in the scalpel's wake. All wounds require edges—these were clean and small. But I heard *heliostasis* and thought instead of the sun immobilized, of winter light suspended. My losses today are virtual, theories only. Sometimes a measured devastation brings relief, the cellular fortress holds. Or a paring knife slips and breaches; we must find a bowl of ice, press a towel to the accident

MamaLu's boys

Chris   Curt Paul Johnny BB

The Washerette

On more than one occasion MamaLu's wringer washing machine "took ill," meaning that it just quit working. On this particular Tuesday, it announced its imminent demise with a jolting walk across the kitchen floor, spewing water everywhere, and making unusual screeching and moaning sounds—then followed by a creepy absolute silence. MamaLu sighed and thought—"Is it time for extreme unction?"

MamaLu was quite talented at fixing just about anything, but the washing machine always pushed her talents to the ultimate limits. She was ready to take an ax to the Kenmore and deliver serious and permanent harm. Before doing so, however, she called upon my brother Curt and me to bundle the dirty clothes, to take them to the nearby laundromat and to wash, dry, and fold them. She presented us with a financial incentive. She would give each of us a dollar, plus any money left after the washers and dryers had consumed most, but not all, of our dimes and quarters. We eagerly complied with her request and stuffed all of the clothes into several pillow cases. We put all the towels, sheets, blankets, and bedspreads into a double sheet that we tied together at opposing corners. We created a very large bundle that gave the appearance of a soon-to-be explosion. Then we put the packed pillow cases on our Radio Flyer wagon along with a gigantic box of Tide. We placed the big drooping sheet bundle on top to keep everything stable. For most people, our wagon was probably a pitiful sight to behold, but not for us. We were off on another adventure, this time to the local, very noisy, and hot laundromat. Our mother had calmed down and was going to give the washing machine one more attempt at resuscitation while we were gone.

Even though we had previously been to this narrow galley of washers and dryers, we detected something different about our presence this time. It seemed that we were being placed under close scrutiny by the patrons who were already there. They watched as we unstuffed our pillow cases and re-stuffed our family's clothes into two rows of small machines, giving them a heavy dose of unmeasured detergent and turning the temperature dial to "hot." There were two large machines and we also stuffed them full, packing them with sheets, bedspreads, and blankets. We were aware of "machine hogs" who took over the entire laundromat, but we didn't consider ourselves as such since most of our fellow washers, all females, had used only a few machines; and there were other ones still available. The looks from the laundromat ladies were not approving; however, they made no comments to us. They appeared as if they, with religious zeal, wanted to provide us with their tried-and-true procedures for such an important aspect of life's demanding duties. In essence, they sought to become our Maytag missionaries.

Curt and I realized that we had violated one of several unwritten laundromat rules by not having the adequate coins for the washers. We had to visit the change machine and insert dollar bills for dimes and quarters. This was not the appropriate protocol. We had initially "claimed the machines" by loading them and dousing them with Tide before we actually had the cash available in coins to start them. Our cleaning colleagues gave us critically disapproving looks and muted comments, delivered with torturously and tightly-drawn faces. We resolved our breech of protocol quickly because the dollar changer was actually working; so we revved ten machines with shirts, pants, underwear, sheets, dishrags, and no telling what else. The place was soon humming with a cacophony of grunts, groans, and clicks from washing machines and screeches and buzzers from the drums of dryers.

We sat down in some very uncomfortable, but strangely appropriate, used and splintered theater seats which lined the front wall of the narrow room. Then we began to observe the performance of the laundromat thespians, who adopted with quiet zeal the role of willing teachers. They were like mimes performing silently with overly-exaggerated gestures and movements. Their well-established and highly refined task analyses led them to the ultimate achievement—the cleanest clothes possible in the least expensive way and in the least amount of time. However, unlike Marcel Marceau, they never flashed the happy face of contentment at the end of their performance. Were we not a worthy audience for such a talented duo of professionals? Perhaps they were amazed at the audacity of two young boys to attempt to wash and dry their family's clothes. Or, maybe they were offended by the boldness of their parents to send them alone to accomplish such weighty tasks. Anyway, they put their doubts aside and performed for us as we sat uncomfortably in their arena. We decided that all the laundromat's a stage and they were the mere actors. We were the mere audience, and a barely worthy one at that, so we watched their multi-act performance carefully and compared it to ours, trying not to miss any theatrical nuances.

Act I. Selecting machines. The laundromat ladies were very specific about what was washed in each machine. They place only white items in one machine, all subjected to very hot water and a touch of bleach. They placed all other clothes into separate machines with warm or cold water, demonstrably shaking each item with vigor and purpose as if to remove extraneous dirt and whatever. They even turned some items inside out. We, however, just stuffed anything and everything into a machine, the more the better. Shame on us! They also monitored their machines closely for the appointed time for the anointing of softeners. We skipped that phase entirely.

Act II. Drying. The loud clicking of the washing machines at the termination of the final cycle of cleansing and rinsing was a critical event. It was time to move to the drying process, an even more meticulous set of movements than previously performed. The laundromat ladies arranged their possessions according to the time required for an adequate drying. Lighter items here, heavier ones there. The first load that completed the drying cycle should be folded before the second load stopped, and so forth—thus maximizing time efficiency. The la-

dies also adjusted the temperature dials on the dryers. Curt and I just loaded the machines as full as possible and put the temperature on as high as possible. Our performers gave us the most severe, stern, and disapproving stares. Where was our mother? Perhaps, she had not taught us the art and science, dare I say the "religion," of washing, drying, and folding?

We proceeded in spite of the bad karma that was being laser-focused upon us. Within a few minutes, we had several dryers full and running. We put several coins in them—also a violation of good practice. Put only one coin in and check afterwards. Some of the clothes might have already dried and could be removed and folded, while other were still drying.

Now with loaded dryers, we had time to assess the laundromat ladies as they had spent a great deal of time assessing us. The most obvious physical traits besides their drawn faces and lips were their hairdos. They had what was generally referred to as "Wesleyan wads," "Wesleyan" referring to a very conservative branch of the Methodist Church. They arranged their prematurely grey streaked hair into a long braid which they wrapped round and round on top of their head and secured it with a mesh net. Curt and I, and many others, thought that it looked like a "cow pile." Were they not aware of Clairol's Loving Care which our mother used so successfully? They were not makeup wearers so there was no hint of rosiness in their cheeks, nor, unfortunately, in their disposition; and they wore long dresses that were grey drab and unremarkable. In fact, the contents of their clothes baskets were completely void of color. Curt and I felt sorry for them. Did they not appreciate the colors of nature? the rainbow? We did not dare express our thoughts to them as they seemed to condemn and pity us with every glance—and the occasional intense stare.

Act III. Folding. We watched carefully as our unofficial mentors demonstrated a boot camp discipline in removing their items, shaking them until they emitted a snapping sound, and then folding them with military precision. They were in automaton mode. Sheets demanded the attention of two actors/dancers; they were folded as if their grand pas de deux had been choreographed by Martha Graham herself. There was a meeting of the hands as these, our luminaries, came together precisely at the halves and quarters, eventually recreating a well-folded mass worthy of gracing Meyers-Arnold's, the finest department store in town. They folded pants and creased them with their hands several times so that very little ironing would be needed. They violently jerked shirts out of the moving dryer, shook them soundly, and put them on hangers as if there were a ten-second limit for each one—including the fastening of the top two buttons. They handled underwear, in contrast to other items, very discreetly, as if no one actually wore it. They folded ever so modestly bras, panties, and men's BVDs. They placed a basket on the clothes folding table so as to shield the view of such intimate items while they were folding them. Curt and I also had no desire to expose our underwear, nor that of any of our family members in this theatre of cleanliness, but our reason was different. Our undergarments were so ragged that they advertised impoverishment. We did not want anyone to see them.

Act IV. Packing up and leaving. The laundromat ladies put all their clothes into strictly-designated baskets. Curt and I, however, put all items into several pillow cases and then placed them into our Radio-Flyer. Separating them by person would occur at home when we dumped everything on the floor and called—"Come and get your clothes." The truth about the entire experience was that we seemed to be equally as content as the Wesleyan women were discontent; or, perhaps they were really happy with their success and just perplexed by our lack of it by their standards.

Our quasi-Methodist mentors shared an old rusting and faded blue station wagon which they loaded with care and exacting precision based upon who would be leaving the car first. Once they placed their baskets into the car, they closed the door securely and took off—leaving a cloud of blue smoke. The final act curtain had been pulled. They had left the cathedral of clean with the righteous satisfaction that their performance was superior to any other actor on the stage, especially the twin boys who would leave with unfolded clothes stuffed into pillow cases. Curt and I should have given them a standing ovation, demanding at least one curtain call.

Evidently, we weren't even appropriate material for proselytization; the ladies did not give us even one religious tract. They did present one (Do you know the Way?) to an older woman who had arrived a few minutes before they made their exit. We obviously had not attained salvation by suds, redemption by rinse, nor forgiveness by folding. Maybe, they were content with ministering to us by example; or, perhaps they just placed us on their permanent prayer list. We left contently soon after they did with an overloaded wagon full of washed and dried clothes and a half-full box of Tide.

Unlike our Maytag missionaries, we arrived home with a number of surprises. Those towels that were moderately white returned as pink, some a subdued baby blue—and there were other surprising color combinations. I liked the tie-dyed effect of my tee-shirts. Underwear wasn't really seen so it didn't matter that it had a dull green or gray, or multicolored look. MamaLu did not complain about the mixing of colors. She always tried to see the positive in any situation, so she found the new colors to be refreshing: "Oh, it looks like some of us have a completely new wardrobe. I always wondered how that blouse would look if it were pink—it's beautiful. Those sheets! Now they match the bedspread." Then there was also the shrinkage issue. Paul acquired new additions to his wardrobe as my clothes, and Curt's, had been subjected to a little too much hot water and heat.

MamaLu praised us for our laundering work as we told her about our close scrutiny by the members of the Wesleyan welfare league. Her response was that she bet that we had probably learned something from them, and that all of us needed as many people as possible to care about us. I had to admit that the next time that we went to the laundromat, I took hangers for the shirts. Anyway, we celebrated a job completed, and we surprised MamaLu with a Dr. Pepper and a Hershey bar, always her favorites. She sat down on the kitchen floor where she had flipped the washing machine on its side. She took a sip of her DP and started tightening a bolt with a pair of pliers. She smiled and said: "I think I've fixed it!"

❖ ❖ ❖

Antonius Roberts. *Rooster*. 1996. Acrylic on paper. 29.5 x 22 inches. Courtesy of The Dawn Davies Collection.

Julie Garcés

Bees and Chickens

One day we found a bee in my brother's room. It was confused, not aggressive, and looking for the nearest emergency exit. My mother cupped it in a glass and set it free outside. The next day there were three bees, buzzing around up in the corner where the ceiling meets the wall and we knew we had a problem. Outside, under the eave, there was a small hole, a portal to a bee super highway. The bees took turns going in and out in an orderly fashion. The avocado trees were in full bloom in the warm Miami sun and they had a lot of work to do.

My father, being brought up in Colombia with maids and nannies, squirmed and said, "I'm allergic," so my mother called her father, my Grandpa Arthur. We loved our Grandfather, an eccentric man full of stories. We could never quite figure out if they were true or not. He was a bit of a mad genius, an inventor, a collector and now an amateur fruit tree farmer. He invented the pull-tab for soda cans back in the 60s and sold the patent to Coca-Cola for peanuts. The workshop on his 15-acre property was a wonder of trinkets and doodads. His most recent obsession at that time was metal. Antique metal bugs, old brass cookware, and random scraps of steel littered a corner of his overgrown yard. My dad called it junk but we knew better. He had big plans for everything.

For the last few years Grandpa had been experimenting with apiculture, a fancy word for beekeeping. He came over dressed in a space suit with a net over his face. I almost always wore my hair in pigtails back then and he would pull one gently to say hello. My brother was greeted with a light punch in the shoulder. He climbed a ladder and peered into the hole with a flashlight.

"Mel, you got a big problem here!" he shouted down to my mother below as we watched from the sidelines.

"Yeah Pop, I know. Can you help?"

"All right, but it's not going to be pretty,"

he said. He got down off the ladder and rummaged around in our garage until he came out with a small power saw. With the bees swarming around his head and covering his suit, he cut the eave open and let the rectangular piece of wood fall to the ground. He reached into the side of the house and pulled out a honeycomb dripping with translucent golden honey. My mouth watered. He looked it over, carefully climbed down and dropped it into a tupperware he had set aside. The bees were more frantic now, we could hear the hum of their buzzing. He climbed back up and this time the honeycomb he took out was covered in much darker goo, mostly a ball of bees. He dropped this into a second container, popped open the trunk to his '79 Oldsmobile Cutlass, placed the open container of bees inside and slammed the trunk shut. We stood there flabbergasted. He said, "Sorry about the mess!" took off his gloves and got in the car. He drove off slow at first, the diesel fuel wafting through the air as the swarm of bees followed like a cloud. We looked at the empty hole, the power saw on the ground, the chunk of extracted wood and the melting honeycomb, but there was not one bee left behind. Later, Grandpa Arthur called our bees "good pollinators." The honey was delicious and I learned the wonders of honey cinnamon toast in the morning before school.

"The bees are a family," Grandpa explained, "and they'd do anything to stay together, even if it means following my old rust trap for eleven miles."

❖ ❖ ❖

A few years later my parents' relationship hit the skids when my father moved in with a girlfriend he had been seeing. Grandpa Arthur never talked bad about my father except for once telling my brother not to "be like him." Instead he talked about our late Grandma Lois, who died before we were born. "I'd swim an ocean to have her back. She'd know what to tell you, Mel. I don't understand people and how some of them don't have feelings." This only made my mother cry harder.

Years later, Grandpa Arthur wasn't able to move around as much. He kept chickens in a large coop under a mango tree, but he wasn't able to tend to them as he once had. For a while I volunteered to muck out the coop, clean up the dead leaves, wash out their water trough and trim branches to let the sunlight through. My reward would be the few gleaming white eggs I'd find in the hay. My grandpa made the best omelets. We'd sit at the table outside and he'd hand me the comics section of the newspaper. As I got lost in my teenage years, I realized how precious Saturdays were, so Mom had to convince Grandpa to give away the chickens before they wasted away from neglect.

❖ ❖ ❖

My mother was having a hard time with me once I reached tenth grade. I went from making straight A's to skipping school constantly or showing up high or drunk. My friends and I all felt there were more important things to do than hear a lame teacher talk about the ground state of an atom. We preferred to listen to punk music and cut up our shirts. Pierce each other with rusty safety pins and drink malt liquor. Jump off bridges into canals and freebase off the top of coke cans.

My hair was cotton candy pink and I had gotten a job at Dunkin' Donuts. I fought with my mom constantly for the freedom to go out whenever I wanted and come home only to sleep. She kicked me out in a barrage of tears and I was staying at my friend Nancy's house.

I was working behind the counter when Grandpa Arthur walked in. I hadn't seen him in close to a year. It wasn't something I had thought about much, lost in my own drama concerning friends and money. I was expecting a plea to call my mother and brother, to stay in school and pull in good grades for college, to consider my future, but I didn't get any of that.

His eyes lit up when he saw me, green eyes that could shine right through droopy eyelids. He wore a ratty baseball cap and a flannel t-shirt.

"Hi, Sammy," he said as he limped up to the counter. He probably needed a cane but refused to carry one. "I'll have two old-fashions and a small black coffee."

I couldn't even smile as I pulled the tray out; my feelings were as jumbled and confused as my life in that moment.

Then Grandpa Arthur took his baseball cap off and threw it down on the tray, almost spilling the coffee. He searched my face for a reaction. One side of his formerly white hair was dyed bright purple with drips running down the sides of his forehead. The back of his head, as he turned I could see, was a dark blue, as if an afterthought. The other side of his head was shaved. I was speechless.

"We belong to the same clan, you and I. When you were born, you were an itty bitty little thing. Hardly ever cried. I bet you still don't ever cry." But it was too late, a tear had slipped down my cheek. He invited me to live with him and I did, until I graduated high school. We bought chickens, took care of them together and every once in a while I would sleep out in the coop. Sometimes, I realized, I didn't want to be free, I wanted to be wrapped up tight, secure in my surroundings, like hens sleeping peacefully in their coop under a star-filled sky, or bees all balled up together, encased in honey.

❖ ❖ ❖

Spindle Loosener

You, who waited in Ithaca
patiently weaving a burial shroud
for your father-in-law
fending off lovers
while your smooth-talking husband
was sleeping his way across the seas.

You must have wanted a lover
of your own
maybe someone to amuse your son,
show him how to be a man.
Your journey spun upon a wheel,
this weaving
pulling together scraps of wool,
patching each day, making
a thing of beauty
and undoing it, only
to sew it again.

And this is where we stand:
in the doing and the undoing
Monk-like with sand,
setting the supper table
like a mandala,
each still life
not waiting for anything
in particular,
saying yes.

The Kidnapped Child, Moved to Welford, England

What kind of a man puts
a gun in the hands of a child?

We were in Welford. I was numb to it.
Ever since I could remember, the large man

had guns in his house, handguns
in his heavy bedroom drawer,

had rifles under the bed, in the closet.
All loaded. His glossy magazine was

The Shooter's Bible, and I saw his religion
enough to cringe. Hallelujah, brother ammo.

He welcomed any intruder. But I was
the intruder he stole into his house.

Years he would sit on the bed, polish
the bluegrey metal and, through his door,

glare at me on the parlour floor
with my quiet pencils.

We were in Welford—when he unsleeved
two rifles and shoved me into the woods—

to toughen me up with squirrel hunting.
We were in Welford and the land was beautiful.

The woods breathed their pastoral art of the earth
as we trampled the underbrush, the crish

crish of my wellingtons. I didn't want
to be there. I didn't want to be in this life.

The man's oily hands forced mine to hold
the bluegrey barrel, to shoulder the gunstock,

and aim for lumps of leaves high
in the tree's thick canopy. I aimed.

I pulled the metal trigger like the movies
and shot lumps of leaves. I shot and recoiled,

shot and recoiled. I hit twenty trees of nothing,
beginning to breathe after each empty thunder.

And then, the tree lived in. And then,
the shot that shuddered out

the furry body of a squirrel,
plunged to the cold ground, thudding through

the bluegrey smoke from the barrel.
We were in Welford, and I couldn't move.

Something more dead in me. Was it possible
to become more numb than usual?

Years. Somewhere in a dead house,
there used to be a photograph of the aftermath:

a looming, smiling man holding a rifle,
a waifish boy holding a squirrel by the tail

and smiling out for the camera.
The world is tentative. I damn that photograph

and pray for its destruction. I pray
for its erasure, its consignment to the garbage.

I cringe from the deadness of its history,
those living dead in that house.

I pray to rise like smoke to the edge of Heaven
where I can, one day, meet the soul

of that squirrel and beg its forgiveness,
and explain that they weren't my hands

and it wasn't my will—
but was only Welford in its English beauty,

in the loved geometric pastures of Welford
stepping over the quilted hills to Chaddleworth,

the carpet of forest that cantered off
into the Newbury haze, the green hills that seasonally

forgave us our trespasses, the yielding forest
that a man could corral and contain anywhere,

that a man could crish through the underbrush
and kill a child by lifting a gun to the air.

Nicholas Samaras

The Kidnapped Child Composes a Last Letter to the Past

This pencil is made
out of the splinters of my life.

This paper is made from a tree
as hammered as my skin.

This page is golden,
as I am golden.

This ink is as blue
as the blood I transfused.

When I break myself open,
my eyes go flowing.

The future comes into the present.
I am gone, I am already gone.

I write this to the dirt.
I lay down the hurt.

I close this pen
to pick up no bags,

just the clothes on my back
to get me out the door.

I mail this to the earth,
nobody's child

but my own signature,
the name I finally am.

John Cox. *Crash & Burn (with Leonardo)*. 1997. Acrylic and silkscreen on paper. 23.5 x 18.25 inches. Courtesy of The Dawn Davies Collection.

Garrett Theige

Blast Radius

"I don't know if it's supposed to mean anything."

— Ronaldi's only on-record interview, shortly after "Shrapnel" incident. *Ronaldi: An Assemblage of Random and Classical Modernica*, p. 374.

Jerry returned to the bedroom with a spool of dental floss he found wedged behind the trap underneath his bathroom sink.

This was fantastic news. He'd finished what he thought was his last spool after fastening the Plexiglas panes together and securing them to the eye bolt screws, which left him with few options for connecting the rest of October. He'd considered scraps of his shirt or jeans, but tearing or cutting them thin enough, and uniformly at that, would take too long, would bungle the whole thing. There was a chance the gas station a few blocks from the apartment would still have some, but a trip was out of the question.

Setting the floss in a coffee can, Jerry picked out a few pushpins and set them on the pile of news clippings at his feet. He'd come across three Dalí-esque clocks drooping over Mt. Rushmore, The Statue of Liberty, and a framed copy of Dalí's own "The Persistence of Memory" interspersed between a checkerboard of news briefs on Thursday's front page. They looked to be rough scans straight out of a sketchbook, and Jerry had been trying to discern if the smudge in the center of each clock was Ronaldi's signature grease pencil. He'd slowly clipped out each clock, careful to make even slices with the scissors, crisp ninety-degree angles at the corners, holding the paper awkwardly so as to not accidentally ignite it with his cigarette.

Breaking his focus, Jerry texted Allison: "Remember when you took me to Spain for our anniversary? You couldn't wait to take me to the Prado, even though you didn't realize that, instead of spending time walking around with you, room to room, talking about what we liked, making up little backstories about all the people frozen in time, I'd spend most of the afternoon in front of that Ronaldi painting of the Che Guevara sticker on the banana (I'm still sorry, by the way). But now imagine it again. I'm so lost in the painting that I couldn't feel the museum guards pulling at me when the exhibit closed, but this time while you're dragging me out, my ankles catch on a dislodged floorboard, severing both my Achilles tendons, my screams startling you so badly that you fall backward, impaling your spinal cord on the floorboard's exposed nails. Instead of calling for help, the museum guards quickly gather poles and velvet ropes in a square to enclose us, writing a sign next to it, calling it 'The Fall of Ronaldi.'" Maybe that would get her.

Jerry picked the Thursday paper back up. The front page featured a nine-column photo of a tear-off calendar page bearing nothing but "14," which hung from its top-left corner and curled up at the bottom. Unlike the days before it, this one appeared to have been burned by something, brushed with toasted marshmallow browns at the edges as if scorched by a distant heat. He scanned the stories beneath the illustration. The only thing of note was the editorializing tucked into the final sentences of each one: "What does it even matter;" "It might as well just happen now;" "As if it comes as any surprise."

Jerry turned to the C section. The top half of the page was dedicated to an illustration of another Dalí clock. This one, however, had little cartoon limbs, and it drooped against a black chain-link fence along a sidewalk. There was a bullet hole where the clock's one used to be, blood dripping through the spider cracks in its face. As the story followed, Ronaldi—an elderly painter-turned-graffiti-artist—had hung a banner over the White House fence and painted contorted versions of Big Ben to spell out "What is Ti" before being shot in the head. Upon hearing the news, supporters of the reclusive Italian painter had come in waves to complete what they believed to be the phrase: "me?"

The honor of completing the job was allegedly so lofty, however, that the would-be-taggers grew territorial, spraying each other in the mouth and eyes as they squabbled, all while trying not to defile the piece with errant paint. The more altruistic taggers positioned themselves between the others and the canvas, dropping their cans, jumping up and down to block the clouds of paint drifting toward the unfinished work. The whole scene was too absurd for the Secret Service's skeleton crew to react in any way.

Eventually, one of the agents shot a particularly aggressive tagger in the head, setting off a brutal retaliation from the other taggers, who were all apparently armed for this exact purpose. Bodies flopped like fish, bearings rattled in cans, and the occasional *paahp* of a can caught in the crossfire sprinkled the bodies with their own artistic caviar. The Secret Service was frantic by this point, all of them instinctively touching their long-dead earpieces as they fired into the fray.

The agent who had originally shot Ronaldi was the only survivor left to survey the damage. He stepped over bodies and kicked cans out of the way as clouds of paint settled on his shoulders. He picked up a can and wiped the blood off on his jacket before finishing the final question mark himself, holding the lapel of his jacket over his mouth. He took a step back to admire the slipshod work, and then shot himself in the head.

Jerry jumped at the sensation of heat. His cigarette had burned down to the filter, singeing the insides of his fingers. Without looking up from the story, he stubbed the cigarette out in a tub of margarine he'd left out from breakfast.

Taking his scissors, Jerry cut out the dying clock and set it on top of the three smaller clocks. He stood up and ducked around the Plexiglas panes hanging in the center of the room by the braided ropes of dental floss. Jerry looked at the wall for a moment before affixing each image into the appropriate square. He stepped back around the Plexiglas, the four panels left swaying as he walked out of the room.

Jerry tried to think up another message to Allison. When they were still together, after spending a winter afternoon binging through all five *Final Destination* films, they'd made a game out of trying to think of the most morbid way to die: drowning; getting eaten by rats; getting set on fire and then drowned; getting eaten by rats that were burning to death, then drowned, then pulled out and shot in the head.

Their little game, which they played via text for the better part of a year, exploded when his mom died of a heart attack, slipping away in less time than it took Jerry to get a cup of coffee. That whole next month, Allison hadn't left Jerry for more than a trip to the bathroom, nodding quietly and rubbing his back as he kept rambling more death scenarios, trying to fill his mind with more horrific things than the reality opening up before him.

"So you know that feeling when you stand up too fast, all dizzy? Imagine you're waiting for the subway to pull up, checking your phone or thinking about the class you have to teach tonight, or the one you just taught yesterday, imagine you're sitting waiting for the train, like I said, and you feel something in your flat, pressing into your arch. So you bend down and try to get it out, except your flat is extra tight today for some reason, even for a slip-on, and once you get it off, you realize nothing is actually on your foot, it's just some mysterious phantom irritant, and when you stand back up it's that dizzy feeling, *bam*, right there, and you stumble forward, and the train hits you as it's slowing down, pulling up to the platform, slowly crushing you, but not enough to kill you like *BLAM* they do in movies and news stories, and so but somehow no one notices you, doesn't hear you screaming, and then the subway, automatic sensor systems failing, still accelerates over you, smearing you across the tracks in deep purples and fleshtones."

Jerry put his phone in his pocket, trying to remember what he meant to do next. It concerned him; he used to go through full days able to focus on just the ticking of his watch, the occasional flipping of the newspaper page, not even checking for texts from Allison, reading the entire paper without lifting his eyes for a moment, drinking coffee from pint glasses without noticing he'd run out of clean mugs, wiping his ass with the hand towel instead of toilet paper, not noting it until he attempted to flush, the toilet protesting with a sad gurgle. His apartment had turned into the psychic backdrop of some new countdown zen he'd developed, both focused and adrift, always moving nowhere.

That focus was the only thing he needed now. He could never figure out how other people did whatever they finally did after cooking dinner, fridging the leftovers, tucking the dishes into the cupboards; how they could watch TV like they did, taking in a litany of shows to fill the segmented 150 minutes between the end of their to-do lists and the hour when doctors recommended they should all fall asleep to get enough rest for yet another day.

That sort of mindlessness used to disgust him, but now he yearned for it, as he couldn't even focus on an episode of *Wheel of Fortune*, let alone the project at hand.

Jerry decided to take the trash outside. He slipped out onto the sidewalk, slinking quietly down the alley where he'd been piling his trash for months. Somehow, despite now having to reach over his head to balance the bags on top of the ones from last week, the piles hadn't yet tumbled onto the sidewalk, been ravaged by scavengers, or been set afire by one of the wandering packs of children. He pressed them down to settle the pile, then checked the bowl of dog food he'd put next to the streetlight.

"You lose Badge, so you frantically try to track him down. You find him inside the dog park, but somehow the gate has been locked from the inside, so you hop the fence to join him, but slip on the way over the top, fracturing your spine and paralyzing yourself from the waist down. In your agony, trying to pull yourself upright, you don't notice that Badge has contracted an impossibly aggressive case of rabies. Just as you see the froth at his mouth, he begins devouring you, tearing flesh from your limbs as if it were cooked, all while you're trying to pull your paralyzed body back over the fence. And then, of course, you die."

The bowl was still full. Jerry put his phone away.

Jerry thought of Ronaldi's trash cans. About five years prior, Ronaldi—just beginning his transition from painting to graffiti—completed a hybrid of the two. Somewhere in Paris, under cover of night, he had painted the outside of a few trash cans to make both the can and liner look completely transparent. Instead of painting empty coffee cups, bruised heaps of banana peels, and chewed, brain-like hunks of gum inside, each item was rendered perfectly whole and intact: lacquered gum balls in lurid reds and greens; full cups of cappuccino complete with fern-leaf foam art; and Ronaldi's watermark of sorts: a Red Delicious apple with

a Roald Dahl sticker on it. Ronaldi had spent most of 2021 painting faces of famous political figures, artists, writers, and celebrities in place of the Dole, Chiquita, and numbered white stickers commonly found on supermarket produce. He never named the series nor displayed all the parts at once, instead opting to randomly hang pieces across Europe, South America and the U.S. one by one — Che Guevara for Chiquita, Hannibal Lecter on Honeycrisp Apples, O.J. Simpson on navel oranges in red mesh bags.

Back inside the apartment, he pulled out the most recent of his Ronaldi biographies. He'd spent the better part of the past five years amassing every book about Ronaldi he could find. He had purchased first editions of the seven unauthorized biographies in publication, pre-ordered every coffee table book he could find displaying his art, even printed and hand-bound collections of message board threads about Ronaldi that Jerry himself had participated in.

In the most recent biography, Ronaldi was still in his sixties, with so little known about his personal life that the biographer had resorted to writing a full chapter about the etymology of his name. Ronaldi was a spin on the French *Renaud*, popularized in twelfth-century Old French literature with Renaud de Montauban, who had impressed Charlemagne by winning a tournament. He then quickly fell out of Charlemagne's graces by killing one of his nephews in a brawl, forcing him to seek refuge with a sorcerer before eventually going on The Crusades. Jerry pulled *Ronaldi—An Assemblage of Random and Classical Modernica* off the shelf and turned to the "ongoing work" section, which ended with the incident that had nearly derailed Ronaldi's career.

He'd delved into the world of non-traditional (some would even say "stunt") art, creating exhibits many critics considered an attempt at career suicide. Among these was a hard-earned spot at an exhibit in the Museum of Modern Art. Ronaldi had agreed to create an interactive, Renaissance-cum-contemporary work the curators believed would re-invent the world of modern art.

Instead, he nearly re-structured the museum.

While he was expected to set up during the three-day pre-exhibition period, Ronaldi was nowhere to be found. Right as the curators were about to fill the empty exhibit with hastily printed Banksy reproductions, Ronaldi walked in carrying three plastic Walmart bags sagging with south-of-pleasant-smelling supplies. He sat them down before removing the three requested seven-by-eleven-foot canvases from the wall. He took out three packs of bone-in, skin-on chicken thighs, an eight-pack of Dannon probiotic yogurt, and a gallon freezer bag of stewed vegetables. After a brief pause to pull on yellow dishwashing gloves, he began splattering fistfuls of the vegetable matter over the canvases.

Within seconds, the nearby curators began frantically pawing at their noses. The weaker ones heaved over the nearest trash cans while the particularly brave-stomached sucked in final breaths of air, puffing out their cheeks with determination as they drew closer. Some took photos as Ronaldi fired up a battery-powered mixer and began hacking at the chicken thighs in their styrofoam trays, flecking little bits of pinkish-white flesh and red fluid onto the white walls and Ironwood flooring. He added cautious dollops of soured yogurt to the chicken, methodically, as one might whisk flour into a roux. He continued splattering the chicken parts, each bit landing with a little fleshy *thwap* in the stiff, meringue-like peaks of Dannon. The Pollackesque canvases took nearly three hours to complete, as Ronaldi kept pacing, apparently immune to the odor that had pushed all but the most ancient curator (a man who had survived the Holocaust as a small boy) out of that wing of the museum.

The smell was so unsurprisingly rank that the head curator called in a Hazmat team minutes after Ronaldi—now slick with a yogurt-and-chicken glaze—had titled the exhibit "Shrapnel" with a grease pencil, re-packed the leftover food parts, and walked out. The museum refused to comment on whether Ronaldi had been fined for his work, and Ronaldi was never heard from, having gone into immediate seclusion upon his exit.

Jerry brought the book into the bedroom and cut out the pages pertaining to "Shrapnel." He looked up at the poster of the Golden Gate Bridge he'd hung above the sixteen-square-foot canvas of calendar squares. The Shrapnel pages were the perfect addition to the final week of October. He pinned them over Sunday the twenty-sixth and Monday the twenty-seventh, which along with the three clock illustrations

and the large, bleeding, anthropomorphic one, completed the month. Jerry took a red Sharpie from the can of push pins and wrote "October" across the underside of the bridge

He grabbed a pair of binoculars and tried to look down the side of the building to where the dog bowl sat on the sidewalk. Aside from a squirrel flitting about in front of the bakery (the first moving creature Jerry had seen in at least two weeks), there was no sign of Badge. Badge, who used to run into the bedroom and jump onto Jerry's pillows before he went to bed, who would manage to wake him up within minutes of his alarm on the days when his phone died. That animal intuition must have been what made him sense what was going on, smelling it in the air, all of it clicking in his little doggy brain as he chewed free of his leash two months ago, probably whimpering as he ran for the hills.

Ronaldi, Jerry figured, had done the same between the post- "Shrapnel" disappearance and his recent death. The only other piece people attributed to Ronaldi during his disappearance was discovered on the side of an apartment building in rural Italy, where his father (a historian from Brazil) and mother (the CFO of a Peruvian financial trust) had moved when Ronaldi was nine. On the white stucco wall of the building, Ronaldi had superimposed Nick Ut's famous Vietnam War photograph of Kim Phuc, the nine-year-old girl running naked in the streets after being nearly burned to death by a napalm bomb. The photo remained largely unaltered except for the words "Blast Radius" running along the top third of the photo, orange letters dripping rather garishly onto Phuc's tiny, bare shoulders. The work had brought the controversial photo back to international conversation, although it was always unclear to Jerry why Ronaldi, a bizarre but seemingly non-random artist, chose to put such a highly political painting in a country with little involvement in the war. The painting, albeit unsigned by Ronaldi and destroyed by vandalism, was photographed and then attributed to him by five of his biographers. Ronaldi, as had become quite common, could not be reached for comment.

"He had to have known something," Jerry had written once on a message board shortly after the painting was discovered. Most people had vehemently disagreed, as the piece had been created three months before news of the failed standoff ever surfaced, long before the paychecks and mail quit coming, before *Wheel of Fortune* began airing an empty studio each day, a pile of transcripts rustling around the studio like a tumbleweed.

Ronaldi, like most everyone else, had probably gone to find family, settle debts, settle into what was coming, before the rioting came sweeping through towns, targeting stores, monuments, wildlife: mowing down deer, squirrels, birds, anything belonging to the earth's natural chorus.

Jerry didn't see the point. These messengers, Allison, all these other people had not studied the meaning of the name Renaud, how it all seemed to be right with Ronaldi's life. They had not read, re-read, committed to memory biographies of Ronaldi, stared at his paintings until they could see the negatives when they closed their eyes. They had not spread their walls with news clippings, paintings, alleged recent sightings of Ronaldi himself, connecting them all with dental floss. They had not spent months in isolation working on this, looking for Ronaldi, trying to pilfer a message out of it all, had not let their dogs loose in the woods, leaving girlfriends in disbelief at backstories about a chewed-through leash. They had not abruptly abandoned girlfriends in pursuit of a new lead.

Two months ago, Jerry had been killing time in the lobby of the building where Allison taught night school, hoping to make things up to her after the Badge incident. In the Community College newsletter lying on the table, he started reading an essay about World Suicide Prevention Day written by a man named Donald Bontamain. Bontamain noted how since the inaugural awareness day, the number of visits to the Golden Gate Bridge on that day increased by two hundred percent. After two or three paragraphs, the writer's anagrammic pseudonym clicked in Jerry's head. He walked out of the lobby and continued reading the whole way home. While the suicide rate didn't correlate with this trend, Ronaldi (he now knew) wrote, it was enough for him to abandon a project he'd wanted to do in San Francisco. He'd planned to hang glass panes from heavy cable beneath the bridge. He'd splatter some with red enamel paint and splash others with swatches of metallic golds and silvers to reflect light. The whole thing would shimmer brilliantly, visible mainly to boaters in the Golden Gate Strait. Jerry taped the essay to a large sheet of blank paper on his bedroom wall and began drawing out what he imagined Ronaldi would make. When Allison called, ending the week-long silence after Badge's disappearance, he wasn't relieved at all, leaving the phone ringing in his pocket. He hadn't seen her since.

He rubbed at his eyes after setting the binoculars down. He had no idea how long he'd had them pressed between his eyes and the window. Just a few months ago, peeping from an eighth-floor window would have been a strict taboo, but the very concept of voyeurism had been wiped out with the complete halt of public life. He wondered what the neighbors he had left were doing, all marooned on their own little islands. As the mail had stopped, stores had shut down, and updates on the standoff had stalled, Jerry figured most people spent their time calling, moving in with friends, scheduling the countdown they had extrapolated from the newspapers: fourteen days, call grandparents; eleven days, dash to grocery store for last can of kidney beans; six days, parents no longer returning calls; five days, parents' phones die. One day. A slight rumble, plates tinkling in the cabinet.

Jerry lit another cigarette. He heard the small thuds continuing. Ripples formed in the water resting in the pots in the sink. He pictured the elongated pools of Ronaldi's blood, rippling thickly, coagulating into something like tapioca pudding. He texted Allison once more:

"Trying to talk me down from the Golden Gate Bridge, stepping out there with me, holding my hand, pulling me back over the ledge, only to fall backward together with an unfortunate gust of wind. Luckily, there's a safety net, but a particularly acrobatic squirrel has chewed through a section of it, so there's a hole just big enough to fit most of us through, but then our necks get caught, snapping them, shitting ourselves, leaving me with the death boner and everything."

Jerry looked up at his calendar, his eyes bloodshot, two months of scruff dangling from his chin like moss. In the presence of his complex string of Ronaldi paintings, stunts, and family history, he didn't want to go anywhere. Renaud remained away at The Crusades for years, only to return to the news that his wife had died. Disillusioned, heartbroken, and alone, Renaud then dedicated the rest of his life to building a church. After some years, he was eventually killed by his workers.

There was no telling what Ronaldi's church was. He'd meant to test the question on the message boards or propose it to Allison, had either party been accessible after Ronaldi's death. He'd been asking Badge for months, slumped on his mattress on the floor, stroking Badge's stomach, intertwining *whosagoodboy*'s with more facts, more strings, more connections. Why Ronaldi was right, why everything was connected, everyone was connected, and how it still might not have mattered or meant anything. The synchronicity of zero was still zero.

Jerry's phone buzzed against his thigh for the first time in months. Allison.

"Jerry?"

Even through a text, he could still hear a gravity in her voice, despite not having heard it in months, if one was, of course, to discount the voice recording on her answering machine, which he had heard upward of fifty times. He considered responses: "I miss you." "How've you been?" "Sorry."

He could also tell her about the clock illustrations, how the combination of the hour and minute hands could've been a loose numerical anagram for today: Oct. 7, 2025. 10/7/25. 1:00, 7:00, 2:05. With a slightly liberal interpretation of the zeroes, it almost seemed too easy.

A pulse of light came through the window behind him. His coffee sloshed against the microwave glass. Jerry felt the heat on his neck this time. Just like they said. He pictured the heat, the concrete rippling down the sidewalks. It would not be pretty, they'd been writing, not pretty as one would hope the unimaginable to be. There wouldn't be warmth, no soft fade to white. Even from a distance there was an unpleasant heat, a thick acrid smell. Jerry imagined modern day Kim Phucs running down the street as the blast scorched their naked bodies, adolescent boys screaming as their downy pubes turned to ash, stumbling over the sine waves of cement under their feet. He felt his colon clench, his own balls rise up toward his stomach. His forehead was damp.

He closed his eyes, trying to think of what to say to her. Instead, his mind rushed with all of the images he'd been picturing for this moment: dust, black clouds, chaotic roars sweeping over the city, combing through neighborhoods of quiet families. Buildings crumbling, disintegrating — falling brick, steel beams bashing the skulls of the charred naked children, spreading them across the sidewalk in elaborate, deathly brush strokes. Foundations collapsing on the homeless, the injured, congealing them together while ash settled on pools of boiling blood, urine, feces. Margarine bubbled in store refrigerators. Badge barked somewhere, running for his life, crushed with a final whimper under massive structures broken up like kindling.

Jerry's breath caught in his chest, his diaphragm spasming wildly. Perhaps things had not yet started where she was, everything still floating in airy anticipation. Or maybe, windows shattering around her, this was it; she had reached out for the last time.

He started typing.

"Allison."

Jerry sat back down on the floor with the paper. The building shook beneath him as he re-read the articles he hadn't yet clipped from the front page. The panes swung violently from the bedroom ceiling. The floor shifted as something pivotal beneath him seemed to buckle.

❖ ❖ ❖

V. P. Loggins

Being Second

You wonder how it happened,
being the second child, how
your parents found the time or
took the chance to conceive you,
launched you into the role
you would always play
of anxious understudy; how
after your father returned —

or your mother — from the office,
they might have set their course
from the kitchen once they had fed
and washed your brother, your sister,
and had taken their own dinner
and put away the dishes; after all
the talk of the day's difficulties,
the need for money, the sad story

of a neighbor's father, the loss of Gray,
their favorite cat, the impending visit
from your mother's Aunt Betty;
after all of this, you wonder, did she
stroke his late-day stubble cheek,
did he take her by the hand
and lead her upstairs, turning
at the landing toward the bedroom;

was it she who said the very words
that needed saying, or was it really
the space created by saying nothing,
your sibling now tucked, asleep,
softly breathing and barely conscious
in the half-light of the other bedroom,
that made it all possible for you,
as Hamlet wonderingly says, to be.

R. Brent Malone. *Famous Dancer: Homage to Vola*. 1984. Acrylic on canvas. 43 x 32 inches. Courtesy of The Dawn Davies Collection.

Embrace Your Pain

After Amnesty International, Save Darfur, and Domicile for Decency had interrupted their first candlelit evening in forever, Jean Desseyn was ready to rip her landline out of the kitchen wall. But her husband, Jerry, had an idea. Leaning over the lily of the valley centerpiece, he pinged the bowl of her cut crystal goblet with the base of his own. "I'll handle the next caller." Then he retrieved the cordless phone from his home office and arranged it alongside his steak knife, as if it were part of the table setting. A few minutes later, when the handset trilled and glowed, he said, "Watch a professional at work."

With nearly a carafe of wine sloshing around in her stomach, Jean was feeling a bit tipsy. "Go for it," she heard herself say.

"Yes, this is the Desseyn residence." Jerry rolled his eyes away from the mood lighting. "Yes, just fine. Until about fifteen seconds ago."

Jean giggled, then hoisted her half-empty glass of Merlot, finishing it in a single swallow.

"My wife's already mailed you a check. In April, I believe."

Jean always sent out the tax-deductible contributions while Jerry was preparing their Form 1040. Then she'd give him an itemized list of the new donations, which he'd file away for the following year. Working as a team, she figured they could serve both God and Mammon at once.

"Look, buddy," Jerry said, while Jean was uncorking a new bottle. "I'm getting sick of you bloodsuckers. What do the 501-C-Threes give you, anyway? Fifty cents on the dollar?" A stammering reply leaked out of the earpiece, until Jerry cut it off. "It's Sunday night, for Christ's sake! You're vampires. Vampires!" He grabbed his knife and raised it above his head, in melodramatic glee. "I'd love to drive a stake through your so-called heart." He plunged the blade into what was left of a medium-rare prime rib.

"Why?" Jean giggle-screamed. "Why?"

"You hear that, buddy? Your actions have consequences. Con Sequences. Before you called, I was enjoying myself at home. With the little woman. And you've ruined my evening. Which means you've ruined her evening. Follow my drift?"

Jean was getting into this. "No, Jerry! Please!"

"Call again. Any time." He bleeped off the TALK button with his thumb before he tossed the phone into the empty breadbasket. Then he high-fived Jean, pulling the knife out of his rib with his other hand. "They all use the same solicitation service. A cubicle farm near that goddamn monument with the Confederate flag sticking out of it like an umbrella drink. Word should get around."

They finished their grass-fed beef without further interruption, then moved on to the crème brulée. Jean hadn't been able to cook a dinner, a *real* dinner, since God knew when. Their daughter, Charity, bounced them all between Lean Cuisine and TakeAway Gourmet, depending upon her body image at any given moment. At fourteen and a half, she'd already lost and regained more weight than Jean had in her entire life. This weekend, she was on a sleepover at the Knoblochs—the newcomers in the Tuscan townhouse at the far end of Belladonna. They'd moved there from a Mc-Mansion out in the country, after the husband had died in a car crash. Priscilla Knobloch had even volunteered to take the girls to school on Monday morning. The poor woman probably welcomed the company, even if it was only a gaggle of eighth-graders. Jean wondered what The Widow Knobloch was feeding them. Amy, Priscilla's soccer whiz-kid, probably had a training diet concocted by a team of professional nutritionists. That girl looked and ran like a greyhound, even if she did have only one hand. . . . Jean closed her eyes and rested her blurry forehead on her thumbs. She wished her own daughter would start doing *something*—soccer, swimming, softball, even cheerleading. Anything other than hanging out at the mall, buying every boy band CD on the planet, staring at her bathroom mirror, and sleeping with her cell phone stuck on her pillow like an engorged tick. . . .

She awoke to her own cottony mouth and opened her eyes. While she'd been dozing over her placemat, Jerry had gone upstairs and changed into a form-fitting Desseyns Unlimited T-shirt she'd never seen before. It was about three sizes too small, with a single pink arrow from the crew neck to the hemline, pointed down.

"Sorry," he said, wiggling everything between his bare navel and his bare toes. "I don't do undershorts."

Jean wished she'd remembered not to put on her panties. "Can I finish loading the dishwasher?"

"Okay," he pouted. "That sounds like a plan."

He walked toward her, into the kitchen, then turned around. On the other side of the T-shirt, something else was flamboyantly pink—but it was pointed up, not down, and it wasn't an arrow. "Just want you to see what you're missing."

She closed the Maytag and embraced him from behind. "I never miss." On her first try, her left hand found what she was looking for. When she pulled him around, he snickered, "It's not rocket science, baby. Just follow the arrow."

God bless Priscilla Knobloch, Jean thought, before opening her mouth.

❖ ❖ ❖

The next morning broke cloudy and cool, perfect gardening weather, and Jean wasn't even hung over. Lying happily in bed, listening to her husband's low moans harmonize with the chickadees' melody from the east window, she felt proud of herself for having had the presence of mind to swallow two Advils and a pint of water the night before. After the birds flew away, but Jerry didn't, she brought him a bottle of Gatorade so he could rehydrate himself and open his T-shirt store on time. "It's not rocket science," she whispered. "Poor baby."

When Jerry finally managed to drag himself into his car and to point his pounding head in the direction of Desseyns Unlimited, Jean decided to pamper her perennials in the front yard. Somehow she'd metabolized Merlot into pure adrenaline. First she watered the peonies, brilliantly blooming in white and pink. Then she clipped the spent blossoms from the Formosa azaleas until they had the uncluttered, dark green look they'd keep throughout the summer months. After lunch, she moved on to the creeping phlox, then weeded nutsedge and quackgrass out of the periwinkle and the lilies of the valley. When she rose from her knees, ready to drag the brimming polystyrene garden bag to the compost heap, she stopped to admire her day's work.

An ivory minivan was parked on the far side of the circular driveway. The logo for The Space of Hope—a mom and two kids standing on a giant blue hand—was stenciled on the driver's door. A woman was watching her through the tinted window.

As Jean approached, the van's door opened.

She was young, in her late twenties probably, with a buzz cut and multiple piercings through the tops of her ears. "Cool shirt," the woman said.

Jean laughed, pulling EMBRACE YOUR PAIN from her damp skin. "My husband silkscreens them. The overruns make good gardening clothes."

"Who'd he make it for?"

"The Triathlon Club. I guess a lot of them didn't embrace it."

The woman nodded vigorously. "Right."

"Are you looking for Jerry? If you want an event shirt, he'd be happy to rough it out for you. He's very creative."

The woman put her freckled hand on Jean's loam-speckled shoulder. "Actually, I came to see you. You're one of our most loyal supporters." She cleared her throat, but her voice still sounded scratchy and deep, as if she had a bad cold. "We'd like to offer our thanks."

"I should be thanking *you*. The Space of Hope does such important work. For families with nowhere else to turn." Jean gestured toward her newly manicured yard. "Not everyone in the world is lucky enough to have all this."

"This spring we're asking all of our donors to tour The Space of Hope. To meet our volunteer staff. To see how we serve women and children in need."

Jean forced herself to smile. "I've made my annual contribution."

When the woman said that she wanted only her time, not her money, Jean told her that she already volunteered at the Food Kitchen, ten hours a week.

"We understand. Everyone's resources are limited." The woman took Jean's left wrist, bare above the cuff of her gardening glove, and gave it a light squeeze. "We'd just like you to see what we do."

Jean looked at the battered, strapless old watch she kept in her pants pocket. "Well, I've got an hour before my daughter comes home. Just let me wash my hands."

"I'll wait outside," the woman said. "You can follow me in your car."

❖ ❖ ❖

Jean Desseyn had been giving to The Space of Hope for over a decade, but she'd never seen it. It was no wonder. The squat two-story building, sided with white vinyl, looked like an apartment complex for kids just out of college. But it was tucked away, between an insurance agency and a law firm, so you had to go down a short private road to get to the gate. The young woman, whose name was Denise—"We only have first names here!"—leaned out of the van's window to punch in the security code. The striped metal arm spasmed upward, to let both vehicles through.

The perimeter of The Space of Hope glistened with bare white gravel, worthy of a construction site. Jean wondered whether she could offer some landscaping suggestions that wouldn't be taken the wrong way. Dwarf nandina, between some Nelly Myers holly, would be perfect, and would be virtually maintenance-free. She'd call Plantadise Nursery tomorrow. She knew the Master Gardeners there—three grandmothers who spent half their time cooing over baby pictures. They'd do it for next to nothing.

Inside, the building smelled clean—too clean, almost, the chlorinated air reminding her of the YWCA swimming pool where she'd rehabbed her knee. Now it was stout enough for jogging—three miles, three times a week—so she hadn't gone to that pool in years. Yet she still remembered to send in her donation, every April, silently praying she'd never need to go back when she signed the check. Indoor swimming made her skin shrivel up like an avocado that had been abandoned on the kitchen counter for a couple of months.

Denise introduced Jean to Sally—in the re-

ception area, which they called The Quiet Room. White and windowless, it had two sofas with throw pillows facing each other, five feet apart, and a play area for toddlers on the side opposite the door. Jean returned the loose wooden shapes—circles and triangles and squares, all in primary colors—to their respective slots. "My daughter used to have these. She called them her Wuddy Buddies. She just loved them."

After Jean sat down, Sally lowered herself into the opposite sofa. Though she was wearing a long, loose-fitting dress, like a sixties folk singer, Jean could tell she was the woman in charge. Sally smoothed her frizzy gray hair, then folded her fingers in front of her pale, thin lips. "How old is she now?"

"Fourteen." Jean smiled. "Excuse me. Fourteen and a half."

"How's she doing?"

"Oh, you know how it is. They change every minute. But she'll figure it out. I mean, we all did."

Jean noticed that the fluorescent bulb above her couch was flickering slightly, as if it were asking to be replaced. "How many women live here?"

"We have room for twelve. And the children." Sally clasped her hands in her lap. "We're just a step on their way. We're here for them until they can find something more permanent. Until they can find what they need to move on. We take the kids to school every morning, and we bring them back every afternoon. In our own vehicles, for security reasons."

Jean nodded. "Safety first."

Sally's cell phone bleeped the first twelve notes of *Ode to Joy*. She put it next to her ear, like a shell at the beach, and listened. "Give me a moment," she whispered to Jean, and left the room.

Now Jean sat alone. Between the sofas, on the low table, lay three big looseleaf binders: pink, blue, and white. She figured they'd be part of the sales pitch, so she picked the white one up, so she could say she'd already seen it. Then her mouth fell open. Behind clear plastic sheets, bruises were glowering everywhere. They'd all been photographed in this very room, on the very sofa she was sitting on. One of the mothers—a coffee-colored woman, about her own age—had a round face speckled with butterfly bandages and a smile that was missing two upper teeth. Jean shuddered, but she couldn't stop staring at the woman's eyes, wide with something Jean couldn't identify, much less understand. How could anyone live like that?

When Jean looked up, Sally and Charity were already inside The Quiet Room. Dark streaks of mascara stained her daughter's cheeks. "The two of you should talk," Sally said, latching the door behind her on her way out.

"Mom, are you out of your fucking mind?"

Jean stood up and tried to hug her, but her daughter pushed her away. "They pulled me out of class, Mom. Tiffany Beegle was in the office when they came to get me. She saw their IDs and she's been texting the whole school. Look at this!" She waved her Yphone in Jean's face. "I'm gonna be SHLTR GRL for the rest of my life!"

Charity started kicking the painted blocks that Jean had put into their proper places. After she'd scattered them, she didn't stop until every circle and triangle and square had disappeared under the sofas. Then she finally stood still, breathing heavily, her manicured hands on her new hips.

"They were saying all this weird shit about Dad. UGH." She pronounced each of the three letters separately, as if she were spitting them onto the floor. "They told me I was in denial."

"This is a mistake, Charity. A terrible mistake."

"Terrible? Mom, you don't know terrible!" Charity's eyes looked like dirty sinks whose faucets somebody had forgotten to turn off. "My life is over. I can't go back to Thornblade. Ever. Not after this."

"I'm just on a tour. You're just on a tour."

Charity threw her purse at the WE ARE FAMILY poster next to the light switch. "They took me to a room, Mom! And they gave me this bag of clothes they must've grabbed from the return bin at Mall Mart. I mean, not that you'd even notice."

Jean saw Denise at the tiny porthole set into the door, and she motioned her to come back inside. "I will straighten this out, Charity, and I will get you home."

Denise walked into the room with an open box of Kleenex.

"Get that Feminazi out of my face," Charity muttered.

Denise put the tissues down on the table. "We all know what you're feeling."

"FAF," Charity snickered. "PIP."

"There's no need to enable him." She swung around her index finger to point at the block lettering on Jean's T-shirt. "Not here."

Jean stepped between her daughter and Denise. "No one's enabling anybody."

"The Space of Hope is a proactive agency. We seize the initiative whenever the police can't. Or won't." She spread open the pink notebook on the table. "Protect your child. We all know what Jerry Desseyn is capable of."

Jean spluttered with laughter.

"We record our calls." Denise smiled slowly, sadly, from one set of ear piercings to the other. "Even on Sundays."

Her daughter grabbed her shoulders from behind and whispered, "Do something!"

"Charity, nothing is going to happen."

"That's the point! Nothing happens! You never *do* anything!" Now Charity was screaming at the flickering ceiling. "You just fuck around with flowers and give away Dad's money! Can't you at least go buy yourself a decent pair of shoes?" She lowered her gaze to snort at Jean's grass-stained sneakers. "You're a mess. Why doesn't he just ditch you for somebody I could shop with?" She swiped her eyes with the back of her hand.

"Charity, go to your room," Denise said.

"Room? You call that pathetic closet a room?"

"Your mother needs—"

"Somebody *needs* to cut off your nuts, lady!"

Now they were both shouting right through her, as if she weren't there. After she'd grabbed Charity by the elbow, Jean looked at Denise. In the young woman's eyes, she beheld the same dark dilation she'd seen right above those butterfly bandages, in that white notebook. But Denise finally moved aside, and Jean spirited her daughter through the doorway, through the long, disinfected corridor, back to their own car.

Charity refused to speak with her on the ride home. Jean tried to explain Sunday's misunderstanding, that it wasn't Denise's fault, that it wasn't *anyone's* fault, that the shelter did good work, but that sometimes people do wrong things for the right reasons. "They were only trying to protect us, honey. That's their job. You have to forgive them." But her daughter just kept inspecting her own face in the illuminated vanity mirror, alternately pouting and kissing the empty air. Jean let her be until they were back inside their own neighborhood, turning the corner onto their own street. "Charity, please. You're acting like a two-year-old."

When they pulled into the driveway, Jerry was already there, waving to the Belladonna Security cruiser pulling out of the other end of the circle. "Thanks, Sandy!" he shouted. "I owe you one!"

"Daddy!" Charity cried. She ran from the car, leaving the passenger's door wide open, and wrapped her arms around him, joyfully, from behind. From her driver's seat, Jean couldn't help thinking that Charity was almost as tall as she was.

Now he was hugging her, spinning her in a tight circle, freeing her two feet from the

ground. Just looking at them made Jean feel a bit dizzy. "No worries, Princess! I'm gonna get a great shirt out of this. Tank top! Ribbed! American classic! Attitude to the max, baby! WIFE BEATER! Rad emoticon! I am talking *way* cool!"

When Jerry finally stopped, with his back to the car, Charity looked over his shoulder and caught her mother squarely in the eyes. Jean had never seen that smile on her face before.

"Daddy, can we *both* wear it?"

Jean felt her own head strike the leather seat behind her—even before her daughter stuck out her tongue, triumphantly, then brought it back behind her bare teeth.

"While Mommy takes our picture?"

Jerry seemed to think it was a good idea.

❖ ❖ ❖

Unicyclist with UM Umbrella

Say you're driving, idling in rush-hour traffic
and the wind has just shared its best open secret.
Say you've come from signing divorce papers.
The palm fronds, streetside, sag as if burdened.

Someone is navigating between cars, busting ass
to get from point A to B in a hellish downpour.
His slaloming of the stopped lines, on a unicycle,
dismantles the distances in a *whoosh* of inches.

A rain-diamonded thoroughfare sings of his tire,
the rooster-tailing arc of spray from it. It seems
impossible that there could be anyone so at ease
with what it takes to just press on. Like a surfer

stepped from an ocean that radiates through him.
They say we're electrons. Particles, wavelengths.
Still, it takes a native Floridian to move like this
with a University of Miami parasol as accessory.

Brad Johnson

Shaken, Not Stirred

Driving home my wife reminds me of what
my mother always said: don't talk about politics
or religion in polite company but how can I not?
When I ask *what's for dinner?* the response's
always singed. Vegetarian lasagna. Free range chicken.
Kobe beef. Foie gras. Hummus. Shark steak. Venison.
Quinoa. There's even a difference between tap water
and bottled. Maybe the hosts have separate
refrigerators, one for meat, one for dairy. Maybe
the husband cooks. Maybe the wife drinks potato vodka.
Or there's bacon served. Or bacon not served.

When Jeffrey showed up late how could I not ask
what happened and when he said he walked
how could I not follow up with *why would you walk*
this time of night this time of year? though I knew
any answer he'd supply would be dogmatic or political
like he didn't own a car and his bicycle had a flat tire
or it was Shabbat or he was protesting a prisoner's release.

What answer could there possibly be, I ask my wife
as I turn off our highway exit, that wouldn't seep
into the dark corners of socially-accepted conversation?
It's a beautiful night she says while placing her left hand
on mine and pushing the automatic window button
with the other. *It's a beautiful night* she repeats as wind lifts
her hair like balloons released from a net at a rally.

Johnny Weissmuller as Tarzan in *Tarzan and His Mate* (1934), one of the Tarzan films shot at Silver Springs, Florida.

Carlos Cunha

In Tarzan's Africa

That weekend we decided to go to the Springs again. Not the ones we'd visited last time but Blue Springs, so-called because the pool they form is indeed blue, as blue as the eyes of my pretty young wife, but, alas, not nearly as warm, because one thing about the cold springs is that they are indeed cold, their temperature never rising above seventy-one degrees, so that no matter how long you're in that water, it never stops feeling cold. Then, of course, you get out and it's summer in Florida, i.e. unbearably hot and sticky.

Our little girls had braved the cold water a couple of times, but so lacking in insulation were their lean, prematurely delivered little twin bodies that they could stand it for only a matter of minutes, and now they were fractiously consumed by the not-so-easy pastime of trying, with their mother's help, to build something castle-like with the white clay found on one shore of these particular springs. On the other side of the natural pool, wild kids and their grown-up versions were jumping off a high platform with screaming abandon, apparently dead bent on landing on those already in the water. Nearer at hand, two big-bellied middle-aged men with vast tattoos and Mohawk hairstyles were recklessly tossing between them a stocky little boy who was not tattooed or obese yet but otherwise looked very much related to them.

I wandered away, wistfully sort of wishing away the last few years of my life and the events that had landed me where I was. And as I dreamed of an alternative existence elsewhere, I followed a raised boardwalk out to the bend where the springs emptied into a slender river. The sounds of nature were more perceptible there: chirps and trills and flutters and cackles and sundry raucous cries, or the effects you might expect to hear in some carnival's "jungle" soundtrack. I even wondered if it wasn't indeed a recording I was hearing, relayed through speakers concealed in the veg-etation. And the lush vegetation itself—tall trees dripping with moss, tangled in creepers and vines, rising amid prehistorically sized ferns—didn't it also suspiciously correspond to the jungle in those old Tarzan movies that were still occasionally shown when I was growing up in South Africa?

They had looked in all ways dated, those films; even Johnny Weissmuller's physique seemed antiquated, falling short of my generation's idea of what a Tarzan should look like (and I say *a* Tarzan because we'd inherited the use of the name as a synonym for "muscle-man," so that if you pulled off a feat of strength, or struck a chesty or muscle-flexing pose, you were complimented, earnestly or sarcastically, as a *Tarzan*), too smooth, too soft-looking, even when he was swinging on vines or during his battles with lions and crocodiles (which battles were themselves strangely smooth, involving a lot of playful-looking rolls devoid of plausible violence.)

But there was something else that diminished the appeal of the Tarzan films: that they took place in Africa. Africa was where I lived, which had the effect of nullifying the exoticism that had to be one of the films's big selling points in America and Europe. To be sure, the Africa in the Tarzan films was not much like the Africa I knew, though I gave it the benefit of the doubt: it could be that Tarzan's Africa did exist somewhere on the continent, perhaps in its central parts, or it had existed in Tarzan's mythic time, a terra-incognita Africa of dense, drippingly humid, primeval, tall-treed, lagoon-spotted tropical jungle, as opposed to what I knew, a well-mapped Africa of tawny expanses of veld and scrubby bush, not to mention high-rise buildings, suburban towns, paved highways, airports, cinemas, sports fields, swimming pools, parking lots, electricity pylons, industrial plants, hospitals, clinics, universities, and just about whatever else was to be expected of a Western country. No part of South Africa was ever referred to as a jungle, and the same may have been true of other African countries. It could well be that the concept of the jungle was actually foreign to Africa, that jungles resembling those in American and European imaginations existed no more in Africa than they did in the United States or Europe.

But in South Africa we took it for granted that people overseas were also aware that the African jungle of myth was indeed mostly a myth, a fantasy terrain akin to the high-noon, dry-gulch, ten-gallon-hatted Wild West of America. We might have been less accommodating had we had an inkling of what it has since startled many traveling Africans to learn: that overseas, and especially in the United States, the primeval Africa of myth is widely taken as actual; that the person in the street is likely to conceive of Africa as one vast and practically unrelieved jungle, an area of darkness where modern engineering, culture, and technology have yet to make inroads.

What Tarzan's Africa did have in common with South Africa was the ubiquity of black servants in the background, and that they were cast as not quite human. They were, in the films, a few rungs in the sympathy ladder beneath Tarzan's menagerie of friendly apes, chimps, monkeys, and elephants. They were mere beasts of burden and lookalike fodder for lions, snakes, and crocodiles, their sweaty sufferings, comical panics, and gruesome deaths rarely causing much consternation among the films's white characters or the films's audiences, serving merely to underscore the perils that Tarzan and his allies had to heroically overcome.

❖ ❖ ❖

So little affected had I been by the Tarzan films that I would not have said my memory retained details of their jungle settings. And if I quickly became convinced that the vegetation at Blue Springs resembled that of Tarzan's jungle, it was precisely because the comparison was not one I should have been able to make. In other words, it must have tapped involuntary memory—and because involuntary memory tends to be accurate, the vegetation must indeed have been like Tarzan's, like it in greater detail than I could be aware of. Why was it so much like Tarzan's? As I walked back, the high probability occurred to me that the Tarzan films had not been shot in Africa. Where then?

Here in America, for reasons of convenience and budget. And it was possible that the films's makers would have deemed the real Africa not dramatically African enough, anyway.

Where in America had the movies been shot? In some Hollywood backlot, no doubt; but could the inspiration for the sets not have been derived from these springs or others hereabouts, perhaps by some Hollywood producer who, while passing through the area, had seen it as a plausible American version of Africa? Had I not just been looking at the original model for Tarzan's silver-screen jungle?

These were thoughts that I bothered to entertain because I found them to be having a bit of a magical effect on me: they seemed to be placing me in earnest communication with my earliest boyhood, making it appear as if it were not long dead but still going on, back there in South Africa, available to be altered by fresh insight or revelation, or even to be resumed: I could still be a twelve-year-old emerging from a weekend cinema's darkness into the South African sunshine, my mind filled with new thoughts about the jungle adventures I had just watched, and nearly the whole of my life still ahead of me waiting to be heroically lived.

❖ ❖ ❖

I may have wanted to convey at least some of this to my wife, but not only is my wife not from South Africa, she is not even from my generation, and whenever I try to draw her into a passing enthusiasm over something that refers back to my youth or childhood in a remote part of the world and in an era before she was born, I have imagined that remote, too, is the look that comes into her blue eyes despite her polite attempts to feign engagement. I end by feeling that mostly I have succeeded in making more patent the gulfs that may persist between our personal worlds, despite our marriage. Besides, she was much too preoccupied with persuading our skeptical kids that what they were building was not a castle, but a much simpler structure: a volcano, with a cavity at the top that they could repeatedly fill with water that would overflow like lava.

❖ ❖ ❖

Six months or so later, around Christmastime, we visited a nearby theme park that my wife had somehow obtained free passes for, and it turned out to be built around another set of springs, Silver Springs. I had heard about the place that it offered glass-bottom boat rides; otherwise, I knew nothing about it. But even in the absence of expectations, it was a disappointment. A haphazard, low-budget mixture of nature park, carnival, and zoo, it was a woebegone place from another time, evidently in its final days and barely operational. In mid-afternoon there was only the thinnest scattering of visitors, and Christmas carols forlornly played through loudspeakers along paths that were mostly vacant. These paths led through lawns and trees (some of these fitfully adorned with Christmas lights among strands of Spanish moss) to becalmed, rusting carnival rides and wildlife exhibits on the perimeter of a large Springs lagoon. Some of the wildlife, including an alligator show, was advertised as being on an island accessed by a bridge, but the bridge was closed, the entire island out of commission. On the mainland, what there was of wildlife was a petting zoo of farm animals, and a couple of blowsy old bears sitting in their open-air enclosures. A strangely narrow and tall, peaked-roof farmhouse with a shuttered window at its apex turned out to be "the giraffe house," preposterously built to shelter an actual giraffe (a cartoonish idea that would never have occurred to anyone in Africa), although it was now condemned since the giraffe had died (possibly of embarrassment).

There was a dock from which two covered, glass-bottom ferries came and went. The skipper of the one we boarded was an excessively courtly elderly black man dressed in whites and a captain's hat, and throughout the cruise he kept up a spooky, singsong prattle, delivered in a barely comprehensible, possibly antebellum black accent, as if he were casting voodoo spells or making voodoo prophecies, so that he redoubled the haunted feel of the entire park. The ferry's glass bottom was in a center well, and what could be seen through it was only fitfully interesting, since much of the lagoon was shallow and its bottom covered with some sort of weed. The water was also, it seemed to me, not quite as crystalline as in the other springs we had visited.

❖ ❖ ❖

But a few days later, at the office, when I happened to mention my Tarzan-jungle theo-

ry about the springs I had visited in the summer, what I had to say did not surprise a native Floridian among my colleagues, who told me it was actually common local knowledge that some of the original Tarzan movies had been shot at the Springs. In fact, he said, at Silver Springs itself there were still monkeys rumored to be descended from those used in the films.

As a little online searching readily established, there are monkeys running wild at Silver Springs but they are probably descended from a troop that, in 1932, was brought in by the operator of a so-called Jungle Cruise at the park. These rhesus monkeys were put on an island on the river that the springs feed, the Silver River. It must have been assumed that the monkeys would remain on the island, trapped by the surrounding water, a fixed attraction for the cruise. But it turned out that rhesus monkeys can swim, or these particular monkeys had soon learned how to, so that they escaped the island to propagate up and down the river to this day.

Yet I suppose that the popular belief that they were brought in for Tarzan is understandable, and it is possible that some of the original monkeys were captured on film: their arrival did coincide with the shooting at Silver Springs of the first Tarzan movie, *Tarzan, the Ape Man*. My colleague had not been misinformed on that score. Tarzan movies had indeed been filmed at Silver Springs, six of them, at a clip of about one every two years. It was at Silver Springs, in fact, that Tarzan met Jane (or so I had to assume from the title of the film, *Tarzan Meets his Mate*,) and it was there, too, that Tarzan acquired a son, in a film called *Tarzan Finds a Son*.

And the Tarzan movies were not the first to be shot at Silver Springs. The park had been the subject of film shorts that theaters would show before the main feature. Produced by Grantland Rice, a famed sportswriter in his time, these mini-documentaries each offered fifteen minutes of footage, many of them having to do with one Newt Perry, a Silver Springs-based swimmer who was regarded as a local Tarzan of sorts and whose stunts—swimming against the river current, diving somersaults, and various underwater tricks such as eating a banana and drinking a soda, or simply remaining submerged for three minutes and forty-five seconds—were one of Silver Springs's main attractions. Perry's fame eventually reached Hollywood, for which he became the man to see whenever a film called for significant aquatic action. He never became an actor himself, but he did become friends with someone who *was* making the transition from swimming legend to movie stardom: Johnny Weissmuller. And when Weissmuller was cast as Tarzan, Perry persuaded Metro-Goldwyn-Mayer that Silver Springs, which he was managing by then, offered all the film needed by way of a plausibly African location.

❖ ❖ ❖

I discovered a photo online, a candid shot taken during a break in the shooting of 1938's *Tarzan Finds a Son*, and showing Perry, Weissmuller, and the actor who played Boy, Johnny Sheffield, taking a break on Silver Springs lagoon dock. All are looking at the camera, Perry and Weissmuller casually, standing in profile to it, as if they had been interrupted in conversation with each other, while Sheffield has turned completely around and is leaning towards us, mugging. Perry, wearing a pair of high-waisted stretch swim trunks, is a broad-faced man with backswept light hair that seems to be receding and graying at the temples. He has a physique that must have been typical of the strongmen of the period: muscle weighed down by a top layer of fat that makes his breasts sag and forms rolls on his waist. No doubt this bit of blubber helped insulate him against the cold of the springs—a cold that young Sheffield is betraying by the fact that he is snugly wrapped in a fluffy white bathrobe. Weissmuller is in full costume. That is, he's wearing nothing but his loincloth, which is more authentic-looking than I remember, not a chaste pair of shorts disguised as a loincloth, but a tanga-like one held at the hip by only a string, leaving the entire side of his leg bare. This must have startled audiences in the 1930s. (Or perhaps not, since that decade was at first a daring, experiment-filled one not averse to risqué fads, nudism among them.) In general, Weissmuller in this picture looks a lot more Tarzan-like than I remember him looking. His hair is long and unstyled and falls about a lean, shadowy face, and his physique, placed alongside Perry's barbecue-and-grits one, looks positively modern in its tan, slender muscularity. The smoother, softer, graying and generally less plausible Tarzan that I re-

Newt Perry, Johnny Weissmuller, and Johnny Sheffield at Silver Springs for the filming of *Tarzan Finds a Son* in 1938.

member from my childhood must, of course, have come from later films in the series, when Weissmuller was older and more jaded, not much caring how properly he embodied a silly character he had played too often. Although he did not look, in those later films, as though he had joined Perry at one too many Southern barbecues, he may nevertheless have acquired just enough subcutaneous fat to render himself more comfortable as he splashed in the cold waters of the springs. That the younger, leaner Weissmuller could swim in cold springs while looking for all the world as though he were in a watering hole in the steamiest reaches of the Congo must have been one of his greatest acting achievements.

But the springs themselves might deserve some recognition. To be sure, attracting the interest of Hollywood and representing the Africa of Tarzan implied something of a cultural demotion for them: back in the late 1700s, William Bartram the naturalist published chronicles about the Florida springs that, in Europe, ostensibly served to inspire the poets of the Romantic Movement, most notably Samuel Taylor Coleridge and his most celebrated poem, "Kubla Khan." Still, the Springs's Hollywood impersonation of Africa is commendable, being perhaps chiefly responsible for the image of the continent that still prevails in many heads throughout the world. Of course, the nations of Africa might themselves not feel very grateful. The Tarzanian image of the world's largest continent might benefit them in the case of tourism, but otherwise it is yet another of the handicaps that it faces, one that leaves the world with trouble picturing modern societies there.

❖ ❖ ❖

More truly if much less cinematically African than Silver Springs was, I remember thinking, the Florida countryside we drove through on the way to the park. In its flatness and tawniness beneath a blue sky, I found it reminiscent of South Africa's Highveld region, where I grew up. Before I could mention this to my wife, though, it was she who used the roadside scenery as a reference to her own background.

I had known that my wife's parents had lived in Florida once, but only now was she making it clear that it had been in this area that they had settled somewhere between Ocala and Silver Springs. And it had occurred not long before she was born. In other words, when we had left my wife's native Connecticut so that I could take up a job down here in Gainesville after a trying period of unemployment, we had come to the very region where she may have been conceived.

"Really?" I said. "You never mentioned this before."

"I didn't?"

"No."

"Well, I did not have a reason *not* to mention it," she vowed, deploying a form a reasoning and syntax that seems peculiar to her generation. "But maybe I also did not have a reason *to* mention it."

"One would've thought our coming to live around here would have been reason enough."

"Are you sure I didn't mention it, though?"

I dropped it.

My wife's parents are divorced. Her father, who lives in Hawaii, is a character who, even at long distance, maintains a tempestuous relationship with his offspring. It was her father, my wife said now, who had kept urging her to take our girls to Silver Springs, which he remembered from his days in Florida. This, too, my wife had failed to mention before, but perhaps only because she was used to dwelling for

only *a hot second*, as she put it, on any advice her father gave her—until the coincidental advent of the free tickets.

I'm sure that my wife has also tried not to dwell on the fact that at times we seem, as a couple, to be moving in uncanny parallel to the life her parents had, with their doomed marriage. But it might explain why she has never been at ease with our move to Florida, although even in this geographical discontent she is unwittingly following her parents' script. Her mother, too, was disgruntled down here and glad to return to Connecticut, where she pursued a master's degree while her husband stayed home to look after their children and indulge sundry unprofitable enthusiasms-du-jour. Our own married life began in Connecticut with nearly two years of my similarly pottering about at home, mostly looking after our infant daughters. Since our arrival in Florida, it was my wife who had stayed home, but she was using some of her time to follow her mother's example and obtain a post-graduate degree.

Sometimes I even had to wonder if we really had not both fallen off the tracks of our respective lives to become trapped, as if by default, in a sort of reenactment of her parents. We were driving to Silver Springs, a place that my wife's father had visited and liked, to which he had, when he lived here with her mother, no doubt thought of taking the child that his wife had been expecting. He had not had a chance to do so, but now I was doing it as if for him, as if I were a mere continuation of him, although the child was now grown up, and a mother herself, a very plausible stand-in for her own mother. And though we were traveling through a countryside that had been referring me back to my childhood in South Africa—in effect reminding me of who I was and how distinct from my wife and her father, distinct enough to be utterly unsuited to whatever "script" he had left imprinted on her—I had now discovered that her father would also have been very familiar with this landscape, that it was *his* landscape, too.

But her father had mentioned nothing about Tarzan's link to Silver Springs—he obviously had not been aware of it or had not been impressed enough by it to remember. So it was my own thing, and I wish I had already been aware of it as we drove to the park. It might have restored that enjoyable sense of being back in my own earlier years, since not only would I have been driving through a landscape that evoked the Africa I'd known, I would have been driving *to* Africa—the Africa of Tarzan, to be sure, but an Africa that had been a tiny part of my childhood in the real Africa. And this in turn would have helped me feel as though I were truly myself and living a life appropriate to myself, however momentary and illusory that feeling might have been.

The most recent years have, for me, been very trying ones, and the sense that I have lost my way has often recurred—lost my way so irremediably that destiny has cast me off from its concerns, leaving me to become a rag-doll in the maws of brute chance, prone to outcomes that have little to do with my essence. In the light of this, my Tarzan epiphany about the Springs's vegetation ceases to seem just a pointless quirk of involuntary memory. When I took my solitary stroll along that boardwalk at Blue Springs and became aware of the campy jungle-like noises, I may as well really have been listening, with hope of rescue, for the only sound that seemed to be missing: a ululating yell that, even today, no one in the world could fail to recognize.

Lauren Tess

Reading Darwin and the News

I've been reading Darwin and the news lately
and looking for a missing link between
the self-solving evolution of all nature and
the state of humanity today. A scientist would dictate
that I wait; the geological scale of modification
is far too great to be measured by calendar dates
like a random November eighth. She'd say
I should expect to die and decay along with
generations of my descendants before the day
the Darwin of a future android race can look back
and proclaim we've changed. Maybe she'd be right.
But I operate in human time and on a scale that,
despite its tiny size, carries lots of weight with me.
I want humans somehow to evolve before I die,
or at least awaken to the possibilities contained
within their 1200cc brains. If only mine could
find some way to effect a change. Maybe someday.
I'm no Darwin, but I still have a little time.

Ars Arachnea

A yellow-black orb-weaver
           has been stringing lines
between the arbor vitae and dogwood
                all morning.
I watched her high-wire act
          from the deck,
  the spider spinning on,
                using one part
after another
          of herself
                to fashion a silken net.
She's a strict revisionist,
          doubling up on lines too thin,
  repositioning breaks
                and end stops.
Then, when she imagines
                her perfomance
          is strong enough,
          she retires
to a browning dogwood leaf.
  She seems to doze,
          one leg on the radial spokes,
                simply waiting . . .
The poet laureate of Aurora Avenue—
          hoping for
                some small attention,
a captive audience of one.

Jeff Worley

Ode to My Unfinished Poems

after Mike Schneider

Like vapor-locked DeSotos, they sputtered,
tried their best to kick-start,
then ran out of breath.

I sequestered them in my bottom drawer
until it occurred to me to take one out
and try again.

I thought the draft last night
(working title "Slug Song")
could start to sing, so I interrogated

imprecise nouns, jettisoned adverbs that
like Sumo wrestlers pushed verbs around.
A pathetic fallacy keeping company

with a cliché (*the angry, pale face of the moon*)
had to go, but still this one, like so many
stacked in their dark Guantanamo,

refused to happen. Still in the rough, the poem
about the singing slug; the poem for Wanda,
my first lover, who was patient with my fumblings

and scrambled us eggs in the morning;
the love song for my Abilene Aunt Fronie
who one winter night—her touch delicate

as feathergrass—stroked the fever from
my forehead; the pair of purple gloves
that tumbled over themselves

from a 6th-story Manhattan window
and landed, side by side,
in a busker's guitar case.

Arjuna "AJ" Watson. *Traffic Pile-up*. 2009. Spray paint on canvas.. 24 x 24 inches. Courtesy of The Dawn Davies Collection.

V – E – X – O

I seldom start a day without a stab at the *New York Times* crossword puzzle, some mornings with more success than others. Recently, I was introduced to a word that surprised me because I had never encountered it in a puzzle. If I had, I certainly didn't recall it. This seemed strange because the word, *vexo*, v-e-x-o, appears to be perfect for filling four white spaces in a puzzle grid. Sounded out, the word possesses an intriguing ring, its first syllable sharp, a bit harsh, while the final one rolls off into space like an Alpine yodel. *Vexo*'s terseness hints at high-tech branding, possibly the name chosen by a start-up that manufactures precision sensors used on satellites or nanotech devices to be implanted by skilled surgeons in life-or-death situations. Maybe it is someone's name—possibly a character in a sci-fi novel or film fantasy; perhaps a robot from an old *Doctor Who* episode or an assassin who proved no match for James Bond. Alas, brief Internet searches revealed only Vexo International, a British firm making water purification products; the Vexo, a hand-held vibration meter; and Johann Vexo, a musician who works the pedalboard, two keyboards, and thirty stops of the choir organ in the famed Notre Dame cathedral. But it wasn't a technology product or an organist, however talented, that introduced me to the word *vexo*. Instead, the word arrived with a severe weather system that dropped unexpected snow into Colorado and Wyoming, generated tornadoes in Oklahoma, and drenched Texas, Kansas, and Louisiana. After being battered by that storm for four harrowing days, I am convinced that if some crossword constructor ever choses to fit the word *vexo* into a grid, there can be only one possible clue: hellish nightmare.

When my wife Marilyn's father died, she inherited his car, a nearly ten-year-old Mercury. We lived in the East, while his residence had been a senior community in the California desert. The car sat in the driveway of his old house for more than two years, an insured, rapidly depreciating yard ornament. It became clear that we had to do something—sell it, have it shipped to Florida where we live, or drive it cross-country ourselves. A road trip sounded appealing. It offered a sense of adventure and would allow us to map out a route that included brief visits with my brother on the Central California coast, our son in Denver, and our daughter in Texas, just outside Dallas. We flew to California, prepared my father-in-law's home for sale, and gave the Mercury a new battery, an oil change, and a full tank of gas. Then our adventure began.

Everything went well until we started across Colorado en route to Denver. It was mid-April, and we hadn't expected snow but we soon ran into flurries, and as the highway climbed toward the state's famous ski areas, the snowfall picked up, sticking to the rocks and grass at the sides of the roads and coating the roofs, hoods, and windshields of cars. As we began to ascend Vail Pass, the snow was falling in sheets, visibility shrank rapidly, and the road turned white and slick. Having lived in upstate New York for twenty years, we were not strangers to driving in wintry conditions. There we always used window washer fluid that contained antifreeze and cut through windshield ice like a welder's torch. But the Mercury, which had spent years in a broiling desert, was ill-prepared for snow and ice, its fluid mere bug remover barely able to resist freezing itself, incapable of dissolving the ice building up on the glass and enwrapping the wipers. The snow abated a bit after we cleared Vail's 10,662-foot summit, but soon returned and was in full force as we climbed again toward the even higher Loveland Pass. The windshield fogged over and the wipers arced back and forth across the ice, failing to push any of it away. The defroster did manage to clear a small opening, no more than four inches high, that spanned a foot or so on the driver's side. If I bent low and peered just over the top edge of the steering wheel, I could see a bit of road in front of our car's hood. We crawled upward as better prepared drivers swept by on the left, their tires kicking even more snow up onto our windshield. Each time a semi passed, a wave of snow blinded us until the wipers, now long thick icicles themselves, could nudge open my spy hole. There was no place to turn off, no spaces at the side of the road. It was harrowing, frightening driving. Marilyn switched radio stations as I fought to keep the car moving and in its lane. A newscaster warned that record snowfalls were expected across Colorado. Four feet, or more. The culprit was something she called Winter Storm Vexo. On another station the reporter predicted six feet, maybe as much as eight feet before it was all over, and suggested that listeners avoid driving if possible. Not so easy for us. We inched over the summit at Loveland Pass and, as we descended, the snow slowed and quickly turned to rain. As we dropped down and closed in on Denver, our destination, even the rain ceased. But the radio reports did not bode well for the future. More snow was coming, they warned. A lot more.

Our son and his girlfriend cautioned us to stay another night in Denver, but our hotel couldn't guarantee a room and the sky was clear in the morning, so we decided to chance it, heading east towards Kansas in hopes of outrunning the storm. Our luck ran out quickly. As we left Denver's suburbs the sky darkened and wet heavy snow began to fall, blanketing the countryside and the roads. The slush on the road surface iced over, and increasing winds swirled the snow, making it difficult to see other traffic and the highway itself. I slowed to twenty miles an hour as the slippery ice made it more difficult to negotiate turns and stay on the highway. Then fifteen. To our right the bed of an abandoned pickup truck stuck out of a large drift. On the opposite side of the highway another accident had several dozen cars stopped in a line, the curtain of snow making them mere shadows, gray ghosts. Soon the falling snow erased any view of the scenery, and road signs only became visible as you passed them. Our speed dropped to five miles an hour, enough to keep our momentum going on the thick bumpy ice that covered the road surface and avoid losing control as visibility dropped to zero. I could, when lucky, make out a tiny bit of the road, never a full lane's width, the sense of pavement dissolving to whiteness five or six feet beyond our bumper. If there was a car ahead of us, I couldn't

see it. If there was someone behind us, he was invisible. Gust-blown snow broke like waves across our path. The icy wipers made a grating sound as they stroked back and forth and the heater's fan droned, struggling to defrost the windshield glass. We seemed encased in a cocoon, plodding ever deeper into its dangerous, featureless white void. Signs marking towns—Deer Tail, Limon, Arriba, Flagler—slipped by, their exit ramps solid white, no tracks or other hints that anyone had even dared try those escape routes. Once, for a moment, the white shrouds parted briefly to reveal an overturned semi, its huge trailer already buried by fresh snow. Further along I thought I saw three motionless police officers standing at the side of the highway. But the scene only lasted a second and took on a dreamlike quality. Were they really there? Eventually, as we prayed they would, the snow and winds lessened and it was possible to see the road as a continuous swath; we exited at Burlington, Colorado, in search of coffee and a restroom. The snow turned to a heavy rain that stayed with us all the way into Kansas. We finally stopped at a motel in Salina, having expended twelve tense hours making the drive from Denver. If it hadn't been for this storm, the one they called Vexo, it should have taken six.

Vexo was not done with us. The next day heavy rains followed us south into Texas, and, after a brief visit with our daughter and her husband, continued to pursue us the following day as we left the Dallas metro area. The sky darkened and rain gushed from the sky, immersing the highway and mercilessly pounding the roof of the Mercury with the fury of a heavy metal drummer. Traffic slowed and some drivers turned on their flashers as they tried to navigate through the deluge. We didn't know it at the time, of course, but less than two hundred miles south of us this rain was devastating Houston, flooding large parts of the city and eventually causing several deaths. The rainfall reached four inches per hour, and a daredevil surfer could have cut back and forth on the waves thrown out from the tires of the big rigs plowing along the Interstate. In the midst of this, our windshield wipers gave out. The arms, thumping back and forth at top speed, suddenly locked up and the blades stopped pushing water away. I fumbled with the switch, fighting to keep the car on an unseen road, and the wipers jumped back to life. Ten minutes later they died again and this time refused to react to the switch. Blind, I somehow found an off-ramp, exited, and pulled over. Stepping outside, water seeping through my shoes, the rain instantly drenching my clothes, I discovered that a tiny push of my hand restarted the wipers. They began swinging back and forth with full force, as if there had never been a problem. We inched back onto the highway. Five minutes later the wipers stopped again, and as I fought to keep us in our lane, Marilyn reached through the open side window and nudged them back into action. It went that way for the next two hundred miles, the wipers lasting five minutes, ten minutes, maybe even fifteen, maybe only two, before they would lock up, and, depending on where they were on the glass, I would try to find a place to pull over, or Marilyn would reach into the rain to urge them back to life. Each time the wipers stalled, we were instantly blinded. It was impossible to make out the flooded roadway, lane markings, nearby cars, or signs. There was no way to tell if there was an open shoulder, a pulled-over vehicle, or a fence to our side. The seconds stretched out, seemingly without end, as we clawed at ways to spur the wipers back to life, our breath locked in our chests, waiting for the sound and jolt of a collision. Somehow, time and time again, luck stayed with us. The heavy rains followed us into Louisiana, finally petering out near Monroe. Two days later we were home, safe.

We had driven into the maw of Winter Storm Vexo. The concept of named winter storms was new to me. During our time in upstate New York, we had been battered by lake-effect snows off of Lake Ontario and visited by storms, like the dreaded Alberta Clippers, that swept through the area from the north, and not infrequent blizzards. Occasionally a news anchor might joke about "Snowmageddon" or a name like "Snowzilla" would pop up in a headline when storms that seemed to have no end disrupted our lives. But I never heard a local reporter use an actual name like "Jonas" or "Ursula," or even "Vexo," for the storms that were regular features of even our mildest winters.

We do expect, however, names for tropical storms. Who will forget Katrina, the hurricane that brought such awesome destruction to New Orleans and the Gulf Coast. Hurricane Andrew resides in my memory because, years earlier my college roommate lost his home when it swept through Florida. As I write this, Tropical Storm Colin is moving through Florida, where I now live, and the governor has declared a state of emergency. The National Hurricane Center, an arm of the National Weather Service, maintains a list of names for tropical storms that arise from the Atlantic. But the government does not name winter storms. In fact, the Weather Service discourages names, as winter weather is variable over time and space, making it impossible to establish a true beginning or end for the storms.

Undaunted, The Weather Channel, a cable television station whose reporters often look as if someone is just off-camera blasting them with a garden hose and leaf blower, began naming winter storms. Names, they reasoned, would allow viewers to personify major winter weather patterns that might disrupt their lives. Rather than nattering on about cold fronts, upper-level lows, unstable air, and omega blocks, the station's reporters needed only warn that Winter Storm Cara, or Jonah, or in this case Vexo, was on its way. The unexpected snows and flooding we encountered arrived in mid-April, well past the meteorological end of winter as well as the Vernal Equinox, but the Weather Channel has no names for Spring storms. So Vexo, a name they derived from the Latin for "I harass" or "I annoy," was assigned to what they deemed was the twenty-second Winter Storm of 2016. It was a doozy.

In the long run, of course, spring storm, winter storm, it doesn't matter. Neither my wife nor I will ever forget our tense drive through a merciless gauntlet of ice and wind-driven snow in the mountains of Colorado, or the rushes of adrenalin that saved us when visibility shrank to zero and the windshield wipers refused to move in the midst of torrential downpours. When terror surrounds you for hours, day after day, and only the most intense concentration, singular focus, and ample doses of pure blind luck keep it at bay, those memories will be indelible. In a few years, however, I doubt that I will recall that the storm we endured had a name, let alone that it had been called Vexo. That might change, of course, if some future morning I am struggling with the day's crossword puzzle, need a word to fill four empty cells and see "hellish nightmare" among the clues. That might spur my memory. It just might.

❖　❖　❖

Love Poem to Kerry Von Erich

Kerry, when you and Kevin strut into the Dallas
Sportatorium, you could be kings—princes at least—
if you'd only lift your chins another inch,
stop grinning quite so big. Speakers blast a song

I can't make out while people clap and cheer,
reach to touch your 80s hair and He-Man shoulders.
It's October 1983, your four brothers
are alive and you still have your whole right foot.

I don't have to watch Kevin as close because
I know he's going to survive, retire,
run the family business and see you all
into the Hall of Fame. Tonight you win against

the Fabulous Freebirds, and the fact that it's on tape
suggests you're the main event—and why
wouldn't you be, wrestling in the league your dad
created? Kerry, please know I'd save you

if I could—from suicide, the painkillers you got
addicted to after the crash that took your foot.
But should I go back further, keep you from ever
entering the ring, give you a father who isn't Fritz,

with his Iron Claw, insistence you be great?
You and Kevin seem to be having a good time,
but I know that once you're out of sight
you might lean hard against each other

or the wall, swallow pills to ease the pain
you'll feel when the adrenaline wears off.
Kerry, I understand why fans confuse your life
with a plot written for the ring. Just before

your suicide, you told Kevin that you couldn't
imagine going on. You'll never know how hard
I've tried, twenty years after your death,
to write a storyline that lets you stay alive.

Not Just With But Through

I feel pain less than I feel other things:
pride, adrenaline, how I can make
a whole arena hold its breath, wonder
what will happen next. They loved me
in Japan because I had more guts
than sense: tables, ladders, thumbtacks,
barbed wire, dynamite and fire.
I wanted fans to understand how great
it was, for a guy no one thought
could wrestle, who's short and often
out of shape, wears flannel shirts
and sweatpants in the ring, to have
his dreams come true. Hardcore
was fun until the crowds turned mean,
fans chanting *You fucked up*
at my friend's swollen brain.
Facing Vader in 1993, I wanted
to kill my career, get hurt so bad
I'd have to hang it up, but he didn't
punish me enough. At Hell in a Cell
against The Undertaker, the roof
of the steel cage collapsed under my weight,
tooth stuck to my lip after I landed,
but I kept getting up because I could.
Sometimes you wrestle not just with
but through: eight concussions,
two herniated discs, torn muscles,
second-degree burns, broken shoulders,
ribs, nose and jaw, 300 stitches,
one ear mostly missing, kidneys
pissing blood. At home I sit and watch
my weight go up, watch wrestling
on TV and think through my old matches,
which ones hurt the most, gave fans
what they were due. My favorite pain
reminds me of applause.

Jared Harél

Best Intentions, 2002

The day I dumped you, I bought you
your own copy of Morphine's *The Night*.
You adored that album, and so before I left, I left
a yellow Tower Records bag on the futon
by your keys. I had yet to learn the cruelty
of ill-timed kindness, or how gutless it is to act
out of guilt. *At least I didn't giftwrap the thing,*
I think these days, recalling how I hoped
those two-stringed, lovesick grooves might ease
your hurt, or your hatred of me, or ease me
out the door, still whispering, *please*.

Jared Harél

Self-Portrait with Gravity

The day before I dove off an airplane,
a hang-glider struck the same green field,
hit the earth like it wanted to hurt it.
The Swede said he heard it from the hostel:
how nothing was wrong until everything was;
cables stripped of rubber casings.
A neon wing pinned in salute. You could still
see the divot, that bruise of dirt
where limbs had splintered, yet there I was
in goggles and jumpsuit, knowing only
I didn't want my parents to know,
and so I boarded the plane, paid in full
before leaving the ground. Against good sense,
I looked down before jumping, but all I saw
softened with distance as I felt how
the pastures might catch me when I fell.

Pseudocyesis

What would it be
to give birth to a memory

each of its fingers and toes
intact, to count them all

aloud with unstrange words.
When I heard

you were dead I numbered
the days and wondered

if maybe I carried your child
and would I keep it.

Nine months later, my stomach
sunken, still I expected

labour pains. If I gave birth
to this grief would it come

with hair or bald, and breathing—
fill its lungs to scream

into the time that's gone:
nine months contract in twisting pain.

There are women who grow pregnant
in their minds and their bodies

follow suit, their bellies swell, sometimes
even a quickening—

who's to say that such a child
isn't real? The morning sickness

comes when I smell gasoline;
a chemical recalls the wake, your body

lying there. I can carry your death
in my belly or my throat.

Re-entry

As I climb the steps to Grandmother's trailer, my family follows behind—husband, son, daughter. It is the day after Christmas, and hot. Even in December, black heat rises from the asphalt driveway, steam swirling up like frost. In damp red sweaters, we've traveled six hours to see my uncle, newly released from the Alabama State Penitentiary. Twenty years for voluntary manslaughter, and now his time is up.

I count the steps. One. Two. Three. Four.

I walk across the porch, holding my breath like I'm crossing a state line. The shooting happened here, forever branding this place the scene of the crime. Feeling irreverent as we clomp across the hardwood, I knock.

The flimsy door swings open, and there stands my grandmother. Her body is hunched and wilted, her face framed by some inches of snowy white hair. I embrace her, inhaling the scent of bacon and hairspray. At eighty years old, her shoulders feel frail under flannel.

"All my family together," she whispers into my shoulder. "First time in twenty years."

The threshold above us is painted Kelly green.

❖ ❖ ❖

The kids push through my legs into the living room, where my father is waiting. Stumbling over furniture, boxes, and knickknacks, they squeal and run into his arms. Dad has flown down from Maine. After thirty years in the Air Force, he retired to a garnet-studded island far from rural Alabama. Sixty years old, and his one act of subversion is his wrinkled Hawaiian shirts and jeans.

He and I exchange stiff hugs. We practice twice a year, the same ritual since kindergarten. This year, we remember that he goes left and I go right, and manage not to bump foreheads. A small victory.

"Can I help you unload the van?" he says, and my husband nods. The kids dart off to the restroom. I follow Grandmother into the kitchen, where she rummages through the cupboard, grabs two dented plastic cups, and fills them with tap water.

Sitting at the dining room table, we drink. The room is piled high with dust and Tupperware, the table spread with month-old loaves of bread and generic two-liter sodas. I search for signs of Uncle Rich, who moved in with Grandmother after his release last month. With the exception of the green threshold, everything looks the same. I find a small space to rest my cup.

"How was the ride up?" Grandmother asks. I tell her about the bare pecan orchards of Butler and the monotonous stretch of highway between Montgomery and Bay Minette. About our lunch at Cracker Barrel, how the kids climbed up in rocking chairs and giggled while we waited for our table.

"That's nice," she says.

We sip.

By now, my daughter is climbing me like a jungle gym as my son runs laps around the table. My children are two and four, and we're in close quarters with a convicted felon. I search for a tactful way to broach the subject.

"Grandma..." I say, then stop. Questions like these are off-limits; my father would think me incredibly rude. Above all, our family is *nice*. Making anyone feel uncomfortable, especially ourselves, is a crime on par with manslaughter.

"Are there any guns in the house?" I ask.

Grandmother doesn't seem to mind my question. Her face remains placid, chest rising slow and steady. Luckily, my father is not within earshot.

"Naw," she says. "We ain't allowed to have guns in the house." She takes another sip of water. "Because of the felony."

That's what she calls it: the felony.

"What about Uncle Daniel?" I ask. Daniel also lives with Grandmother. He moved in soon after my grandfather died. At night, he works as a guard at a maximum security prison. During the day, he takes Grandmother to doctor's appointments and Walmart.

"Daniel moved all his guns to Junior's place." Junior: my other uncle. The youngest brother of the bunch. Also a security guard.

That my prison guard uncle would hand over his firearms without keeping one tucked away in the recesses of this trailer is doubtful, but I drop it and change the subject. I decide to corral the kids in the main part of the house and keep close watch over them, make sure they don't venture into bedrooms or strange cabinets.

"Where's Uncle Rich?" I ask.

"He'll get up around two," Grandmother says. "He likes to sleep late."

❖ ❖ ❖

Felony. I suppose it rolls off the tongue easier than voluntary manslaughter, but still: Twenty years ago, on the front stoop, Rich shot a man point blank. My uncle was drunk, in the middle of a bad divorce, when his brother-in-law came looking for him. Things got heated. Rich went into the back bedroom and came out with a gun.

I was ten years old. I remember Dad phoning me. It was a Monday night, and his voice was deep and heavy, void of its usual buoyancy.

"Jenny, I have something to tell you."

I twisted curly phone cord around my finger and looked up at my mother, who was hovering uncharacteristically near the nightstand. Too young to be apprehensive, I expected news of an upcoming visit—maybe an impromptu trip to the beach, or an amusement park.

"Uncle Rich shot a guy," Dad said.

For a moment, I just breathed into the tiny holes of the mouthpiece.

I'd seen dozens of action movies. Bullets flew; men clutched bleeding limbs. Through gritted teeth, they muttered vows of revenge. Usually, a quick-witted sidekick turned a t-shirt to a tourniquet or called 911. The wounded sometimes survived.

"Did he kill him?" I asked.

"Yeah. He killed him." My father sounded irritated.

"Oh," I said.

My father never spoke of it again.

❖ ❖ ❖

In the dining room, I ask Grandmother how Rich is adjusting. She says he keeps himself busy, mowing the lawn twice a week, fixing things around the house. Her only concern is Rich's diet: three peanut butter sandwiches per day. Sometimes a fast food hamburger. "And he won't go nowhere," she says. "Won't even ride with me to town. Says he's afraid of seeing someone he knows."

My uncle's fears are probably well-founded. Bay Minette, Alabama is small—around eight thousand people. His ex-wife is long gone—married a pediatrician—but the rest of her family still lives here, including the parents of the man he shot. Not someone he wants to bump into at the supermarket. It's one of the many things working against my uncle. When it comes to facilitating reentry for released prisoners, Alabama ranks at the bottom of the nation. People with criminal records face restrictions on everything from food stamps to public assistance, public housing, student loans, and drivers' licenses. As with most states, Alabama laws allow employers to discriminate against applicants who've been convicted of crimes, making it nearly impossible to obtain jobs. Convicted felons are even barred from voting for the rest of their lives.

Rich at least has a place to live, and family. He'll never be destitute, not as long as Grandmother's alive.

"I'm glad he's here," Grandmother says. "He's always been a mama's boy." She sips again and smiles. "Just like you were a daddy's girl."

❖ ❖ ❖

Daddy's girl. The words are like forgotten song lyrics or laughter heard from another room. I know I once sat in my father's lap, preferring him over my mother. My grandmother's house is lined with photographs of our early years—Dad and me posing on the front porch, or holding fishing poles in front of Mays Creek, or eating ice cream cones at Dairy Queen. But I don't remember the events captured in the pictures. My memories *are* the pictures.

My parents divorced when I was eighteen months old. Soon after the paperwork was filed, my mother moved us from Washington, D.C. to Georgia. Dad immediately requested a transfer to Keesler Air Force Base in Mississippi. Once a month, he drove to Georgia to pick me up for a long weekend. We drove together to my grandparents's place in Alabama, arriving on Fridays and leaving on Mondays. He did that every single month, until I started kindergarten.

On those monthly trips to Alabama, I must have spent time with Uncle Rich. Grandmother says he used to tease me with a straw hat, one with faux flowers and a price tag hanging off the brim. He'd perch the hat on my head and call me Minnie Pearl, much to my relatives' delight. I'd never seen an episode of *Hee Haw*, so I didn't get the joke. "That's Jenny Pearl to you!" I shot back, pretending to be offended but enjoying the laughter.

In addition to being a jokester, Uncle Rich was attentive to me—laid back, affable, kind. I was born before his own children, and he gave me giant stuffed animals and Barbie Dolls on holidays. Rich always looked at me when I talked to him, seemed to care what I had to say. I remember liking that.

A picture of an old Alabama Christmas sits on Grandmother's mantle. Artificial tree twinkling in the background, the four brothers pose together, along with Grandmother and me. I'm probably four years old, dark-haired and grinning, red-faced from the euphoria of new toys. There's Dad in the recliner, the only one of the brothers to go to college and move away. Daniel stands with an arm around Grandmother, and Junior kneels beside them, mouth open mid-laughter. The three boys all look the same—dark hair, broad shoulders, prominent noses. Rich stands behind the group, the only one with that tall lanky build, hair the color of a dirty penny. Everyone is smiling, pulsing with holiday adrenaline, arms around each other. Uncle Rich smiles, too, but his smile doesn't quite reach his eyes.

❖ ❖ ❖

At two o'clock, I hear thuds from the spare bedroom, then footsteps. By now, we're gathered in the cramped living room, killing time until dinner. My husband and I stiffen; my father thumbs through some magazine. The children's toy cars screech to a halt and they both turn toward the hallway.

Suddenly, there he is. Rich. I expect wrinkles, regret and loss burrowed into his skin, grief tattooed around his eyes, but his face is smooth as sanded pine. Still tall and lanky, his shaggy hair buzzed short. Everything still brown—eyes, hair, teeth. He moves easily, fluidly, with no trace of entropy.

"Hey, Jenny," he says. No one's called me by my nickname since childhood.

I give him a quick hug and introduce my husband and children. The kids cling shyly to my knees.

"Woo wee, what purdy babies."

On the trip up, I googled it: conversation starters for released convicts. The first website said not to discuss sensitive subjects: prison life, family ties, politics or religion. "One of the most important things former prisoners require of their friends and family is help maintaining personal dignity," the article said. Avoid anything, it instructed, that draws attention to the person's formerly incarcerated status, like comments on how good food must taste, or how nice it must be to take hot showers and sleep in. Instead, the article suggested opening with a neutral observation like "it's good to see you." Then, it said, let the other person direct the conversation.

"It's good to see you," I say.

I sit down and let my uncle fill the silences. He asks questions: How old are the kids? What kind of work do we do? How was the trip up? I answer, trying to elaborate as much as possible. Still, the conversation peters out.

"What about you?" I say. "Grandmother says you've applied for a job on an oil rig. Right off the coast of Louisiana?"

"I hope to some day," he says. "Right now I'm still waiting on my work permit, which could take six or nine months."

"Oh," I say helpfully.

"They won't let me apply without it. You know. Because of the felony."

"Right," I say. "The felony."

Uncle Rich shifts. Then he fishes in his pocket and pulls out a cell phone. "Smile, kids," he says, snapping their photos. "Look," he says with a tobacco-stained grin, holding up a picture of my son. He's downloaded some kind of free app, a Snapchat knockoff, one that distorts faces. My son's forehead is wide and his chin is small. He's deformed, caught in a funhouse mirror. Rich shows me one of my daughter next, nose stretched like Pinocchio, eyes disappearing into slanted lines.

"I do this stuff all the time," he says. "Look what I did to your Grandmaw." He hands me the phone and I scroll through five or six pictures. He's Photoshopped Grandmother's eighty-year-old face onto the body of a baby. There she is, holding a rattle, sitting in a highchair, crawling around in a diaper.

I've seen these types of pictures before. Shortly after Rich was released in November, he started sending me the same weird photos. My phone dinged at 2:30 in the morning with a distorted picture of my father—huge forehead, pointy chin, slanted eyes. Shaken, I'd blocked Rich's number and deactivated my social media account. The next week, he texted me again using a different number.

❖ ❖ ❖

Grandmother shoves leftovers into the oven, half-empty pans of dressing from yesterday's holiday meal. I help dump vegetables from plastic containers to pots, sitting them on the stove to warm. There's still some time before dinner. The children are restless from the long drive; some fresh air will do them good. I could use some, too.

"We're going to take the kids for a walk," I tell her. "We'll be back in a bit."

"Y'all don't be too late. You know Julia's coming tonight." Julia, Rich's youngest daughter, is visiting tonight to open gifts with the family.

"We'll be back in plenty of time."

My husband and I each grab a kid and head out the back door. We pass a garden of five gallon buckets holding withered beets. Rich has undertaken several such projects—the bare bulb mounted above the living room recliner, the front threshold painted Kelly green. He installed a tinfoil-wrapped brick as a doorstop, and duct-tape wall-bumpers to silence doorknobs hitting bathroom walls. Like Grandmother's broken dishwasher, which serves as a drying rack, Rich's projects serve a purpose, sort of.

We walk through naked farmland, cutting through old cornfields that have long since yielded harvests. A half-mile and a few shoulder rides later, we reach a winding dirt road. The land in front of us planes out into red clay, flanked on all sides by thorny pines. A two-story wooden house sits in the clearing. The house belongs to Daniel. He began construction shortly before Rich's incarceration. It looks like a log cabin, the kind seen in the Smoky Mountains. There's a wraparound porch and a slanted roof. Plenty of windows, though they're covered in grime and cobwebs. My uncle finished the house years ago but never moved in. It sits empty now, deteriorating.

I remember being ten years old, biking to the house through rows of green stalks. My cousin Aaron, Rich's oldest son, often pedaled behind me. His fair face turned red as watermelon meat, burning and streaming sweat. "Wait for me," he'd call. At seven years old, he always struggled to keep up.

The last time Aaron and I biked here, the house had just been dried in. We stomped across the plywood floors and threw handfuls of sawdust at each other. "Uncle Daniel says he'll be finished by spring," he said. "He says I can come here anytime I want, and maybe we'll even go camping together." I could think of nothing less pleasant than spending quality time with Daniel, with his strange twitches and year-round allergies, but I could see the excitement on Aaron's face.

"That sounds like fun," I said.

I circle the house now, noting termite damage and poison ivy. The porch steps have dry-rotted, and there are wasp nests in the rafters.

"What a shame," my husband says as the kids run around in the yard. "Such a waste, isn't it?" His eyes linger on the roof and porch and plank siding, as if his attention can restore the house's lost dignity.

We turn around and head for home, back through the brown cornfields. Dinnertime is approaching. After dinner, we'll open our gifts.

❖ ❖ ❖

As sun sinks low, bathing the living room in a mossy green glow, we gather around the artificial tree. A styrofoam angel sits at the top of Grandmother's crooked fir, which is strewn with Dollar Store ornaments and salvaged gift bows. She's long since stopped wrapping presents; the arthritis in her hands makes it painful. Instead, she sticks flannel shirts and socks in patterned cardboard boxes. Dozens are piled under the tree.

We balance plates of tepid leftovers in the living room, eating and sometimes talking. The conversation is governed by a set of unspoken rules. Grandmother talks to everyone. That one's easy. My father and Daniel don't talk to Rich. Junior, the other brother, speaks to Rich occasionally, but when he does, the other brothers's eyes bulge like bullfrogs. The dust has to settle before they will speak to him again. The palpable tension is made worse by the fact that no one acknowledges it. Grandmother alone seems oblivious. She's blissed out and giddy, looking around the room and smiling, eyes passing over us one at a time.

"All my boys," she says again. "Together for the first time in twenty years." As if they've been separated by forces beyond their control, as if Rich is a prisoner of war who's been plucked from enemy hands and delivered home.

A knock at the door. Julia, Rich's youngest daughter. His other daughter refuses to speak to him. And Aaron, the boy I chased through cornfields long ago, died in a motorcycle accident shortly after high school. Police found him facedown in a stream of water. Incarcerated at the time, Rich could not attend the funeral.

Julia enters with some kids—one on her hip, one holding her hand, one trailing behind her. We shuffle to make room for the new guests, standing and clearing spots on the sofa.

Rich greets and hugs her. She doesn't reciprocate.

"Julia, you want something to eat?" Grandmother asks, and Julia just shakes her head. Her children scatter and start playing with my two. Now that she's not holding kids, I can see that she's pregnant. She sits on the edge of a love seat, wide-eyed and silent. I sit at the nearest end of the sofa. We're knee-to-knee. She must be in her early twenties. She has the same fair skin and cornsilk hair as Aaron, the same blue eyes and overbite. I don't want to assume that she remembers me, so I reintroduce myself.

"I know who you are," she says.

I tell her that her children are beautiful, ask how old they are, and when her baby's due. She tells me May. It's one of many one-word responses. Eventually, I give up.

Grandmother tries, too, patting Julia's knee and smiling with moist eyes. When Rich's kids were young, Grandmother looked after them, seeing to it that the older ones made it onto the school bus, giving them sandwiches when they returned home each afternoon. But there's no love or nostalgia in Julia's eyes. Grandmother is just an extension of Rich. Guilty by proxy.

For the rest of the visit, Julia speaks only when spoken to and doesn't meet anyone's eyes. Soon, she leaves. Uncle Rich follows her to the driveway. Grandmother, too. I hear her

call from the porch. "Julia? Don't y'all want to stay and open presents?"

"She was having a hard time," I say to my father as my children continue to play. Other relatives clang around in the kitchen, rewarming pies for dessert.

"She doesn't want anything to do with Rich," my father says. Anger breaks through his usual calm façade, darkening his cheeks and revealing the tendons in his neck. "And who can blame her? He should've thought about that before . . ." He regains his composure; his eyes rest on my children. "Before the felony."

His anger should repel me, but I feel the urge to sit in his lap. I want to be taken into his mind, to know who he is and who he thinks I am. Somehow transcend time, space, and distance. I wonder if Julia feels the same way.

A memory comes back. Me, seven years old and flying by myself from Atlanta to Boston, where Dad was newly stationed. At thirty thousand feet, I ate a personal pan pizza and colored outlines of Delta airplanes. The plane landed, and I stepped onto the tarmac, holding a flight attendant's neatly manicured fingers. A dark airport greeted us.

"Where's your father?" the stewardess said.

"I don't know," I said.

We waited. I felt the slow, embarrassed panic of a forgotten child. Like being the last kid picked up after a sleepover or summer camp. An inconvenience. A burden.

Dad arrived an hour later, apologizing and pumping the stewardess's hand up and down. He'd fallen asleep. I am so, so sorry, he said— to me, to the flight attendant, to everyone. He embraced me, as though I might disappear in a cloud of smoke.

Because of his cross-country transfer, I hadn't seen him in months. Hugging him felt strange, and he smelled funny, too. His laundry detergent had changed or something. And when did he start using aftershave and chewing pale green gum? The menthol mingled with spearmint, burning the insides of my nostrils.

The following day he took me to Salem, Massachusetts. I understood that the trip was an apology. I was fascinated by witches and he was a history buff; it was the perfect outing. We ducked in and out of dark gift shops selling candles, amulets, and potions. Touring the mock gallows, we listened to the wisdom of a teenage tour guide. On cobblestone streets, I curled my fingers into grotesque formations, cackling and pretending to be a witch.

"Look at these white specs on my fingernails," I told him, momentarily breaking character. "My friend at school says they're called sweethearts."

"You're my sweetheart," he said. He patted my back.

I looked up at him, not knowing what to say. Even at seven, I understood that he was sustained by a storehouse of memories to which I had little access—my first eighteen months of life, the monthly trips to Alabama, summer vacations, Christmases. As an adult, he held those experiences in his consciousness and sifted through them whenever he felt lonely or sad or disconnected. He felt close to me even when distance separated us. I was desperate for that kind of connection, too, though I wasn't sure how to articulate it. So I ran away, cackling like a witch, toward some vintage ice cream shop.

❖ ❖ ❖

A few moments later, Grandmother and Rich return. Outside, a minivan crunches across gravel as Julia drives away. Uncle Rich studies my daughter and fishes through the boxes under the tree. He produces a wrapped gift, covered in crinkled reindeer paper. It appears he's wrapped it himself.

"I don't think Julia's coming back, do you, Ma?" he asks Grandmother.

"Naw," says Grandmother. "I don't think so."

Rich hands my daughter the present.

"Are you sure?" I protest, but my daughter is already tearing open the box. She tears off the paper, revealing a boxed baby doll. She looks at us and smiles, clutching the box to her chest.

"Baby!" she says. "Baby!" Untwisting little plastic ties, I help her remove it from the box. She squeezes its middle and it laughs and kicks its feet. She laughs, too.

Uncle Rich bends down and softly pats her back. I feel him wanting to hold her. I feel myself wanting to hold them both.

Later that night, we unwrap flashlights and flannel shirts, and cheap plastic toys for the kids. Grandmother looks on, smiling. Daniel and Junior take their leave, mumbling something about swing shifts and early mornings.

Rich sits in the armchair, elbows on knees, tight and ready as a coiled spring. Every few minutes, he pops up—to the restroom, the kitchen for a soda, to pick a piece of lint from the floor. My father crouches on the floor with the children, playing and hugging. Every now and then, his mouth reverts back to that grim, straight line.

Reentry into society is hard, but reentering a family is harder. There are resources to help former prisoners—government programs, parole officers, guidebooks. I think back to the websites I read on the drive up, the articles and columns and how-to guides. But there's no manual for putting a family back together.

"I ain't never done Julia wrong," Grandmother whispers to me under the noise. "I loved her—loved all them babies—took care of 'em like they were my own. That just ain't right, for her to leave like that," she says. "It just ain't right."

Grandmother's demeanor is different now. Julia has broken some enchantment, and all that's left are aging, angry sons in a broken-down singlewide.

I pat her knee, the same way she patted Julia's. "I'm so sorry," I say. "Maybe she'll come around." My words sound hollow.

❖ ❖ ❖

The following day, it is time for goodbyes. Our minivan, sagging with gifts, idles in the asphalt driveway. Above us, another hot blue sky. My father hugs the children tightly, and they hug him back. They love him, despite the distance. My grandmother and I embrace, and I hug Rich, too.

"Y'all don't be strangers," he says. "And you enjoy that baby doll, sweet girl."

My husband straps the children into car seats, and Grandmother and Rich disappear inside the singlewide. My father lingers on the porch.

"Be careful on the road," he says. "It's not you I'm worried about, it's the other drivers." His eyes turn glassy, and I see myself reflected in them—small, shiny, faraway. My throat tightens, and I refuse to blink. There will be time for tears on the trip home.

"I love you," I say.

As we pull away, brown cornfields fill the van's mirrors, vast expanses of shriveled stalks. I am creating distance—distance between myself and the barren land, between me and my fractured family. I miss my father already. I miss Grandmother and Uncle Rich. Even as the broken circle repels me, I yearn for it. Like a magnet in a vortexing field, spinning and searching for north.

Ten years ago, I stood at a green tin mailbox and tore open a number-ten envelope. In the upper left corner: Baldwin County Juvenile Detention Center. Heart thumping, I read a crinkled three-page letter, written in loopy cursive and signed by my cousin Aaron: *Do you remember when we rode bikes as kids?* he wrote. *When I get out next month, I wanna come see you.*

That evening, I phoned my father. My cousin and I were strangers—I hadn't seen or heard from him since the felony. Why was Aaron in jail? Was he dangerous? Would he hurt me? Steal from me? Or worse? Dad answered only that Aaron had been in and out of trouble. "He's family," he said before we hung up. "He needs you."

The receiver remained at my ear until I heard a dull, steady beep. I thought of Aaron and Uncle Rich, how they sat serving time in neighboring counties in Alabama. Aaron would be released shortly; Uncle Rich would be in prison for another decade. In their cement cells, did father and son feel some small sense of solidarity? Did the shared confinement bring any measure of connection? And I thought about my father, how he chipped garnets from Maine's rocky coastline and sent them to me in January birthday cards. I pictured him hunching in the bitter cold with a hammer and screwdriver, a thousand miles away, breaking up stone for his long-distance daughter.

I opened a kitchen drawer, one filled with pens, ketchup packets, and old coupons. Folding Aaron's letter in half, then fourths, then eighths, I slid it into the back corner of the drawer. Then, I closed it.

❖ ❖ ❖

At the Monterey Bay Aquarium

after Marianne Moore

World
in a world
      where fish swirl overhead, mad race of
      mackerel—it's dizzying,
          this place of ocean art where we stand

packed
shoulder-to-
      shoulder. Tentacles beckoning, fringed
      jellies spread across
          your vision like eye floaters, up and

down;
a blink, then
      gone. Some sequence iridescence while
      others pulse transparent.
      Here the deadly wait to receive their

prey
by hand from
      the diver who submerges twice a
      day to please the crowd.
      Children lean into the swirling kelp

for
a better
      look at the leopard sharks, the blunted
      foreheads of dolphin fish,
          bloated bluefin tuna. The big fish

ate
yesterday,
      the guide tells us, so they are full. Here
      come the sardines—giant globes
          of silvery souls that move as one.

From
somewhere just
　　　beneath our vision, they navigate
　　　the tank like a single
　　　　　creature; hungry, careful, a million

eyes
that do not
　　　see so much as feel the offering
　　　that shivers the surface—
　　　　　then descends, like motes in a shaft of

sun,
a glitter
　　　of stardust in a turquoise sea—a
　　　revival. Enough to
　　　　　feed a wavering immensity.

Why Today Was a Good Day

I spent the morning splitting
and stacking wood. For years,

I've let the orchard of two trees
drop its small windfall apples
to deer, worms, and freeze.

But today I collected the globes
in a white cloth bag. I shook hands
with the relieved limbs.

In the afternoon, I sat on a rock
beside a shallow lake. A moose
raised and lowered her anvil head, waded

to her haunches, nose pressed
across the algaed surface. I know
what's to come. I can feel it inside

like the turning of a moon,
how the cold and the dark will last
longer than a season. But today

was a good day. I gathered
wonder and food. And tonight

I will light the season's first fire.

Eric Roy

First Rain after a Dry Spell, a Sunshower

First rain after a dry spell, a sunshower
slicks old oil in the streets.
From the sidewalk I watch the light turn yellow,
hear brakes locking up as a car slides
sideways through the intersection
past a police cruiser in the onlooking lane.
The cop is white, the woman sliding through the red light
is black, and walking toward the scene
I see the officer get out and direct traffic
so she can get turned around
and headed back like nothing ever happened.
Everything is slippery.
The whole planet is glazed to go either way.
There has to be a better expression than
The Devil is beating his wife for a rain-shower in the sun, I think
before the thought is sideswiped by another:
Lord, I'm thirsty. The noontime summer rain
has turned to sauna-steam over asphalt.
Every street and sidewalk blurs like skin of ghosts evaporating,
and, like a ghost, wherever you are headed you're not there.
Wherever I am headed you're not there.
It wasn't, or isn't always so. It's slippery I tell you.
It's the smell of Magnolia trees in bloom and gasoline.
Not so easy to slide in and out of that residential cemetery
over there. Lichen-capped stones askew
trying to hide in the sun like the crooked bottom teeth
you would cloud with a hand
whenever there was 100% chance of scattered laughter.
I walk by our old white wooden house,
see the glider bench on the porch, how it once moved
against our planted, perfectly situated feet.
Some things never leave your mind—lemon seeds
you can't pinch from the tea. When you're not sliding
you're steadying yourself. Everything is slippery.

Lillian Blades. *Civilization*. 1998. Assemblage. 51 x 27 inches. Courtesy of The Dawn Davies Collection.

Hotel Du Nord

Vera checked herself in the mirror of the café at the Walker Art Center in Minneapolis: a pale face with dark lipstick, a white rose in her lapel. *Rosa rosae rosam*, James liked to say, teasing it between his thumb and index finger like a fruit.

She asked the bartender at the Walker for espresso, poured sugar in, stirred. When she was a child her mother in Italy told her that she knew how to read the future in coffee grounds, but it turned out she did not see her own husband leaving her, only a new job for him, a new city. The grainy coffee smudges could not tell about the suitcase, the train station, the drinks with a different woman. They knew no secrets.

James was late. It was part of his charm; whenever he rushed in at last, light seemed to flood the room. The frescoes in Italian chapels resembled him: young men standing upright, windswept curls and full lips.

He had suggested they go to the Walker Art Center to celebrate Vera's birthday as there was an exhibit of works by Joseph Cornell, an artist she loved. The first time she had seen his boxes, she wept in front of his tiny rolls of printed paper held by a string in a cardboard container, and still dreamt of rose petals and seashells scattered like delicate fossils in another.

The bartender had to ask twice if she wanted milk in her coffee. No, she did not.

She drained her espresso. The cup was now smudged with coffee dregs in the shape of feathers: long, delicate; something caught in the instant before taking flight. She stirred them away with her finger. She thought of Joseph Cornell the moment before he had placed a shiny sphere inside a box the first time, changing his life forever. She thought of his meticulous attention to everything small.

When she looked up, James was walking to her in the reflection of the mirror. He had the blue scarf on, the one his sister gave him, or so he claimed. He went nowhere without it.

"Vera." He leaned down and kissed her cheek. "You waited, thank you." She always did.

"Oh, the Cornell exhibit won't take off," she said. She liked how she sounded. Not really jaded, but almost. "Coffee for you?"

Her mother in Italy had been fond of a Turkish poem that said, *A friend is what the soul longs for, coffee is just the excuse.*

"No, I had two cups already," he said.

"You had two?" she asked, as if it was of significance. She was irked by his precision.

"At the hospital. Shall we go?"

She nodded. Words being what they were, she did better without.

"I wanted to wear the shirt you love but couldn't find it," he said. It was their shared joke. They had met two years earlier in a small clothing store where she worked on weekends. She was exhausted from deadlines for her Master in Graphic Design and had pressed on him a sorry polyester thing. He bought it, counting dollars and dimes, taking his time. While he did, he told her stories, and she listened to his voice rise and fall, she watched his hands move with the words. They were the most beautiful hands.

"More," she said later over a glass of wine, "more stories." While he talked she imagined a room just for the two of them. No mirrors, an aroma of blossoms and tea, and furniture like one comes across in an attic, with a whiff of dust.

"Oh dear," he said, "shall we talk about movies, instead? How to make the perfect gin and tonic?"

"Anything," she said. She just wanted his voice.

❖ ❖ ❖

It had been a long winter in Minneapolis; ferocious wind chills and now snow, but walking through The Walker Art Center with James, Vera felt a calm joy. The Cornell boxes were here, too. James chided her that she was fond of his works like a kid, as hiding places. Only, Cornell's existed.

"Secret places do, too," she said.

"And where are they?"

"Anywhere." She remembered the cracks in time she slid through as a child when lost in thoughts.

"Vera . . ." James said. "Only in the imagination."

"Oh, well . . . We see numbers all over, but where are they? We invented them."

Since the time her husband had left, the mother found pleasure in writing expenses in columns, admiring the order of the non-existent. She used to cry at the bathroom mirror every morning like a man shaves.

"You truly believe that different realities exist at the same time?" James asked.

When she was studying for confirmation, the more an answer did not make sense, the more *Suor* Agnese demanded it to be embraced in full.

"I do," Vera said.

"It would be crowded," James said. "Don't you think?" She felt tenderness for the way this seemed to make him nervous.

"Cozy, maybe." She smiled.

The first night she spent at his home, looking at a photo of him as a child Vera had seen his future bike rides, summers, a little dog, then drinks, planes, and lovers. The images brushed lightly against each other fast, then a schoolboy remained alone, squinting at the camera.

The light from the windows at The Walker was fading and James mentioned he did not like watching things lose definition.

"It's nothing to worry, really," Vera told him. "One time I vanished altogether for a day as a baby, and here I am."

"What!? How?"

"I wouldn't know," she said "I don't remember much." Just an intensity of silence, and the shadow from a tree like an island, seen from a distance. "Maybe I became something else: a fly, a bird," she chided.

"Please don't do it again," he said.

They passed by a window. It was now snowing outside the Walker, and James said his energy was diminishing.

"I wish I could help you," she said. She was afraid he'd leave.

"You can," he said. "Don't take off and be a fly, a bird."

"I won't, if it's what makes you happy," she said, and laughed.

"How can I please you?" James had asked the first time they spent the night together, only half joking. She liked to feel his chest under her fingertips, inhaling and exhaling.

"Tell me my fortune, foreign gypsy," he said afterwards.

"I don't know how," she said.

"Tell me whatever, and I'll believe you." He gave her a pencil and a piece of paper. "Make it good."

"No," she said. "What comes, comes."

"Oh, all right." He looked down, lips tight. She was to learn that he liked to set the rules. One was that lying was a game.

She wrote on the piece of paper with her wrong hand, the left. It couldn't do anything useful, not even cut bread. She thought it might be the one to tap the unknown. Whatever came, came. It was fast and strange, like a dream of falling. Afterwards James put the paper in an envelope and licked it shut. It remained in a drawer, as if something forbidden they both were weary to return to.

The first Cornell box had an apple inside, a die that once might have amused a child, a thin pipe. The apple was in the upper shelf; it gave her the sense of an apparition, with a loneliness that cut.

"Why an apple?" said James.

"Oh, I think he just wants us to grow curious of simple things," she said. "I love it."

"Okay . . . why?"

"It makes me remember."

"I don't remember apples." He kissed her. "Make me." She always found terribly exciting how attuned he was to *now*: no fragments, no bric-a-brac from the past.

"All right." She started to laugh. She kissed him softly, and then hard and light again, with whispers in between. He smelled faintly of biscuits. "You will remember the apple now?"

"No, you," he said.

"Perhaps the apple too."

Her parents had gone on honeymoon to Paris, at a tiny hotel where there was a fruit basket in the room. The mother did not remember the name, but Vera called it Hotel Du Nord from a Cornell box she loved. Whenever she ate an apple, her mother mentioned the special time in Paris. The grandmother said it did not exist, there had been no trip. There had been no place in time without fear, sadness, loss. But Vera knew every detail: the piano, the wine and the smell of fruit, the mother murmuring *promise me* and the father responding *forever*. When Vera ate an apple, she did it slowly to make it last.

"Interesting artist," James said. "He locks up forever what he loves."

James had been intrigued by her fondness for dolls and little toys. She kept her old ones huddled on top of a bookcase. They gave her the same sensation as being close to tiny animals.

"Do they tell you bedtime stories?" he had mused.

"Yes, " she said. "But I don't know anymore what they say." The dolls spoke with no desire to be understood; the sound was like a drizzle of rain.

Refugees, James called them.

"Feed them," he had chided the last time. "Give them a shot of tequila." She sensed that when he pulled her to sit in his lap that night he still had the excitement of another woman in him. This time, she must have liked tequila.

The next Cornell box had a *nocturnal feel,* as James put it, and when she turned to him in surprise he smiled and said, "See? I do my best."

"Your best is *eccellente,*" she said.

"You are too generous," James said, moving on to the next exhibit.

"Well, of course: it's my birthday."

"Yes it is," he said.

"That's all?"

James stopped and turned.

"Vera," he said. It seemed the beginning of a long sentence. Behind his shoulders she saw the street through a glass window, the park with trees.

A friend had told her that James never loved just one person. He simply could not. "It's really not so bad if you can live with it. You are the one he likes special." Vera did not speak to the friend again.

Recently James had been evasive about evening plans. A few nights, he had cancelled because of an emergency at the hospital. The phone, off all night.

The Walker galleries were almost empty.

"I love you, James," she said. In English it sounded more authentic. Un-poetic.

He took her in his arms and held her. There was comfort in resting her face against his chest. It was a bit like talking, only better.

"I wanted to take you out for dinner tonight, but something urgent came up. He touched her chin with delicate fingers. "I am terribly sorry." He always was.

"Ah, my luck." She pulled back. Her eyes misted.

"Oh dear. *Vera . . .* " he sighed. Once he had told her that there was nothing wrong with tears but, just like flies, one did not truly need them. She admired flies. Bread, garbage, they liked what they liked. "No . . . no. Vera, are you crying?"

"I am."

"I'll arrange to be free on Friday, rain or shine," James said. His fingers trembled, rising to his lips. Pity made him look sappy. The word *arrange.*

"Friday?" She laughed a little. *Ha ha.*

He raised his eyebrows.

"Saturday, then," he said.

"I hate both," she said. They had meant no James, as in their two years together he had rarely been free on weekends. He was busy at the hospital or exhausted. One Friday evening she had passed by his home; the curtains were fluttering, the lights were on.

"How much do you hate them?" he said.

"A lot."

In a dream, they were married and getting a divorce. It meant packing away in boxes everything they ever loved. The cardinal they had admired on Lake Harriet resisted, hurling itself at the cardboard, *toc-toc-toc.* There was a silent whiteness of snow that would not fit anywhere.

"I care about the dinner, *and* the birthday," James said. He seemed to carefully select ordinary words. He had in fact mentioned how important a kind of routine even in emotions was to him, it had an almost mystical power. "The issue is to choose a different date from today. What's so terrible?"

"That you are loved by me," she said.

"It's wonderful."

She gave him a little smile. *Ha ha.*

During their dinners she had started to notice that James disliked not only butter but questions. She found herself asking all sort of silly things. Because it made him unpleasant. Each time, he looked up from the plate with the eyes of a crazy bird. His mouth was twisted. She would try to fix on these details to miss him less, and one day perhaps not at all. But she did, even when he slept next to her. His breathing, soft like a child's, his arms raised above his head, the butterflies of her lipstick all over his skin. James.

"I choose Saturday," she said.

Friday would come, and Saturday after that, of course. This had happened ever since she could remember, but she had always sensed in any sequence something frightening rather than reassuring. Births, Christmases, marriages and funerals came. But she only remembered the funerals, the deep mystery of absence, bowed heads with snowflakes melting in the hair.

"Saturday. Perfect," James said.

There was a light beep, he checked a message on his phone.

"Oh. Vera . . . maybe Friday?" he seemed entranced by the text. He read it again moving his lips with the words. "Please take Friday, Vera. I'm so sorry, it's better for me." She saw his excitement, his hope. "Please."

❖ ❖ ❖

This morning a common friend, a nurse, had taken Vera out for a nice birthday breakfast. She told Vera that she was very happy, as this Saturday her sister was planning to come to town from LA again. James had met her on her most recent visit, and liked her very much. A dancer, she taught him complicated steps in the kitchen.

"You are free on Friday, James? Let me think about it," Vera said. The night she had passed by his home, the lights were on, there was music.

"Please do," he said. "Please?"

She liked how James existed within the space he occupied. The light so sharp. His eyes filled with tenderness. The hush of the room. He stood still, and she did too, a few steps back as if taking a picture of him with her eyes. James here, now. There was only one version to the story: this.

"I'm going to freshen up," she said. "It will take but a minute."

❖ ❖ ❖

When she left the restroom it was near closing time and the rooms at the Walker Art Center looked larger with no visitors.

Her mother had told her that one died a little in the moment between sleep and wakefulness, and in the instant you know that something is going to happen just before it does.

Vera strolled through the galleries in the evening light, savoring everything more. She wished she could dip her hands in paintings like in water and splash about, say, in the red of a Rothko.

She applied herself diligently to the act of walking back to James but kept drifting off with no apparent direction. He was a man who did not like to wait, said that God only created time to makes us suffer. But she wandered still.

She walked by the first Cornell box and admired it again. The objects inside were doing something beautiful simply by being together. There seemed to be a quiet understanding between them, the bond of the unsaid. It was a pleasure familiar to her. How strict was the narrative of life. She had found true company as a child in found objects and the pointless trifles she chatted about with them. How delicate these conversations were, and so comforting, no visible traces afterwards; a fly walking over glass. Still, the emotion was vivid. "Memory is love," her mother said.

She lingered in front of the box. Oceans, islands, even attachments were continuously changing, and not for the better, but everything in the box withstood time. There was a purity to them. She had often imagined Joseph Cornell sharing his passion with her. Side by side, they chose mementoes from her hours spent alone and placed them in a special box. A glass of wine from one evening, an earring from another. People would admire the work and be touched by a strange memory, the way torn pages make you miss something you never read.

The Walker gallery was empty except for an old male guard near the door. She stopped to look at one more box, wishing it was Hotel Du Nord, where she had been often in her imagination, and had fantasized of listening to her mother's honeymoon story.

It was time to go to James. She was already very late. She would apologize, whisper *mi dispiace*, kiss his fingertips saying it. It's the little things that matter.

Still, she did not move. She felt a heavy weariness wash over her at the thought of going back. She saw images of what was to come. Here were she and James in restaurants and cinemas all over the city. Often there would be no James. She would wait out the weekends, quietly and tirelessly as she always did.

A subtle aroma of fruit reached her nostrils. It seemed to come from the Cornell box itself, the one with the apple. She grew restless and moved closer to peer inside. The fragrance grew stronger, now mixed with one of flowers.

"Miss " The guard raised a hand in admonition. "Miss!"

She moved even closer and leaned in, placed her palms on the glass. The closeness was making her feel dizzy. Her hands tingled.

"What . . . ?" She panicked. *What, what?* The tiny objects were holding her in a spell. The rest was fading.

The guard was rushing over.

"Move back, *move back.*"

"Okay," she said. But she could not.

"Miss! Move away! Now!"

Instead of stepping back she pushed through, and in. A fine dust covered everything. There was a low hum, like voices singing in unison at a very great distance. She was smaller than the apple and possibly transparent, as guards going back and forth in front of the glass did not notice her. She felt a bit disoriented like a child with a fever. Perhaps she had always been so tiny, and living in here, as she felt at home.

The lights dimmed. There was now a soft noise of the sea. The word *refugees* came to her when a man with a blue scarf walked by quickly. He seemed agitated and in need of direction. Back and forth he went, back and forth.

The man came back. He did not seem to remember how to walk in a straight line, close to the glass and then away. She wondered if people could forget everything. She pondered over that. Her thoughts were as light as waves of static. She could catch them on the tip of her fingers and thread them again, differently.

Days came and went. Guards walked by, people walked by. Some of the visitors pushed strollers, some did not. Occasionally, men and women stood and watched for a long time. Their eyes went soft, lips smiling.

A few minutes before closing, when the halls were emptying, a man with a blue scarf came and stood in front of the glass. He had curly hair like a cherub, only he was much older, with some gray. He talked and talked to the apple, it seemed. His cheeks were pale, bloodless.

The only other people in the room were two young women who kept whispering in each other's ears, laughing. They had on winter hats and gloves, while the man did not. His eyes were wide open, and he came to the glass as if looking for something important. She had never seen such interest, and moved close to him. His lips formed a name and he teared. *Era . . . era . . .*

Her fingertips traced his features, miming something she had seen in a dream. The man closed his eyes as if he felt her touch. He seemed trapped outside the glass, tapping hard with his fingers.

A guard came over, spoke to him severely. This might have happened many times, as the guard shook his head and threw his arms up, seemingly in exasperation. The man told the guard some complicated story, moving his hands while he did. They were beautiful hands. She wanted the man to stay forever.

The Bus

On that occasion, it was carrying
only women—
with the exception of the driver—
a fact that
passes through us like a secret,
something that might have gone,
in any other circumstance, unnoticed.

In those minutes, on the bus with the glass missing
where a window would have been in the door,
the city passes,
and we see the world as if waking
from a particularly vivid dream—
where the waking world lacks color.

In those minutes, I knew who I was; they knew who I was;
I knew I was good and they knew I was good and I they;
and I knew I would not die young, nor in a bus,
nor in the afternoon, nor alone.

A man boards. The quiet shifts its weight
and its presence. And I remember
that I've forgotten my keys and I lose
one language and then another.

//

It is necessary at times to board a bus you've never been on
to know how the day sits with faces you've never seen,
with streets you've never walked, with dogs you've never passed,
and most importantly, with those fates you've never lived—

and sometimes you must ride that bus to the end
until one by one all of the others have gone where they needed to go
and you are sitting squarely with the fact
that you're not going where you need to go
but where you don't know,

and when you finally get down from that bus
you'll just keep your eyes up
and walk as if you know exactly where you are,
and you won't dare turn around
until absolutely no one, not even you,
is looking.

There you sit,
dead quiet,
until it arrives: a wave
between the bus and what passes
expanding and contracting:
el mar, la mar,
la mar, el mar.

Peter Meinke

One Year Later

On June 12, 2016, a deranged 29-year-old security guard killed 49 people and wounded 53 in Pulse, a gay night club in Orlando, Florida. It was the deadliest massacre in America since 9/11/2001.

Time passes Sleep ravels A smile might start:
the mind can weasel out of any trap
but there's no real healing of the heart

A Sauer automatic can tear apart
a face or year pealing like a thunderclap
Still time passes sleep ravels smiles can start

She sang each morning He ran our supermart:
each memory stings sharper than a slap
How can there be a healing of the heart?

Our blood slows thickened by a poisoned dart
My bluebird my beau when you nestled by my lap
time passed sleep unraveled sly smiles might start

Now time's tipped over like a broken cart
that carries nothing forward not a scrap
Nothing much to heal in an empty heart

And what of kindness mercy music art?
O how we all could dance tango and tap!
Time passes Sleep ravels A smile can start . . .
but there's no real healing for a stricken heart

Notes on Contributors

Gilbert Allen's most recent books are *Catma* (a collection of poems from Measure Press) and *The Final Days of Great American Shopping* (a collection of linked stories from USC Press). In 2014 he was inducted into The South Carolina Academy of Authors, and he is the Bennette E. Geer Professor of Literature Emeritus at Furman University.

John A. Beadle, is the son of a Bahamian mother and Jamaican father who lives and works in Nassau. He studied at The College of The Bahamas; received a BFA in painting from the Rhode Island School of Design; studied in Rome, Italy, as part of RISD's European Honors Program; and earned an MFA from the Tyler School of Art of Temple University. He has been a member of several of the Bahamas's most prominent artist collectives including B-CAUSE, Opus 5, and the art groups B.B.B and Jammin'. He has lectured in art at The College of The Bahamas and exhibited widely nationally and internationally at the Biennial of Painting of the Caribbean and Central America in Santo Domingo, and at various venues in Japan, New Zealand, France, Germany and the United States. He has served as a principal designer and sculptor for the Junkanoo Group "One Family." Beadle's work has been accepted for each of the eight National Exhibitions through 2016 at the National Art Gallery of The Bahamas, and he was one of the artists representing The Bahamas at the 2010 Liverpool Biennial. In early 2010 he completed a short residency in Zambia, sponsored by Gasworks/Triangle Arts Trust of London; participated in the Master Artists of The Bahamas Exhibition in Waterloo Centre for the Arts in Iowa in 2011; and in 2013 at the National Art Gallery of The Bahamas, in *40 Years of Bahamian Art*. He held solo exhibitions Nature's Lines in 2012 at the Central Bank of The Bahamas Art Gallery, and The John Beadle Project at the National Art Gallery of The Bahamas in 2013. His work was shown in EN MAS': Carnival and Performing Art of the Caribbean in New Orleans, Cayman, Nassau and Chicago. In 2016, he reunited with Stan Burnside and Antonius Roberts to create works for Jammin' 4, both to produce commissioned work for Baha Mar and for an exhibition held at the D'Aguilar Art Foundation.

Mark Belair's poems have appeared in numerous journals, including *Alabama Literary Review, Atlanta Review, The Cincinnati Review, Harvard Review, Michigan Quarterly Review, Poetry East* and *The South Carolina Review*. His latest collection is *Watching Ourselves* (Unsolicited Press, 2017). Previous collections include *Breathing Room* (Aldrich Press, 2015); *Night Watch* (Finishing Line Press, 2013); *While We're Waiting* (Aldrich Press, 2013); and *Walk With Me* (Parallel Press of the University of Wisconsin at Madison, 2012). He has been nominated for a Pushcart Prize multiple times. Please visit www.markbelair.com

Roy Bentley is the author of five books: *Boy in a Boat* (University of Alabama), *Any One Man* (Bottom Dog), *The Trouble with a Short Horse in Montana* (White Pine), and *Starlight Taxi* (Lynx House). He has received a Creative Writing Fellowship from the NEA, six Ohio Arts Council fellowships, and a Florida Division of Cultural Affairs fellowship; his poems have appeared in the *Southern Review, Prairie Schooner, Shenandoah, Blackbird, RATTLE* and

elsewhere. *Walking with Eve in the Loved City*, a finalist for the Miller Williams Poetry Prize, is due out in 2018 from the University of Arkansas Press.

Lillian Blades was born in Nassau, attended The College of The Bahamas, and received the Chris Blackwell Junkanoo Scholarship enabling her to complete a BFA from Savannah College of Art and Design and an MFA in painting at Georgia State University. Additionally, she studied at the Skowhegan School of Painting and Sculpture in Maine and at the Caversham Centre for Artists and Writers in the Kwa-Zula Natal Province, South Africa. She resides and works in Atlanta, Georgia, where she has completed commissions for Hartsfield-Jackson International Airport and Jean Childs Young Middle School. Her artwork is in the collection of the Birmingham Museum of Art and the National Art Gallery of The Bahamas, among other public and private collections. She was the 2016 Visual Artist awardee for the National Black Arts Festival and received an Award for Excellence in Visual Arts in the Bahamas.

Renée Branum recently graduated with an MFA in Creative Nonfiction from the University of Montana. She received an MFA in Fiction in 2013 from the Iowa Writers' Workshop, where she was a Truman Capote Fellow and a recipient of the Prairie Lights Jack Leggett Fiction Prize. Renée's fiction has appeared in *Blackbird, The Long Story, Georgia Review,* and *Narrative Magazine*. Her nonfiction essays have been published in *Fields Magazine, Texas Review, True Story, Chicago Quarterly Review, Denver Quarterly, Hobart,* and *The Gettysburg Review*. Her essay "Certainty" was awarded first prize in *The Los Angeles Review*'s Fall 2016 Nonfiction Contest. Her essay "Bolt" received first-place recognition in *The Florida Review*'s 2017 Editors' Awards. She currently lives and works in Phoenix, Arizona. Her story in this issue, "Night Moves," is a 2017 AWP Intro Journals winner selected by Brendan Kiely.

Claudia Buckholts received Creative Writing Fellowships from the National Endowment for the Arts and Massachusetts Artists Foundation and the Grolier Poetry Prize. Her poems have appeared in *Alaska Quarterly Review, Harvard Magazine, Indiana Review, Minnesota Review, Prairie Schooner, Southern Poetry Review,* and other journals; and in two books, *Bitterwater* and *Traveling Through the Body*.

Polly Buckingham's collection *The Expense of a View* won the Katherine Anne Porter Prize in Short Fiction (2016), her chapbook *A Year of Silence* won the Jeanne Leiby Memorial Chapbook Award (2014), and she was the recipient of a 2014 Washington State Artists Trust fellowship. Her work appears in *The Gettysburg Review, The Threepenny Review* (reprinted at PoetryDaily.com), *Hanging Loose, Witness, North American Review, The Poetry Review,* and elsewhere. Polly is founding editor of StringTown Press. She teaches creative writing at Eastern Washington University where she is also the editor of *Willow Springs* magazine.

Chris Carbaugh encouraged his high school students to write and publish their best work in the literary journals they created, *Possum Kingdom* and *Sekaishugi*. Both journals were recognized with the highest awards by scholastic press associations. Now retired, Chris is writing the short stories that his children and grandchildren have asked him to tell, and retell, numerous times. They are the adventures of five boys, Chris and his four brothers, as they meander through life in a small town with their incomparable mother, MamaLu. As a new writer, Chris is honored that his work has appeared or is forthcoming in *Kestrel, Broad River Review, Valley Voices, The Bitter Southerner, Broad Street Review, The Dead Mule School of Southern Literature, THEMA, The Heartland Review, Colere, The South Carolina Review, JMWW,* and *New Southerner.* He has been named a finalist in the Alex Albright Creative Nonfiction Contest as well as a Nonfiction finalist in *New Southerner.*

Bill Christophersen's debut collection of poems, *Two Men Fighting in a Landscape,* was published in 2015 by Kelsay Books's Aldritch Press; his second collection, *The Dicer's Cup,* was published by Kelsay in 2017. He plays traditional and bluegrass fiddle and lives in New York City.

John Cox attended the Rhode Island School of Design, earning a BFA in Illustration and an MAT in Art Education. He has taught in the Art Department at The College of The Bahamas and has worked at The National Art Gallery of The Bahamas, first in the Education Department and later as Chief Curator, until leaving to become Creative Art Director at Baha Mar. A mixed media artist, he is known for his large-format paintings, found object assemblages using familiar and ordinary objects to reference distant places and ideas, collage, and non-traditional printmaking. In 1999 Cox founded Popopstudios International Center for the Visual Arts in Nassau, a dynamic evolving hub for the Bahamian community with artist studio spaces; a gallery; international, local, and student residencies; and education and programming. He remains on the Board, helping Popopstudios to support the growth of contemporary Bahamian art. In 2005, he spent a month in Pietrasanta, Italy, working in marble and granite as part of the International Professional Artists Symposium and Exchange. He has exhibited in solo and group shows in Europe, Asia, the United States, the Caribbean, and The Bahamas, including each of the five National Exhibitions through 2010 at The National Art Gallery of The Bahamas, and his artwork was installed at the expanded Lynden Pindling International Airport in Nassau. He curated the exhibition *The Unseen Structure—A Response to the Work and History of Bahamian Civil and Structural Engineer George Victor Cox* at the National Art Gallery of The Bahamas in 2017.

Carlos Cunha's stories, essays and poetry have appeared in *The Kenyon Review, TriQuarterly, The Los Angeles Review of Books, The American Journal of Poetry, The Seattle Review, The Manchester* (U.K.) *Review* and elsewhere. He is a past winner of the Pirate's Alley William Faulkner writing contest in New Orleans, and *Gulf Coast* magazine's annual contest. Born in Portugal, he grew up in South Africa and lives in Florida, where he works as a copy editor for *The New York Times International Weekly.*

Holly Day has taught writing classes at the Loft Literary Center in Minneapolis, Minnesota, since 2000. Her poetry has recently appeared in *Big Muddy, The Cape Rock, New Ohio Review,* and *Gargoyle,* and her published books include *Walking Twin Cities, Music Theory for Dummies,* and *Ugly Girl.* She has been a featured presenter at Write On, Door County (WI), Northwoods Writer's Festival (CA), Spirit Lake Poetry Series (MN), and Hampton Roads Writers Conference (VA). Her newest poetry collections, *A Perfect Day for Semaphore* (Finishing Line Press) and *The Yellow Dot of a Daisy* (Alien Buddha Press), will be published in 2018.

Gregory Djanikian has published six collections of poetry with Carnegie Mellon, the latest of which is *Dear Gravity* (2014). His poems have appeared in numerous journals including *American Poetry Review, Crazy Horse, Boulevard, New Ohio Review, Poetry, Poetry Northwest, The Southern Review,* and in many anthologies and textbooks. He teaches poetry workshops at the University of Pennsylvania.

Shawna Ervin is a Pushcart nominee and has taught writing workshops for both adults and children. She is a member of Lighthouse Writers Workshop in Denver, where she graduated from the Book Project, a two-year intensive mentoring program. She also attended the Mineral School residency last fall. Recent publications include poetry in *Forge, Jelly Bucket,* and *Hiram Poetry Review;* and prose in *Existere, Superstition Review, Willow Reivew, The Delmarva Review, Front Porch,* and *Apalachee Review.*

Alicia Fuhrman is a graduate of the UMass Amherst MFA for Poets and Writers, at work on her first novel, *Rabbit Moon.*

Daniel Gabriel's published work includes a novel (*Twice a False Messiah*) and two story collections (*Wrestling with Angels* and *Tales from the Tinker's Dam*), in addition to hundreds of nonfiction articles on travel, baseball, rock 'n' roll, and the like. His piece "Syria Before it all Went South" appeared in *Tampa Review* 49. He is also editor of several volumes in COMPAS's anthologies of student writing: *This Bursting Sound Within, The River Starts Flowing,* and *Punch at the Wild Tornado.*

Julie Garcés, born and raised in Miami, Florida, graduated from The University of Miami's creative writing and screenwriting programs. Her work is also forthcoming in *New Plains Review.* She lives in Los Angeles and works as an editor on films and documentaries.

Meredith Davies Hadaway is the author of three poetry collections. Her most recent, *At the Narrows,* won the 2015 Delmarva Book Prize. She is a former Rose O'Neill Writer-in-Residence at Washington College, where she taught English and creative writing in addition to serving as vice president for communications and marketing. www.meredithdavieshadaway.com

Ceridwen Hall is pursuing a PhD in creative writing at the University of Utah and reads poetry for *Quarterly West.* Her work appears or is forthcoming in *The Moth, Hotel Amerika, Prairie Fire, Rattle, Tar River Poetry,* and elsewhere.

Jared Harél is the author of *Go Because I Love You* (Diode Editions, 2018). He's been awarded the Stanley Kunitz Memorial Prize from *American Poetry Review,* as well as the William Matthews Poetry Prize from *Asheville Poetry Review.* His poems have appeared in such journals as *Tin House, The Threepenny Review, The Southern Review, Massachusetts Review, Bennington Review* and *32 Poems.* His narrative long-poem, *The Body Double,* was published by Brooklyn Arts Press. Harél teaches writing at Nassau Community College, plays drums, and lives in Queens, New York, with his wife and two kids.

Rage Hezekiah is a MacDowell and Cave Canem Fellow who earned her MFA from Emerson College. She is the recipient of the Saint Botolph Emerging Artist Award in Literature and was nominated for Best New Poets, 2017. Her poems have appeared or are forthcoming in *Fifth Wednesday, Hayden's Ferry Review, The Cape Rock, Carolina Quarterly Review, Salamander,* and *West Branch,* as well as other journals. Her writing is featured in various anthologies including *Other Tongues: Mixed Race Women Speak Out* and *All We Can Hold: Poems of Motherhood*. You can find out more about her work at ragehezekiah.com.

Erin Hoover's debut collection of poetry, *Barnburner*, was selected by Kathryn Nuernberger for the Antivenom Poetry Prize and will be published by Elixir Press in late 2018. Her poems have appeared in the 2016 edition of *The Best American Poetry*, and in *Prairie Schooner, Crab Orchard Review,* and *Narrative,* as well as numerous other magazines. New poems are forthcoming in *Alaska Quarterly Review, Grist,* and *Pleiades*. Until recently she served as editor-in-chief of *The Southeast Review* and as a volunteer for VIDA: Women in Literary Arts. She lives in Tallahassee, Florida.

Brad Johnson's full-length poetry collection *The Happiness Theory* (Main Street, 2013) is available at bit.ly/BradJohnsonBooks. Work of his has also been accepted by *Hayden's Ferry Review, J Journal, New Madrid, Meridian, Poet Lore, Salamander, Southern Indiana Review, Tar River Poetry* and others.

Kimberly Kruge is the author of a collection of poetry, *Ordinary Chaos* (Carnegie Mellon University Press, 2018) and the chapbook *High-Land Sub-Tropic*, which won the 2017 Center for Book Arts Chapbook Prize. Her poems have appeared or are forthcoming in *Ploughshares, The Iowa Review, The Denver Quarterly, Copper Nickel, RHINO,* and many other publications. She is the recipient of a residency fellowship at the Millay Colony for the Arts and the founder of Comala Haven, a retreat for women writers. She lives and works in Guadalajara, Mexico. kimberlykruge.com

Moira Linehan is the author of two collections of poetry, both from Southern Illinois University Press: *If No Moon* and *Incarnate Grace*. Each of those books was named an Honor Book in Poetry by the Massachusetts Center for the Book. Linehan's poem "Enter the Cill Rialaig Landscape" was the Grand Prize in *Atlanta Review*'s 2016 International Poetry Contest. Other work of hers appeared recently, or is forthcoming, in *Crab Orchard Review, Innisfree, Poetry Journal* (online), *Nimrod,* and *Salamander.*

V. P. Loggins is the author of *The Fourth Paradise* (Editor's Select Poetry Series, Main Street Rag, 2010) and *Heaven Changes* (Pudding House Chapbook Series 2007). He has also published one critical book on Shakespeare, *The Life of Our Design,* and is co-author of another, *Shakespeare's Deliberate Art.* Loggins won the 2016 Cider Press Review's Editors' Prize for *The Green Cup.* His poems and articles have appeared in *The Baltimore Review, Crannog* (Ireland), *The Dalhousie Review, English Journal, The Formalist, The Healing Muse, Memoir, Poet Lore, Poetry East, Poetry Ireland Review,* and *The Southern Review,* among other journals.

Erika Luckert is a writer from Edmonton, Alberta, and a winner of the 92Y/*Boston Review* Discovery Prize. She holds an MFA in Poetry from Columbia University and was nominated for the Canadian National Magazine Award in Poetry. Her work has appeared or is forthcoming in *Denver Quarterly, The Indiana Review, CALYX, Room Magazine, Measure, Atticus Review, The Boston Review,* and others. Erika lives in New York City, where she teaches creative and critical writing.

Ron MacLean is author of the novels *Headlong* and *Blue Winnetka Skies,* and the story collection *Why the Long Face?* His fiction has appeared in *GQ, Narrative, Fiction Interna-*

tional, Best Online Fiction, and elsewhere. He is a recipient of the Frederick Exley Award for Short Fiction and a multiple Pushcart Prize nominee. He holds a Doctor of Arts from the University at Albany, SUNY, and teaches at Grub Street in Boston. Learn more at www.ronmaclean.net

R. Brent Malone, a graduate of Queen's College High School, was the first Bahamian to receive a distinction in "A" Level Art in the Cambridge General Certificate of Education. He studied at Don Russell's Academy of Fine Arts and was an apprentice at the Chelsea Pottery in Nassau. In England he attended the Beckenham School of Art, and then obtained a National Diploma in Design from the Ravensbourne College of Art and Design. As a graduate student, his first exhibition was at Oxford College, England, after which he returned to The Bahamas in 1964. Over the years, he established several art galleries to highlight the works of emerging Bahamian artists and in which he mounted eighteen exhibitions of his own work: Bahamian Pottery (1964-65), The Loft Art Gallery (1965-70), Matinee Art Gallery (1977-80), and The Temple Gallery (1981-87), which merged in 1987 with Marlborough Antiques. In the early 1990s he studied etching and printmaking at Bob Blackburn's Printmaking Workshop and at Nyle Press in New York. He held important solo exhibitions at The Central Bank Art Gallery: *Retrospective (1962-1992)* in 1992, an official Quincentennial event; *The Nude* in 2001; and *Journey* 2003 (with photographs by Sabrina Lightbourn). Internationally, Malone presented a one-man show at the Black Music Association of America Conference in New Orleans in 1982, various other exhibitions in the 1980s and 1990s. Seven of his etchings are in the Royal Library at Windsor Castle in the private collection of Queen Elizabeth II, and his paintings were presented by The Bahamas government to the leaders of Canada, Mexico, Republic of China, St. Kitts, and South Africa. Malone was a recipient of the Distinguished Citizens' Award for the Visual Arts from The Bahamas Chamber of Commerce; the E. Clement Bethel Award for Excellence in the Visual Arts from The College of The Bahamas in 1991; an M.B.E. Award in the Queen's Honours of 1993; and a Silver Jubilee Award from The Bahamas government in 1998. He was a founding member of B-C.A.U.S.E., a group dedicated to the exploration and development of Bahamian art, and he is considered a "founding father" of modern art in The Bahamas.

Peter Meinke is Poet Laureate of Florida. He's had over twenty books published, including eight in the Pitt Poetry Series, most recently *Lucky Bones* (2014). The University of Tampa Press has published six of his books, including a guide to writing poems, *The Shape of Poetry* (2012); a collection of his Poet's Notebook essays, *Truth & Affection* (2013); a children's book, *The Elf Poem* (2015); and a collection of short stories, *The Expert Witness* (2016)—all illustrated by his wife, the artist Jeanne Clark Meinke, who also illustrated his latest book, *To Start With, Feel Fortunate,* a collection of essays which received the 2017 William Meredith Award, published by Poet's Choice Press.

Tom Moran's stories and essays have appeared in numerous publications, including *Brevity, Stone Canoe, Reed,* the *Los Angeles Times, Seattle Times,* and *Washington Post.* He recently retired as professor emeritus from Rochester Institute of Technology in upstate New York and currently lives in Ormond Beach, Florida, with his wife, artist Marilyn Groch. He is at work on several writing projects, including a novel set in Venice, California, where he lived for many years.

Lisa Mullenneaux's forthcoming collection, *Keep Talking to Her, Private* (2017, Post Traumatic Press), details the devastation of our "endless wars" on soldiers and civilians. Lisa's poems and essays have appeared in *American Arts Quarterly, The New England Review, The Tampa Review*, and others. When she's not writing, she teaches writing for the University of Maryland UC.

Patrick J. Murphy's short stories have been widely published in journals like *The New Orleans Review, The Cream City Review, Confrontation, Fiction, Other Voices, The Sycamore Review*, and twice each in *The New England Review* and *Buffalo Spree Magazine*. A story was published in the anthology *100% Pure Florida Fiction* published by The University Press of Florida, and a short story collection of his entitled *Way Below E* was published by White Pine Press. He has worked as an assistant pastor in a Presbyterian Church, as an electronics engineer for NASA at the Ames Research Center, as an adjunct professor teaching English and creative writing at Florida State, the University of Texas, and Eastfield College, and currently works for the Florida Department of Law Enforcement as a Human Performance Toxicologist.

Doug Ramspeck is the author of six poetry collections and one collection of short stories. His most recent book, *Naming the Field*, is forthcoming from LSU Press. Four books have received awards: *The Owl The Carries Us Away* (G. S. Sharat Chandra Prize for Short Fiction, forthcoming), *Original Bodies* (Michael Waters Poetry Prize), *Mechanical Fireflies* (Barrow Street Press Poetry Prize), and *Black Tupelo Country* (John Ciardi Prize for Poetry). Individual poems have appeared in journals that include *The Southern Review, The Kenyon Review, Slate*, and *The Georgia Review*.

Thomas Reiter's latest book, *Catchment*, is his tenth collection of poems. His poems have recently appeared or are forthcoming in *Kenyon Review, Georgia Review, Hudson Review, Southern Review, Sewanee Review, Shenandoah*, and *North American Review*. He has received fellowships from the New Jersey Council on the Arts and the National Endowment for the Arts. He is Emeritus Professor of Humanities at Monmouth University, where he held the Wayne D. McMurray Endowed Chair in the Humanities.

Antonius Roberts is a graduate of Philadelphia College of Art (now the University of the Arts) with a BFA in Painting. As the former coordinator of FINCO Summer Art Workshops and as a teacher and lecturer at Government High School and The College of The Bahamas, Roberts has mentored a generation of young Bahamian artists. He served as the Curator of the Central Bank of The Bahamas' Art Gallery until the end of 2017, and was the architect and coordinator of their annual Competitions and Exhibitions until 2006. He also played a supportive role in the restoration of the former Villa Doyle and its conversion to the National Art Gallery of The Bahamas. In recognition of his contribution to national development in the arts he was a recipient of a Commonwealth of The Bahamas Silver Jubilee Award and of the E. Clement Bethel Award from The College of The Bahamas, as well as the Ministry of Tourism's Cacique Award for the Arts in 2000. In recognition of his contribution to national development in the arts, he was a recipient of a Commonwealth of The Bahamas Silver Jubilee Award and of the E.

Clement Bethel Award from The College of The Bahamas, as well as the Ministry of Tourism's Cacique Award for the Arts in 2000. As an artist, he has participated in exhibitions around the world and has mounted many within The Bahamas. As a sculptor, he is best known for the first *Sacred Space* project at the historical Clifton Heritage site, which was followed by the installation at the Blake Road Welcome Centre. His ethos connecting man's spiritual and emotional nature and the nature itself, and his desire to record and honour Bahamian heritage is inherent in all of his paintings and sculpture. Most recently, He participated in *Art Africa Miami* during Art Basel (2017) in Miami Florida. In the Queen's 2018 New Year Honours, Roberts was made an Officer of the Most Excellent Order of the British Empire —O.B.E. for his services to education, the arts, and the community.

Robert Rothman lives in Northern California, near extensive trails and open space, with the Pacific Ocean over the hill. His work has appeared in *Atlantic Review, The Alembic, Existere, The Meridian Anthology of Contemporary Poetry, Westview, Willow Review*, and over thirty-five other literary journals. https://robertrothman.wordpress.com

Eric Roy has poetry forthcoming in *Spillway, Minnesota Review, Rhino, Maine Review*, and *Tar River Poetry*. He gets paid to watch the fire.

C. T. Salazar is the editor-in-chief of *Dirty Paws Poetry Review*, and a 2017 AWP Intro Journals poetry winner, selected by Leona Sevick. His writing has appeared or is forthcoming in *Cosmonauts Avenue, The Matador Review, The Harpoon Review, Bad Pony, Ink & Nebula, FLARE: the Flagler Review, The Broke Bohemian*, and elsewhere. He's an MFA candidate and children's librarian.

Nicholas Samaras is from Patmos, Greece (the "Island of the Apocalypse") and, at the time of the Greek Junta ("Coup of the Generals") was brought in exile to be raised further in America. He's lived in Greece, England, Wales, Brussels, Switzerland, Italy, Austria, Germany, Yugoslavia, Jerusalem, thirteen states in America, and he writes from a place of permanent exile. His current book is *American Psalm, World Psalm* (Ashland Poetry Press, 2014). He is completing a new manuscript of poetry and a memoir of his childhood years lived underground.

Katherine Schaefer is a writer of creative nonfiction and memoir. Her essay "Edna, With Her Mouth" won the 2016 Hunger Mountain Creative Nonfiction Prize and was published in *Hunger Mountain*. Her writing also has appeared in *The Matador Review, The Talking Stick*, and *Minnetonka Review*, among others, and has received grants and awards from the Minnesota State Arts Board, Key West Literary Seminar, and Brainerd Writers' Alliance. A resident of Minneapolis, Minnesota, Katherine is currently writing a series of personal essays.

JD Scott is a writer, editor, and educator. Recent and forthcoming publications include *Best American Experimental Writing, Best New Poets, Denver Quarterly, Prairie Schooner, Salt Hill, Sonora Review, The Pinch, Ninth Letter*, and elsewhere. Recent accolades include attending the Poetry Foundation's inaugural Poetry Incubator and being awarded residencies at both the Millay Colony and Writers at the Eyrie. See more at jdscott.com.

Carrie Shipers's poems have appeared in *Crab Orchard Review, Hayden's Ferry Review, New England Review, North American Review, Prairie Schooner, The Southern Review,* and other journals. She is the author of *Ordinary Mourning* (ABZ, 2010), *Cause for Concern* (Able Muse, 2015), and *Family Resemblances* (University of New Mexico Press, 2016), as well as two chapbooks.

Rosanna Staffa is an Italian playwright and author published by *The Sun* and *The Baltimore Review* among others. Selected as a finalist for the New Rivers Press 2015 Short Story Prize, her story "Brazil" appears in the press's American Fiction Anthology, *The Best New and Unpublished Writers Vol. 15* (released December 2016). She holds a Phd in Modern Foreign Languages from Statale University in Milan, Italy and an MFA in Fiction from Spalding University. Her plays have been staged in Tokyo, New York, Los Angeles, Seattle and Minneapolis. She has been awarded fellowships by the McKnight and Jerome Foundation, and an AT/T On Stage Grant.

Adam Sullivan's stories and essays have appeared in *Monster Children*, *The Binnacle*, *Pregnancy*, and a few other places. He is the winner of the 2010 Los Angeles Comedy Festival's Screenplay Competition, as well as the 2011 Atlanta Film Festival Screenplay Competition. He is currently enrolled in UCR Palm Desert's Creative Writing M.F.A. program.

Paige Sullivan completed her B.A. at Agnes Scott College and her M.F.A. at Georgia State University. While at Georgia State, she served as an assistant editor at *Five Points*, then as the poetry editor of *New South*. She has participated in the 2015 Kentucky Women Writers Conference Workshop, the 2017 Tin House Winter Workshop for poets, and most recently the Poetry Foundation and Crescendo Literary's 2017 Poetry Incubator. In addition to essays and reviews, her poetry has appeared in *Arts & Letters*, *Ninth Letter*, *American Literary Review*, and other journals. She lives and works in Atlanta.

Maxwell Taylor was born in Nassau in 1939. He studied at Don Russell's Nassau Academy, later apprenticing at the fabled Chelsea Pottery as a ceramic designer alongside Bahamian artists Brent Malone, Eddie Minnis, and Kendal Hanna. He left home for the U.S. to study at the Art Students League in New York from 1968 to 1972, and worked in photo silkscreen at The Pratt Graphic Center and printmaking at Bob Blackburn's Printmaking Workshop from 1969 to 1977. He was awarded the Southern Arts Federation Fellowship award for works on paper by the National Endowment for the Arts, and in 2009, the National Art Gallery of the Bahamas mounted a major retrospective of Taylor's work entitled *Max Taylor: Paperwork, 1960-1992*, which featured a great number of his emotionally charged large-scale woodblock prints. More about his life and work can be found on page 55 of this issue.

Lauren Tess currently lives in Los Angeles. She has poetry forthcoming in *Saranac Review* and *Tar River Poetry*.

Garrett Theige grew up in the suburbs of Detroit and graduated from the University of Missouri with degrees in magazine journalism and English. He has worked as a freelance magazine writer, newspaper reporter, ad sales man, and as the door guy at a bar in North Dakota. He is currently an English Instructor, house counselor, and basketball and track coach at Phillips Academy Andover in Andover, Massachusetts, where he currently lives with his wife and their dog. This is his first fiction publication.

Jesse Wallis's poems have appeared or are forthcoming in *CutBank*, *New Ohio Review*, *Rhino*, *Southern Poetry Review*, *The Southern Review*, *Zone 3* and *Tampa Review* 43/44 ("Setting the Track Record"). He studied writing and film at the University of Iowa and, prior to that, art at Syracuse University and the California Institute of the Arts. After living in Japan for nine years, he returned to his hometown of Phoenix, where he works in human resources for a public school district.

Abigail Warren lives in Northampton, Massachusetts, and teaches writing, literature, and poetry at Cambridge College. Her work has appeared in print and on-line, in *Hawai'i Review*, *Tin House*, *Monarch Review*, *Brink Magazine*, *Gemini Magazine*, *Sanskrit*, *Emerson Review*, *The Delmarva Review*, and *Serving House Journal*, among others. Her essays have appeared in *SALON*, *Northampton Media*, and *The Huffington Post*. Her book, *Air Breathing Life*, was published by Finishing Line Press in 2017. Her webpage is abigailwarren.org.

Jennifer Watkins, MFA, is an essayist with work appearing in *The Chattahoochee Review*, *Hippocampus Magazine*, and *SFWP Quarterly*, among others. She writes and teaches in Milledgeville, Georgia, where she lives with her husband and two children. Her essay in this issue is a 2017 AWP Intro Journals winner selected by Benjamin Busch and nominated by Georgia College.

Arjuna "AJ" Watson is the son of an Australian mother and a Trinidadian father. At the age of five, he moved with his mother to Melbourne, Australia, where he became a keen skateboarder, greatly absorbed with gritty, rebellious street-style graffiti. Obsessed with creating and spraying stencils, he became one of the most prolific graffiti artists of his age, with resulting encounters with the law. At the age of eighteen, on the insistence of his mother, he stopped. In 1997, he returned to Trinidad, worked as a sailor, and in 1998, arrived in Nassau to stay. It was not until 2007, following the gift of a book on Melbourne graffiti, that his interest in art was reignited. He started painting again, this time mostly on canvas and occasionally on skateboards. His first solo show in 2007, *Decypul*, was a collection of urban images. It was followed by *Hit & Run, Part One* and *Hit & Run, Part Two* in 2008, *Muse* and *Crux* in 2009 and *Muse II* in 2010. He has participated in group shows at the Cube West Gallery, Albany Resort, and at the Ladder Gallery during *Transforming Spaces*. His work reflects his interest in urban art, worldwide and current news, but his shows have also included the nude form and portraiture. He held a solo exhibition *I Get Jealous Even When the Sunlight Touches You* (2015) at Popopstudios Annex. In 2016 Watson moved to Australia, where he now lives and works.

Ellen Doré Watson's fifth collection, *pray me stay eager*, will be published by Alice James Books in 2018. Her work has appeared in *The American Poetry Review*, *Tin House*, *Orion*, *Field*, *Gulf Coast*, and *The New Yorker*. Among her honors are fellowships to the MacDowell Colony and to Yaddo, and a NEA Translation Fellowship. She has translated a dozen books from the Brazilian Portuguese, including the work of poet Adélia Prado. Watson serves as poetry editor of *The Massachusetts Review*, director of the Poetry Center at Smith College, and teaches in the Drew University Low-Residency MFA program in poetry and translation.

Charles Harper Webb's latest book, *Brain Camp*, was published in 2015 by the University of Pittsburgh Press, which will publish his next collection, *Sidebend World*, in

2018, *A Million MFAs Are Not Enough*, a collection of essays on contemporary American poetry, was published by Red Hen Press in 2016. Recipient of grants from the Whiting and Guggenheim foundations, Webb teaches Creative Writing at California State University, Long Beach.

Kevin West is an MFA candidate in poetry at Virginia Tech. His poetry has appeared or is forthcoming in *Blue Earth Review, Sycamore Review, Sierra Nevada Review, Qu*, and elsewhere.

Thomas A. West Jr. has had over 200 poems published in little and literary magazines such as *The Aurorean, Bryant*

Literary Review, California Quarterly, The Listening Eye, The Literary Review, The New Renaissance, POEM, Wisconsin Review, etc.

Jeff Worley's latest book is *A Little Luck*, which won the 2012 X.J. Kennedy Poetry Prize from Texas Review Press. A former NEA Fellow, he has published poems in *The Gettysburg Review, New England Review, The Threepenny Review, Poetry Northwest, Black Warrior Review, The Southern Review, The Georgia Review, The Sewanee Review*, and others. Jeff lives in Lexington, Kentucky, and spends as much time as possible at his cabin at Cave Run Lake.

❖ ❖ ❖